Mysteries
& Intrigues
of the Bible

Mysteries
& Intrigues
of the Bible

HOWARD BOOKS
A DIVISION OF SIMON & SCHUSTER
New York   London   Toronto   Sydney

Our purpose at Howard Books is to:
 • *Increase faith* in the hearts of growing Christians
 • *Inspire holiness* in the lives of believers
 • *Instill hope* in the hearts of struggling people everywhere
 Because He's coming again!

Published by Howard Books, a division of Simon & Schuster, Inc.
1230 Avenue of the Americas, New York, NY 10020
www.howardpublishing.com

Mysteries & Intrigues of the Bible © 2007 The Livingstone Corporation

Library of Congress Cataloging-in-Publication Data
Mysteries and intrigues of the Bible.—1st ed.
p. cm.
Summary: "A nonscholarly, nonfiction presentation of hundreds of unusual facts from the Bible"—Provided by publisher.
Includes bibliographical references and index.
(pbk. : alk. paper)
1. Bible—Miscellanea. I. Howard Books. II. Title: Mysteries & intrigues of the Bible.
BS534.M97 2007
220—dc22
2007005214

ISBN-13: 978-1-4165-4356-5

1 3 5 7 9 10 8 6 4 2

Cover design by David Uttley, The Design Works Group
Interior design by Davina Mock-Maniscalco

Produced with the assistance of The Livingstone Corporation (www.LivingstoneCorp.com).
Project staff includes Linda Taylor, Dana Veerman, Rachel Hawkins, Sara Korber DeWeerd, Michael Kendrick, Jonathan Farrar, Bruce Barton, Greg Asimakoupoulos, Cecil Cole, Kari Barton, Betsy Elliot, Steve Hawkins, Mark Fackler, Amy Ronne, Randy Southern, Dawn Jett, and Neil Wilson.

Contents

Introduction   xi

SECTION ONE: STRANGE BUT TRUE

Shrinking Life Spans   3

Giant Questions   5

Without Beginning or End   7

Desert Visitors   9

The Saline Fräulein   11

The Deception   14

The Interpreter of Dreams   17

Crimson Tide   19

First Born, First to Die   21

Bread from Heaven   23

The Lost Ark   25

Swallowed Alive   29

The Venom of the Viper   31

Balaam and the Beast   33

Mountains of Blessings, Mountains of Curses   41

The Valley of Fire   44

Gideon's Army   47

A Curse for the Tyrant   49

Jephthah's Vow 51

Ghost Town 53

Samson's Amazing Strength 55

Hemmed In 57

The Prophet's Parable 59

The Queen's Visit 61

The Prophet's Mistake 63

Fire from the Sky 67

Elijah, World-Class Runner 69

The Flying Prophet 71

The Queen of Heaven 73

Babylon, Then and Now 75

The Fourth Man 77

How the Mighty Have Fallen 81

The Handwriting on the Wall 83

Dinner Bell at the Lion Pit 85

Mountaintop Encounter 89

The Shadows of the Crucifixion 91

The Mysterious Death of Judas Iscariot 96

Hog Wild 100

Road to Recognition 102

The Best for Last 105

The Prince of Darkness 107

Rushing Wind 110

Death Times Two 112

Strange Lights and Mysterious Voices 114

Dungeons and Disciples 118

The King's Last Boast 120

Midnight Deliverance   122

Shipwreck   124

SECTION TWO: CURIOUS CONNECTIONS

Binding Curses   129

Armed Angels   131

Signs and Shadows   134

Urban Decay   137

The Race for Children   139

Miraculous Births   141

Brushes with Death   143

Left Standing at the Altar   146

Memorable Meals   149

What a Way to Go   152

Twisted Sisters   154

God's Mountain   156

Ordinary Objects   161

Instant Leprosy   164

Circumstantial Circumcision   166

Sorcerers' Apprentices   168

Water, Water Anywhere   170

Winning Against All Odds   172

Animal Tales   175

Sudden Death   178

Stoned   180

Tall Tales   182

A Throw of the Dice   184

One-Man Wrecking Crews   187
"Idol" Hands Are the Devil's Workshop   192
Unlucky Seventies   194
Temples of Doom   200
Pernicious Priests   202
Demonic Possession   204
Tragic Ends to Twisted Tyrants   206
Scripture Streakers   208
Liars' Club   210
The Rise and Fall of the Temple   212
Kings and Jokers   215
Fabulous Food   219
Fantastic Healings   224
People Raised from the Dead   226
Firestorms from Heaven   229
Poison-Pen Letters   231
Listen Up!   234
Fishy Stories   237
Puzzling Parables   242
Church Creeps   244

SECTION THREE: FAQs
Angels   251
Collective Judgments   254
Demons and Demon Possession   258
Family Customs   263
Fire and Brimstone   266

Miracles   269

Prophecies   274

Topical Index   281

Scripture Reference Index   293

Index to the Charts   301

Index to "Did You Know?"   303

Introduction

FOR MANY PEOPLE, the Bible is like the pyramids. Those who live along the Nile take the massive stone triangles for granted. Their design, complexity, and origin are steeped in mystery, but because they are so obviously there, they go largely unnoticed.

In the same way, the Bible is everywhere. With so many versions, so many translations, so many options—often on our own bookshelves—we too begin to take it for granted. But having Bibles and reading the Bible are two very different experiences. Open the pages of the Bible with a curious mind, and mysteries leap off every page. The Bible is a boring book in the same way that a massive archaeological dig is boring to someone with undeveloped curiosity. The boredom is in the beholder. Even repeated readings of the Bible never seem to prevent the attentive person from occasionally uttering, "I didn't know that was in the Bible!"

The Bible has been with us for nearly two thousand years, and the early books of the Old Testament have existed almost twice that long. Its enduring life attests to not only its great spiritual treasures but also its amazing stories, astonishing miracles, and intriguing facts that continue to grip readers today. *Mysteries and Intrigues of the Bible* simply retells those stories in a fast-paced format.

Despite its questioning and sometimes lighthearted tone, *Mysteries and Intrigues of the Bible* seeks to uphold the value of Scripture. Even today, the modern scholar or scientist is hard-pressed to provide a logical, natural explanation for the events described in the Bible. We must rely on the Bible authors' interpretations to shed light on otherwise inconceivable happenings. Their confident understanding of these events points us beyond ourselves to consider the One who created all things.

The entries in this book present hundreds of fun facts and astounding stories in three main sections.

- **"Strange but True"** investigates unusual stories in a thought-provoking style. Written newspaper-style by "investigative journalists," these articles describe the many unusual stories in the Bible. Each article has a fun title, a headline-style subtitle, and then a news story describing the event. These are arranged canonically.
- **"Curious Connections"** brings together a series of related events that all share a puzzling or astonishing similarity. These lists are presented canonically by the first entry in each list—and then canonically within the lists.
- **"FAQs"** (Frequently Asked Questions) provides answers to common questions about the supernatural and miraculous. Each question or set of questions has a topic, and the topics are arranged alphabetically.

In addition, other kinds of notes give you even more information:

- **"Did You Know?"** sidebars present unusual facts about the Bible.
- **Charts and lists** are sprinkled throughout the text, further demonstrating the wonders of the Bible in a wide context, taking in the sweep of Scripture.

Scripture references are provided with each feature for the reader who wants to further examine the facts. We would encourage you to reread these Bible passages to grasp the full impact of God's work among his people. We hope you enjoy the wonders described in this book and pause to consider the great truths they reveal.

In the back you will find several indexes that will allow you to locate (or relocate) stories by their topics or scripture reference.

SECTION ONE

Strange but True

Shrinking Life Spans

Why did human life expectancy decline sharply in early Bible times?

ENOCH WAS A MERE CHILD when his life on earth ended at age 365. Today, at the ripe old age of thirty, most people find they cannot run the mile quite so fast as those younger kids they used to compete against. At forty, fathers begin to lose arm-wrestling matches with their sons, and at fifty with their daughters. At sixty, you may be feeling young but a look in the mirror prevents self-deception. At seventy, you have qualified for every senior-citizen discount ever invented, and people say, "You're so young looking," only to coax you for a walk around the block. How did those people in the Bible live so long, when in comparison many of us grow tired and old so soon?

One of the oldest people in the Bible was Methuselah, a man who lived 969 years, nearly a full millennium. Most of these people had begun raising kids when they reached our age of retirement. How did these ancients live so long? Did they have a purer air and water? Was their some type of enzyme or protein in the food they ate that gave them immunity against diseases that plague our populations, such as cancer? What secret did the ancients possess that enabled them to live superhuman lives? Was there actually some Fountain of Youth, the same one that Ponce de León searched for in Florida in the sixteenth century?

Although the Bible lists the names and ages of these ancient heroes, it does not provide any explanation for the longevity of the

3

people. We can well imagine that in those days stress wasn't as prevalent, food was purer, the environment was less toxic, disease was less virulent, and the air was less adulterated than it is today. The agricultural pace of life was most likely slower, giving the ancients time to achieve mental peace. The rat-race pace of life was still to be invented by distant descendants who would look back disbelievingly at the incredible life spans once enjoyed. Perhaps environmental and lifestyle factors explain much of the disparity between the modern person's life expectancy and that of the ancients of old. The fact that these extremely old people existed before the biblical account of the flood might account for some of the differences in life expectancy. An extensive flood may have changed prehistoric atmospheric and climatic conditions that supported human existence much more readily than the environmental conditions we endure today. Still, a person's body must be unusually strong to last seven, eight, or nine centuries.

A more theological explanation is that the life expectancies declined according to a divine plan; as the earth became more populous, the need for such long life spans disappeared. God's displeasure with human behavior enters into the explanation as well. Genesis 6:3 contains this terse comment: "Then the LORD said, 'My Spirit will not put up with humans for such a long time, for they are only mortal flesh. In the future, their normal lifespan will be no more than 120 years.'" The life expectancy after Noah indeed drops sharply; Noah himself lived 950 years, his son Shem only 600; six generations later, Terah, the father of Abram, died after 148 years of life.

The reason why these ancient people lived so long continues to be a complex puzzle, and we may never have the pieces necessary to provide a complete answer.

For some ancient genealogical data, read Genesis 5.

Giant Questions

Who were the mysterious "sons of God" described in Genesis 6:1?

IN A CRYPTIC PASSAGE just before the story of Noah's ark, the writer of Genesis tells us that "sons of God" looked down on "the beautiful women" on the earth and took them as wives. Their offspring became a race of giants called the Nephilites (some Bible versions say Nephilim), who became the heroes of ancient lore.

That is the extent of our knowledge of this moment in early history, a puzzle that raises more questions than we have answers. Who were these sons of God? What do we know about the Nephilites?

One theory suggests that these giants were descendants of Seth, a godly line of people, who had intermarried with the wicked descendants of Cain. You'll recall that Cain murdered his brother Abel; Seth was born later to Adam and Eve. A problem with this theory is that Genesis seems to draw an obvious difference between mere mortals and supermortals in this story, a difference too plain to avoid.

Another theory proposes that these sons of God were great men—rulers and kings. The appeal of such an explanation is that it smoothes away the difficulty of imagining that angels (or some other spiritual beings) were intimate with women. The impression we infer from the passage is that of extraordinary, supernatural beings who somehow entered earth's realm to choose earthly wives.

A third theory is that these sons of God were unlike anything seen on earth, then or now. They were from another spiritual realm—some would say a demonic one—but had certain physical capacities. They had a sex drive, and their offspring were giants, powerful men—the stuff of legends. That might be too difficult to fathom: part-angelic, part-human beings. But whatever the Bible was speaking of in this mysterious chapter, it is clear from the books of Jude and 2 Peter that any angelic being who sins by transgressing the gulf between human and angelic will endure the full wrath of God. These angels can only expect the gloomy dungeons of God's judgment (see 2 Peter 2:4; Jude 6).

And what of the Nephilites? We encounter them again in Numbers 13:33 when the spies reporting from the Promised Land spoke fearfully of a race of giants that inhabited the land. Were they related to these giants of old? We can't say. But we do know that the Israelites encountered giants during their early history, Goliath of Gath being the most famous example. Second Samuel 21:15–22 includes a brief chronicle of Israel's battle with these large men.

For a firsthand account of the "sons of God," read Genesis 6:1–8.

Without Beginning or End

Who was the mysterious priest who ministered to Abraham?

H E SHOWS UP ONLY ONCE during Abraham's life, but he became an archetype of the high priest to whom Jesus himself is most often compared. Despite his remarkable association with Jesus, we have scant biographical data about him. This interesting and little known character in the Bible is the ancient king and priest named Melchizedek.

According to Hebrews 7:2, "The name Melchizedek means 'king of justice,' and king of Salem means 'king of peace.'" Most Bible scholars believe Salem was the ancient city that became present-day Jerusalem. He is the first priest named in the Bible, and though his priesthood was not necessarily connected to the Israelites' priesthood descended from Aaron, Melchizedek is honored as God-fearing and even an exemplar of Jesus.

Melchizedek's name survives because, unlike many other ancient king-priests, he did not exploit his subjects—in particular Abraham. When Abraham offered 10 percent of what he conquered to Melchizedek, the mysterious ancient priest gave Abraham a blessing and a banquet. By contrast, the king of Sodom, another ruler who accepted gifts from travelers and subjects, took nine times the tithe money and provided nothing in return.

The author of the New Testament book of Hebrews makes

much of Melchizedek, calling him "a priest forever, resembling the Son of God" (Hebrews 7:3). These are extraordinary words of praise in the Bible for a mere ancient priest. Melchizedek is called "a priest forever" because he has no father, mother, or ancestors. Indeed, in a book like Genesis, where the whole human race's ancestry is mapped out, there is no mention of Melchizedek's ancestors. Who was this mysterious priest-king? Who were his parents? What is his complete story? These questions have confounded biblical scholars. Was Melchizedek an angelic appearance like others described in the Bible? Or was Melchizedek merely a righteous priest who became a symbol of the righteousness the Israelites could expect from a coming Deliverer? Was Melchizedek merely a righteous leader who represented for all time a greater truth than even he imagined? Whatever the facts, we recognize that Melchizedek symbolized the covenant relationship that would come to completion in Christ.

For Melchizedek's story, read Genesis 14, Psalm 110, and Hebrews 5–7.

Desert Visitors

Who were the mysterious travelers who told Abraham about future events?

THE SUN SHONE HIGH one hot afternoon in ancient Canaan. Three dusty travelers slowly approached the several tents that had been placed amidst a pleasant oak grove. These were Abraham's tents, and his family lived among these oak trees at Mamre. When Abraham saw the three approaching, he encouraged his wife, Sarah, to prepare a meal. Hospitality in this ancient culture was paramount; when even uninvited and unexpected guests arrived, they were greeted and fed.

Abraham ran to meet the men and welcomed them. They exchanged greetings, and Abraham urged them to stay as his honored guests. The three travelers agreed, and Abraham was delighted.

After a hearty meal, the men headed out toward Sodom. Since Abraham knew the way well—his nephew Lot lived in that city—he went with them part of the way.

But the talk of these three grew strange. One spoke of the city of Sodom with great displeasure. He had heard of the unspeakable perversions that thrived in that city. He even spoke of destroying the city for its wickedness. Abraham pleaded with the man to spare the city, bargaining down to the point of asking that the city be saved if only ten righteous people could be found there. The man agreed and Abraham returned home.

But the next day, Sodom was a smoldering ash heap. Had

armies come and destroyed it? Had the trio sabotaged the city by torching it in the middle of the night?

These were all plausible explanations for the sudden destruction of a thriving city. But the villagers of the nearby towns told a far different story. They spoke of fire and burning sulfur raining down on the city, licking up all its inhabitants—save one man and his daughters.

The one man who had barely escaped this appalling plight was Lot, the nephew of Abraham himself. Filled with great fear, Lot lived the rest of his days in the caves of the region.

The tale Lot told of that harrowing night filled everyone who heard it with dread. He told of two visitors who insisted that he leave his hometown that instant. After some hesitation—it was their home, after all—Lot's family fled, only to barely escape the hot sulfur that rained down from the sky. Lot's wife stole a quick look back and with that glance, lost her life (see the next story, "The Saline Fräulein").

We may never know with complete certainty whom Abraham hosted on that hot day—although Scripture makes it clear that one of these men was the Lord himself. Given the sudden fiery destruction of Sodom and nearby Gomorrah—by means unavailable to ancients—it's obvious that Abraham's visitors were from another realm.

For more on Abraham's visitors and the subsequent destruction of Sodom, read Genesis 18–19.

The Saline Fräulein

What really happened to the woman who looked back at Sodom?

L OT IS ONE of the Bible's most famous husbands, not for anything he did to win points with his wife, but for the distinct
and unusual honor of being married to a block of salt. Here's how it
happened.

Ancient Sodom crawled with seedy behavior. Its name has come
to stand for debauchery. Its character was worse than daytime TV
soap operas. One night around the year 2050 B.C., Lot was instructed
to evacuate the city, for the anger of God was about to fall upon it.
He had too little time to arrange for the sale of his residence, but at
least he had his life. The one condition: "Don't look back."

So Lot and his family got away before fire poured from heaven
on the sorry city of Sodom. But Lot's wife did glance backward, a
quick look over the shoulder. After all, her home, her possessions,
her friends were back in the city. As the deafening noise came from
the heavens, as screams rose from the city, she turned around to
look. In the next instant, her body became a block of salt. How can
such a dramatic chemical change happen so fast?

Maybe she was hit by debris from the firestorm—hot lava that
turned her corpse into crystalline salt. A more literal interpretation
suggests that God turned her body into an inert block of sodium
chloride.

No wonder Lot and the rest of his family moved on hastily and
never looked back.

For more on Lot's wife, read Genesis 19.

HOLY VENGEANCE

Scripture outlines the fates of families, nations, and peoples who died defying or neglecting the power of God.

GROUP	FACT	REFERENCE
Sodomites	Obliterated for their corruption and evil.	Genesis 19:24
The firstborn of the Egyptians	Perished because Pharaoh would not allow the Israelites to leave Egypt.	Exodus 11:1–10
Egyptian soldiers	Drowned in the Red Sea in a vain attempt to recapture the Israelites.	Exodus 14:21–28
Three thousand Israelites	Executed by the Levites for worshiping a golden calf.	Exodus 32:15–28
Many Israelites	Killed by a plague resulting from widespread complaint about their food.	Numbers 11:31–35
Ten Israelite spies	Fell ill and died from a plague after delivering fearful reports about the Promised Land.	Numbers 14:36–37
Many Israelites	Killed by poisonous snakebites; the cause was complaints about Moses' leadership.	Numbers 21:4–6
Twenty-four thousand Israelites	Died of a plague that ravaged the camp because the Israelite men were consorting with Moabite women.	Numbers 25:1–9
Korah and his followers	Swallowed by the earth for rebelling against Moses' authority.	Numbers 26:10

GROUP	FACT	REFERENCE
Amorites	Decimated by a ferocious hailstorm for opposing the Israelites.	Joshua 10:11
One thousand Philistines	Struck dead by Samson in an amazing show of strength.	Judges 15:14–15
Philistines	Killed by tumors and plagues after seizing the ark of the covenant.	1 Samuel 5:1–12
Seventy men of Beth-shemesh	Died after looking into the ark of the covenant.	1 Samuel 6:19
Amalekites	Crushed by Saul's army for their repeated hostility toward Israel.	1 Samuel 15:1–7
Seventy thousand Israelites	Swept by a plague after David ordered a census contrary to God's commands.	2 Samuel 24:10–16
Twice, captain and fifty men	Consumed by fire from heaven for confronting the prophet Elijah.	2 Kings 1:9–12
Ahab's family	The last of his relatives exterminated by Jehu, in accordance with Isaiah's prophecy.	2 Kings 10:1–17
Ethiopians	Destroyed for attacking Asa, king of Judah.	2 Chronicles 14:12–13
Moabites and Ammonites	Long-standing enemies of Judah—killed each other off in a flurry of confusion.	2 Chronicles 20:22–24

The Deception

A father's blessing and curse that couldn't be undone.

WHY—WHY CAN'T YOU BLESS ME?" The loud cry pierced the silence. "Bless me, too," came the anxious plea again. The wrinkled and gray old man was sitting straight up, a troubled look on his face. His son, a livid young man named Esau, was pacing back and forth in the tent. "Please bless me, father," he cried. "Please bless me." Isaac stared straight ahead, seemingly unaffected by the commotion. Blind for many years, Isaac could not see his anguished son; but he certainly could hear his loud pleas.

Finally Isaac spoke, "Your brother was here, and he tricked me. He has taken away your blessing. . . . I have made Jacob your master and have declared that all his brothers will be his servants. I have guaranteed him an abundance of grain and wine—what is left for me to give you, my son?"

Esau collapsed, weeping bitterly, "Do you have only one blessing?"

As Esau sobbed, his face buried in his hands, Isaac slowly stretched out his bony hand and placed it on his son's head. In quiet monotones, Isaac pronounced, "You will live by your sword, and you will serve your brother. But when you decide to break free, you will shake his yoke from your neck" (Genesis 27:34–40).

These were not the words Esau was looking for. They fell on his ears like pelting rain. His heart sank. His stomach churned. Finally he stormed out of the tent, vowing to kill his brother Jacob. That brother of his had stolen his blessing and left him with his father's curse.

How could the words of a feeble old man hold so much power? Why couldn't Isaac take his blessing back from his conniving younger son, Jacob? How could mere words change the destinies of these two young men?

Isaac's curse did come true. King David, a descendant of Jacob, conquered the Edomites, Esau's descendants, around 1000 B.C. For centuries after that, the Edomites lived to the south of Israel in a desert region under Israel's dominion (see 2 Samuel 8:14).

Why did Isaac's words hold so much power? The ancients believed that a spoken curse contained inherent power to accomplish itself. This explains Esau's reaction. But it does not explain why Isaac's words came true or why Isaac couldn't take his blessing back. Could Isaac, although physically blind, see centuries into the future? Did Isaac hold the future of his sons in his wrinkled hands?

The key to this mystery lay in the heart of Rebekah, Isaac's wife. Decades earlier, she had buried a secret deep within herself. When she was a young woman pregnant with twins, her days and nights had been filled with great pain. The two babies she had been carrying in her womb were continually struggling, kicking, and fighting. The pain kept her up late into the cool desert nights and filled her days with agony. Finally in desperation, she sought out a place to be alone. There, she poured out her grief to the God of Abraham. Why this pain? Why her?

God spoke to her: "The sons in your womb will become two nations. From the very beginning, the two nations will be rivals. One nation will be stronger than the other; and your older son will serve your younger son" (Genesis 25:23).

It was obvious to Rebekah that God had ordained Jacob's and Esau's fates long before their father had pronounced his words of blessing and condemnation. Isaac's dying words did not hold any power over his sons' lives; God had determined their destinies long before.

For more on this curse, read Genesis 27.

BLESSINGS

God's people have been asking for and giving blessings since the first generations walked the earth. Here are but a few of the biblical blessings . . . and their sometimes unusual results.

BLESSER	PERSONS BLESSED, CIRCUMSTANCES, OR RESULTS	REFERENCE
God	Noah and his sons, after the flood; God established a covenant with them.	Genesis 9:1–11
Melchizedek, priest and the king of Jerusalem	Abram, whose devotion to God increased and who then gave a tenth of his possessions to Melchizedek.	Genesis 14:18–20
Isaac	Jacob stole his brother Esau's blessing from their father; years of sibling rivalry ensued.	Genesis 27:1–40
Moses	The Israelites set up the tabernacle exactly as God had commanded.	Exodus 39:42–43
God	Job; the last part of his life, after all his trials, had more abundance and joy than the first part.	Job 42:12–17
God	Person who follows God's ways; grows and prospers.	Psalm 1
God	Several rather surprising kinds of people, such as the humble, those whose hearts are pure, mourners, and the insulted; according to Jesus, they receive various blessings.	Matthew 5:1–12
Christians	Other people; those who bless instead of insulting or repaying evil with evil will in turn inherit a blessing from God.	1 Peter 3:8–14

The Interpreter
of Dreams

A man's unique supernatural gift propels him to power.

H ATED BY FAMILY, thrown into a pit, sold into slavery, tossed into prison. These are not details of an ordinary life. Perhaps no other account in all of Scripture illustrates the strange vicissitudes of life than the biography of Joseph, a sage of dreams.

Joseph was born into privilege. He was the eleventh—and favorite—son of Jacob, one of the patriarchs of Israelite history. Though Joseph was loved by his father, he was hated by his brothers because of his favored status. Joseph stoked his brothers' hatred by telling them of dreams he had—dreams in which his brothers bowed down to him.

One day the brothers could not contain their rage anymore. They seized Joseph and threw him into a pit. Their first thought was to kill him, but they changed their minds when they saw a caravan heading for Egypt. Instead of murdering Joseph, his brothers sold him as a slave to members of the caravan. Afterward, they returned home and told their father that Joseph had been killed by a wild beast.

In Egypt, Joseph became the servant of Potiphar, an official in Pharaoh's court. Unfortunately, Potiphar's trust was shattered by his wife's false accusation against Joseph. Without so much as a court hearing, Joseph was thrown into prison. He was doomed, or so he thought. But then a perplexing turn of events raised him to unexpected heights.

In prison, Joseph met the king's cupbearer and the chief baker. Both men were troubled by strange and mysterious dreams they had recently experienced. When they told Joseph their dreams, Joseph interpreted the strange visions for them. Days later his words came to pass, in precisely the way he had announced. What kind of special powers did Joseph possess? How could he interpret these dreams? Joseph merely attributed his ability to the God of Israel, a God not worshiped in Egypt.

Two years later, Pharaoh had a dream. His advisors could not even start to interpret it. Joseph was summoned from the pit to decipher the strange, troubling images. After a moment of silence, Joseph declared that the visions meant that Egypt would be blessed with seven years of abundance, followed by seven years of famine. In grateful response, Pharaoh appointed Joseph second in command. Again, Joseph downplayed his own abilities and spoke instead of the power of God. And just as he predicted, the seven years of abundance came, as well as the seven years of famine.

In Bible times, God often used dreams to communicate his purpose to particular people. We must keep in mind that without books and the conveniences of modern telecommunications, the supernatural vision may have been the preferred way of conveying truths to God's followers. But does God still communicate this way today? Many would say he does.

Joseph's appointment to second in command remains an astonishing moment in ancient history. How do we explain his journey from an impoverished foreigner and prisoner to imperial leader? Joseph himself would explain it to his brothers later as part of a divine plan. "You intended to harm me, but God intended it all for good. He brought me to this position so I could save the lives of many people" (Genesis 50:20). And perhaps that is the best explanation of all.

For more on Joseph's story, see Genesis 37; 39–50.

Crimson Tide

What caused a sudden catastrophe in the Nile River?

IMAGINE A HOT DAY in the tropics. How far will you go to get refreshed? Swim in pristine, clear waters? Certainly. How about brackish water? Sure—anything to cool off. Yet, one such scorching day in Egypt had bathers scampering out of the Nile River as if they had seen a shark. The waters had suddenly turned red. Blood red.

The Nile is a big river. It stretches 4,160 miles from central Uganda to the Mediterranean Sea. Nine countries share its basin of 1,150,000 square miles. That's a lot of water, but it was much more than H_2O on the day Moses went to Pharaoh demanding that the Hebrew slaves be freed.

For four hundred years, the descendants of Jacob had lived in Egypt, first as guests, but eventually as unpaid workers roughly handled by the powerful Egyptian dynasty. Around 1300 B.C., God broke through to a man named Moses, a Jew who had been raised as an Egyptian in Pharaoh's own palace. Moses became the Hebrews' great leader from slavery to the Promised Land. But first, Pharaoh had to be persuaded that releasing a half million brick-making Israelites was a politically correct move.

Moses used a variety of persuasive tactics. This one struck at Egypt's most precious natural resource. To demonstrate God's determination that Pharaoh free the Hebrew slaves, Moses changed the Nile River from water to blood, effectively closing the world's greatest waterway to all barges, ships, and bathers—not to mention an entire Egyptian nation that needed drinking water. How did Moses do it?

Blood is composed of a complex combination of plasma, platelets, red and white cells, hormones, protein, carbohydrates, and fats—so let's rule out the theory that Moses sprinkled a trickle of blood into the river and changed its entire chemistry. Let's also rule out red dye. A person could ponder a long time about the bag of tricks up Moses' sleeve—unless there were no tricks. We could take Moses' declaration at face value: God himself had determined to rescue his people, and every element of nature was marshaled to serve this end. No wonder the mystery of the Nile is a wonder that chemistry textbooks cannot explain!

To learn more about the Nile's red-letter day, read Exodus 7:14–25.

First Born,
First to Die

The last of the plagues on Egypt was the worst.

PHARAOH HAD SEEN the Nile turn to a river of blood. He had walked on a land covered with frogs, then gnats, flies, and finally locusts. He had watched livestock fall down dead and boils cover his people. Hailstones and then great darkness had descended on his kingdom. All these things had come through the hand of Moses.

So why did he not believe the threat on his nation's firstborn sons when he again refused to free Moses and the Israelites? The Bible explains that, over and over, Pharaoh hardened his heart.

It was at midnight that the firstborn males—animals as well as humans—were struck down dead because of Pharaoh's hard-heartedness. They died mysteriously and without warning. The biblical account of the tragedy is more direct. It reveals the firstborn were "struck down" by the Lord, killed by a death angel that passed over the land. Yet just as mysterious is the fact that a select few of the firstborn males living in Egypt were spared.

Who survived? And why? The children of the Israelites were not killed; their parents had followed the strange instructions communicated by Moses and Aaron. They took perfect male lambs, slaughtered them at twilight, and wiped some of the blood on the sides and tops of the doorposts of their homes. They roasted and ate the meat with bitter herbs and bread made and eaten in haste, without yeast.

When God's hand of death moved over the land, it passed over the homes marked with the lamb's blood. That night Pharaoh finally released the Israelites from 430 years of slavery, and they left the country as quickly as they could. And Jews to this day remember the night that God's final plague passed over their homes when they celebrate Passover.

The complete account of the Passover can be found in Exodus 11–12.

DID YOU KNOW?

What was the pillar of fire?

The Israelites who fled from Egypt to their Promised Land witnessed many wonders. Perhaps most memorable were the manna that rained down from heaven (see Exodus 16:31) and the water that gushed from a rock (see Exodus 17:1–7). The most mystifying phenomenon, however, was the pillar of fire that guided the Israelites at night (see Exodus 13:21–22). Some have wondered whether the pillar of fire described in the Bible was actually volcanic eruptions in the Sinai region. But the descriptions of the pillar of fire seem to preclude such an explanation. How could a volcanic eruption shine light on the Israelites but at the same time cover the Egyptians in darkness (see Exodus 14:19–20)? In the end, no one can offer a natural explanation for the column of fire that followed the Israelite camp during those forty years in the desert. But it is clear from the Bible that the fiery pillar represented God and his holiness. It was both a brilliant light that provided physical safety and a luminous reminder of the source of all spiritual enlightenment.

Bread from Heaven

What was the food that sustained the Israelites in the wilderness?

THE DESERT FLOOR east of the Red Sea was white with a mysterious substance. Like snow, it lay evenly on the ground. Like frost, it began to crystallize and evaporate in the midday sun. "What is it?" the famished Hebrews asked one another. No one was sure. But because everyone was asking the same question, the strange milky white ground cover was called manna (in ancient Hebrew, *manna* means "What is it?" as noted in Exodus 16:15, 31). The Lord had told Moses he would "rain down food from heaven" (Exodus 16:4), and food arrived. The wandering Israelites harvested the manna each day of their forty-year trek in the wilderness.

On the day it first appeared, Moses told the people to gather enough for their household needs for each day—but only enough for one day—and to trust the Lord to provide more for the next day.

The manna tasted sweet like honey. It resembled coriander seed with a waferlike consistency. What is more, it satiated their desert-driven appetites. Strangely, those who tried saving additional quantities for subsequent days were disappointed. Any surplus of manna not eaten on the day it was collected began to rot by the next day. Leftover manna was an oxymoron.

Because the seventh day of each week was a day of rest for the Israelites, no manual labor was allowed. Therefore, no manna could be harvested on the Sabbath. Even though manna not eaten at the end of a given day would be crawling with maggots by the next morning, on the sixth day this was not the case. Moses gave the Israelites permission to collect enough of the "Jewish dew" on the sixth day of the week to last them for two days. And sure enough, on the morning of the Sabbath, the manna gathered the day before was as fresh and tasty as if it had just been gathered. This peculiar putrefaction pattern made manna even more puzzling. Was it the atmospheric condition of the weekdays that made the manna rot so quickly? Or did the manna gathered on Friday contain some chemical that retarded its deterioration and repelled maggots?

The manna was nutritious enough. Men and women and children survived on this bread substitute. But was it really a miracle food? Since these two million slaves had never traveled in this region before, how did they know this was not a natural phenomenon of the wilderness? Perhaps it was a convergence of moisture and desert plant particles that routinely coated the ground. Wild animals of the desert quite possibly had lived on the morning flakes for thousands of years. But to call it "food from heaven"? Wasn't that a bit presumptuous? Would God create a customized never-before-heard-of food just for a homeless extended family of nomads?

Well, actually, yes he would. He had said he would rain down food from heaven—and he did. This food from heaven kept a whole nomadic nation alive when their survival seemed in jeopardy. And he continued to provide for them until the day the Hebrews entered the Promised Land (see Joshua 5:12).

You can read more about manna in the books of Moses. Begin with Exodus 16.

The Lost Ark

What happened to Israel's most holy object?

IN 1981, *Raiders of the Lost Ark* took movie viewers by storm. The plot related the adventures of an inquisitive archaeologist who wrests the ark of the covenant from the evil intentions of the Nazis, only to lose it again. Though entirely fictitious, *Raiders* resurfaced interest in one of the most puzzling mysteries of the last two thousand years—namely, what happened to Israel's most holy object?

It is amazing that a simple box of acacia wood four-by-two-by-two-feet could inspire so much fear and reverence. That box is, of course, the ark of the covenant—the box that occupied the Most Holy Place, the inner sanctuary of the temple of God. Built when the Hebrews were still nomads in the wilderness, the ark of the covenant was the centerpiece of Israel's worship. In it were stored the two tablets of the Decalogue (the Ten Commandments), a bowl of manna (the food during Israel's long march to the Promised Land), and Aaron's rod (which facilitated the miracles in Egypt that led to the exodus). For many years it stayed in the tabernacle, a large tent that traveled with the Hebrews. Later, Solomon placed the ark in his magnificent temple, and it rested in a chamber known as the Most Holy Place.

The precise time when the ark of the covenant was lost remains an intriguing mystery. Many believe that the Babylonians destroyed it when they sacked Jerusalem in 586 B.C. Others say that Shishak of Egypt destroyed it when he plundered the temple. But others say that the ark was taken and hidden somewhere else and still exists at some unknown location, even today.

One theory is that Shishak stole the ark and took it to Egypt. This idea emerges strongly in the film *Raiders of the Lost Ark*. Unfortunately, there is no evidence or even legend to support this theory. Others believe that the ark is somewhere closer to Jerusalem. Some suggested sites include Jordan or the region of Qumran where the Dead Sea Scrolls were found. But again, there is no evidence that the ark was ever taken to either site.

Still others say that the ark is actually in Jerusalem, buried in a cave or under the stones of the old city. A group of ultraorthodox Jews believe that the ark is under the Temple Mount. Others say it is in a tunnel under the city streets.

Perhaps most intriguing of all is the theory that the ark was taken to Ethiopia in the days of Solomon. This view was made popular by the book *The Sign and the Seal: The Quest for the Lost Ark of the Covenant* by Graham Hancock and is based on Ethiopian folklore that Solomon fathered a child by the queen of Sheba. Ethiopia is one possible location of the land of Sheba. The legends say that this son, named Menelik, whisked the ark away to Ethiopia for safekeeping. But as with all the other theories, no one has seen the ark or produced any evidence beyond the folklore that the ark is safely tucked away in northern Africa.

Whatever the case, the ark has been lost. The second temple, erected under Ezra and Nehemiah, contained no replacement or facsimile of the ark. There was truly only one of its kind, and it could not be replaced.

Could the ark have survived? May it still be found somewhere in the desert sands of the Middle East?

If you travel near Axum in northern Ethiopia, you will hear that the ark is kept under lock and key and out of sight in the Maryam Tsion Church. That is the lore among the people of that region. No other place or people claim to know its whereabouts.

To learn about the ark for yourself, read Exodus 25, Joshua 3, 1 Samuel 4, and 1 Chronicles 13.

ARK OF THE COVENANT LINKED TO MYSTERIOUS DEATHS

CASE	CIRCUMSTANCE	RESULT
Eli and his family (1 Samuel 4:4–22)	Eli, judge and priest, failed to stop the detestable behavior of his sons, Hophni and Phinehas. Both young men were priests but used their position to extort bribes and favors.	A series of disasters followed, each related in some way to the ark, each resulting in death. Hophni and Phinehas carried the ark into battle thinking it would protect them. Instead, both died at the hands of the Philistines, and the ark was captured. When Eli heard that the ark has been taken, he fell from his chair and broke his neck. His daughter-in-law went into labor after hearing that the ark had been captured. She died shortly thereafter.
The Philistines (1 Samuel 5:1–6:18)	Having captured the ark, the Philistines celebrated their victory and put the ark in a shrine to their god Dagon.	The triumph dissolved into terror after a plague broke out. The pestilence became so widespread that the ark was moved to two other cities, with the same results. "Those who didn't die were afflicted with tumors; and the cry from the town rose to heaven" (1 Samuel 5:12). So anxious were the Philistines to end the plague that they placed the ark on a cart and guided the animals to return the ark to Israel.

CASE	CIRCUMSTANCE	RESULT
Seventy men of Beth-shemesh (1 Samuel 6:19–20)	The people of Beth-shemesh rejoiced that the ark was in Israel's possession again. But seventy curiosity seekers made the mistake of looking into the ark.	The men of Beth-shemesh certainly would have known about the penalty for looking on the holiness of God (see Numbers 4:20); no person could see God and live. Consequently, all seventy died.
Uzzah (2 Samuel 6:6–7)	King David was moving the ark to Jerusalem using an oxcart. During the journey, the oxen stumbled, and a man named Uzzah reached out to steady the ark.	Uzzah ignored clear warnings about touching the ark. It was a holy dwelling place for God and could not be touched by human hands. Uzzah died instantly.

Swallowed Alive

Conspirators, fire, earthquakes, and the plague

THE EARTH began to tremble. Slowly, the Hebrews backed away from the desert tents of Korah, Dathan, and Abiram. The men had come out and were standing with their wives and children when suddenly the ground beneath the families split apart. The earth opened its mouth and swallowed them, their households, and all their possessions. Screaming, they tumbled alive into a yawning grave.

Filled with fear, the rest of the Hebrews fled to their own tents. But then, from out of nowhere, a raging fire arose and licked up 250 more men. Smoke and the smell of burning flesh filled the air. Why had this happened? According to the Scriptures, those ancient Israelite nomads asked the same questions many of us ask today: Why did God strike down these people?

The day before this calamity, Korah, Dathan, and Abiram had challenged Moses and Aaron. They accused Moses and Aaron of placing themselves above all the people, lording over them as great high priests. According to these challengers, everyone had a right to approach God and the sacred objects of the tabernacle on an equal footing. In fact, it was their right to do so. But now, these defiant challengers of the status quo and their followers were dead. The people could not help but cringe in fear as they remembered the words of Moses that still rang in their ears, "Tomorrow morning the LORD will show us who belongs to him and who is holy" (Numbers 16:5). That morning, the earth opened its mouth and swallowed alive Korah, his coconspirators, and their families.

The people fumed and fretted about the disaster. Why did these men have to die? What did they do wrong? Blaming Moses and Aaron and challenging God's authority over them only brought more horror—soon afterward a plague ravaged the camp, killing scores more. By the time it was all over, the twelve clans of Israel had been decimated. The decomposing bodies were stacked outside the camp. Everyone knew of a father or mother, a brother or sister who had succumbed to the plague.

Those who rush to the conclusion that the men were victims of an angry God overlook the patience the Hebrew people had been afforded. They saw the plagues that ruined Egypt but had not touched them; they witnessed the Red Sea collapse around the pursuing Egyptian armies; they had their food and water provided daily by a loving God. Seeking only their own pleasure and comfort, they repeatedly turned away from divine guidance. The divine judgments can thus be seen as the sad but fitting punishment for stubborn rebellion.

For more information on Korah's rebellion, read Numbers 16.

The Venom
of the Viper

A bronze snake produces miraculous healings.

M OST SNAKES are thinner than people, slower, shorter, and not
nearly as intelligent, but we fear them much more than they
fear us. Figure that out! Face-to-face with a snake, people give way.
In the Bible, a serpent led the first humans into big trouble. But
in a surprising turnaround during their wilderness years, the Israelites were saved from a deadly invasion of poisonous snakes by a
snake made from bronze. A symbol of what the people feared most
became their deliverance from the venom of the viper. How could a
snake made of metal diffuse toxic chemicals already inside a snake-
bite victim's bloodstream?

Some of the Bible's mysteries might be explained by the laws of
nature, but this one seems to defy them all. Lethal chemicals circu-
lating through a person's body seem unlikely to be altered by visual
sightings of any kind. But perhaps we're not really *seeing* the issue
here. Can even the most tough-minded scientist doubt that a powerful and largely unexplained connection exists between the mind
and the body? Cancer patients are told that laughter, joy, and merriment are related to longer survival rates. The effects of neurological
diseases are oddly postponed by positive mental attitudes. We don't
know how or why, but something is going on behind the scenes that
connects what we believe with how our bodies actually respond to

the microscopic vermin inside us. In this case, it seems clear that a "little extra" antidote helped the bodies of those who obeyed Moses and looked at the bronze snake—for all who looked lived.

The bare facts stand by themselves. We know that Moses prayed and put the snake up on the pole (see Numbers 21:7–9). The miracle of prayer and faith is the only explanation given for the recovery. Perhaps, then, we must take seriously the intention of the writer of Numbers: God brought about a mighty miracle among his people.

But wait; there's more. As weird as this prescription may sound, remember that God always has a purpose. Looking at a snake on a pole may not have made a lot of sense, but it worked. Centuries later, however, Jesus would refer back to this event and say, "As Moses lifted up the bronze snake on a pole in the wilderness, so the Son of Man must be lifted up" (John 3:14). Salvation from sin happens when we look up to Jesus, believing he will save us.

For more on the Israelites' detox program, read Numbers 21:4–9.

Balaam and the Beast

Directives from heaven come from an animal's mouth.

A s KING BALAK looked out over the Jordan River, Israelites covered the landscape as far as he could see. He trembled in fear.
Balak, the king of Moab, was terrified of the Israelites because of the
news he had recently received. King Sihon's people, the Amorites,
and King Og's people of Bashan had been wiped from the face of
the earth. The Israelites had utterly destroyed them; there wasn't a
single survivor.

And now, these same Israelites were camped along the Jordan,
too close to his own people. Fighting the Israelites did not seem to
work so well; they were too powerful. Balak wondered what else
might work. The Israelites would certainly want his land as well.
And so he decided to put a curse on them. He wanted all the help
he could get. Perhaps the curse of an old prophet would weaken
them in order to give him victory!

Balak knew of a man named Balaam. Some people called
Balaam a prophet, and some called him a sorcerer. All Balak knew
was that Balaam seemed to have magical powers. Whoever Balaam
blessed seemed to do extraordinarily well. Whoever he cursed was
doomed. Balak had to get this man to curse the Israelites, so he sent
his elders, along with a great deal of money, to get Balaam and bring
him to this spot to place a curse on the invaders.

Several days later, the elders of Moab returned—*without* Balaam.
Balak couldn't believe it! So he sent other men, more distinguished
than the first group, to persuade this old prophet to come. Along with

them, he sent a message to Balaam: "Don't let anything stop you from coming to help me. I will pay you very well and do whatever you tell me. Just come and curse these people for me!" (Numbers 22:16–17). This time, Balaam came. However, Balak was angry at the delay and therefore did not notice Balaam's odd behavior.

Balak brought the distinguished old prophet to a high point looking down over the vast Israelite camp below. Balak waited expectantly to hear the curse, the curse that would doom this people. But as Balaam opened his mouth, only words of blessing came out. Balak couldn't believe his ears. "What have you done to me?" he cried out. But Balak would not give up.

Balak took Balaam to another high point that looked over the Israelites. Once again, as soon as Balaam opened his mouth, words of blessing poured out. A third time, from another spot, Balaam blessed the Israelites—except this time he also cursed Moab! Balak, filled with anger and completely confused, was furious with Balaam. What was he doing? Every time Balak rebuked the old prophet Balaam responded, "I will speak only the message that the LORD puts in my mouth."

What had gotten into this old prophet of Canaan? Balaam knew better than to mess with God, for when he had been on his way to curse the Israelites, his loyal donkey began behaving very strangely. The donkey veered off the path into a nearby field, crushed Balaam's foot against the wall of a vineyard, and even lay down in the middle of the road. Donkeys are known for being stubborn, but Balaam's donkey had never done anything like this before! All three times, Balaam did what any owner would do to a disobedient donkey—he beat it again and again to get it moving. But as he was beating the animal a third time, Balaam couldn't believe his own ears. His donkey started talking to him! "What have I done to you that deserves your beating me three times?"

Balaam was dumbfounded! A talking donkey? But then he saw something even stranger: a terrifying angel with a drawn sword. The angel's words sounded like a thunderclap: "Three times the donkey saw me and shied away; otherwise, I would certainly have killed you by now and spared the donkey" (Numbers 22:33). The donkey had saved Balaam's life.

Realizing that he had sinned, Balaam willingly followed the angel's next instructions: "Go with these men, but say only what I tell you to say."

The talking donkey? The work of God, the Creator. He will get his message heard—whatever it takes.

For more information on Balaam and his donkey, read Numbers 22–24.

MYSTERIOUS MESSENGERS

According to Hebrews 13:2, some people have entertained angels without knowing it. This is certainly true of many people in the Bible. Throughout history, God used these "mysterious messengers" to bring messages of hope, life, and death to his people.

PERSON VISITED	REASON	REFERENCE
Hagar	This former servant of Sarah was visited twice by angels: once when she ran away from Sarah's cruelty and once again when she and her son, Ishmael, were driven away from Abraham and Sarah.	Genesis 16:7–13; 21:14–19
Abraham	Three men, two of whom were angels and one possibly God himself, appeared to assure Abraham that he and his wife would have a child in their old age. An angel later appeared to him on Mount Moriah to prevent him from sacrificing his son.	Genesis 18; 22:11–18

Person Visited	Reason	Reference
Lot	Two angels were sent to destroy the cities of Sodom and Gomorrah. He and his daughters were saved. His wife was turned into a pillar of salt.	Genesis 19:1–29
Jacob	He saw an angel of God in a dream about spotted goats. Jacob later struggled with a mysterious man who dislocated Jacob's hip and changed his name to Israel. The man was God himself in the form of an angel.	Genesis 31:10–13; 32:22–32
Moses	The angel of the Lord appeared to Moses in a burning bush.	Exodus 3:2–4:17
Balaam	He was summoned by Balak, king of Moab, to curse the Israelites. On his way to visit the king, an angel blocked his path, but he didn't recognize it until his donkey spoke to him.	Numbers 22:21–35
Israelites	An angel was sent to the Israelites to warn them of the consequences of their disobedience.	Judges 2:1–5
Gideon	The angel of the Lord was sent to Gideon to call him to battle against the Midianites.	Judges 6:11–24

Person Visited	Reason	Reference
Manoah	An angel appeared first to his wife, who was childless, to tell her she would have a son (Samson). The angel reappeared to Manoah, who heard those words confirmed.	Judges 13:2–25
David	His disobedience led God to send an angel to bring a plague to the people. Seventy thousand people died.	2 Samuel 24:15–17; 1 Chronicles 21:12–30
Elijah	A depressed Elijah was visited twice by an angel who brought him food and drink.	1 Kings 19:5–7
Hezekiah	The angel of the Lord put to death 185,000 men in the Assyrian camp to bring victory against Sennacherib, king of Assyria.	2 Kings 19:34–35
Daniel	He claimed an angel shut the mouths of the lions when he was thrown in the den of lions. Later, he had a number of visits from a messenger called Gabriel who had been sent by God to interpret Daniel's visions of end-times.	Daniel 6:22; 8:15–27; 9:19–27; 10:1–12:13

Person Visited	Reason	Reference
Joseph	He saw angels in three dreams of life and death: one to help him decide to marry Mary, the second to get him to take the child Jesus to Egypt, and the third with a message of their safety.	Matthew 1:18–24; 2:13–23
Women	An angel was sent to roll back the stone from Jesus' tomb. At the tomb, he told the women that Jesus had risen.	Matthew 28:2–7
Zechariah	The angel Gabriel appeared to Zechariah to announce that he and his wife would have a child in their old age.	Luke 1:11–20
Mary	The angel Gabriel appeared to Mary to announce that she would have a child, Jesus.	Luke 1:26–38
Shepherds	First one angel, then a host of angels, appeared to the shepherds proclaiming the birth of the Savior and where he could be found.	Luke 2:8–15
Apostles	Two angels spoke to them after Jesus ascended into heaven, telling them that Jesus would one day return in the same way they saw him go.	Acts 1:6–11

PERSON VISITED	REASON	REFERENCE
Apostles	They were arrested for preaching, but an angel released them from prison.	Acts 5:17–20
Cornelius	Cornelius, a righteous Gentile, saw a vision and heard an angel speak.	Acts 10:3–8
Peter	He was freed from prison by an angel.	Acts 12:1–11
Paul	While on a ship about to sink, an angel appeared to Paul with the message that his life and the lives of the others on the ship would be spared.	Acts 27:21–26

DID YOU KNOW?

Who were the Nicolaitans?

In Revelation 2:6, Jesus commended the Ephesian Christians for hating the evil deeds of the Nicolaitans. He even threatened to use "the sword of [his] mouth" (Revelation 2:16)—a metaphor for judgment—against this group in Pergamum. Who were these people? No one knows exactly, but Revelation does give us some clues. Christ likened the Nicolaitans to the pagan prophet Balaam, who in Moses' time had been hired by an enemy king to curse the Israelites. Later Balaam encouraged Moabite women to seduce the men of Israel (see Numbers 25:1–4; Revelation 2:14). Today most scholars concur that the Nicolaitans, whoever they were, likely encouraged sexual immorality and idolatry among the early Christians. According to Revelation, this group would experience the full wrath of God.

Mountains
of Blessings,
Mountains of Curses

A great prophet's dying command

WIZENED AND THIN, the aged Moses spoke to the assembled tribes of Israel. His voice, though noticeably weaker, still resonated with the authority he had possessed for decades. Earlier, he had summoned the people of Israel to a great gathering. They knew something of great importance was going to happen—but what? Adding to the drama was the army of followers who stood with Moses. For the first time ever, the elders of Israel had joined Moses publicly as he addressed the nation.

Moses had scant time to finish his work on earth. Nearly 120 years old, he knew that he would not be with his people when they entered the Promised Land. Yet he feared that they would slide into disobedience as they often had during their forty-year trek through the desert. So he instructed the people to remember God in the new land by going through an elaborate—and somewhat mysterious—ceremony.

Once the people crossed the Jordan and into the Promised Land, they were to pause and remember God's words. To do this, they were to place large stones on Mount Ebal and coat them with plaster. The leaders were to write the law (most likely the key points) on the stones as a visible reminder of God's demands for a holy life. After the stones had been set up, the people would feast and offer sacrifices.

When the feasting was over, a great ceremony would mark the inheritance of the new land. Moses instructed the tribes to assemble near two mountains once they had crossed the Jordan. The tribes of Simeon, Levi, Judah, Issachar, Joseph, and Benjamin would gather at the foot of Mount Gerizim and announce blessings to the people, while the tribes of Reuben, Gad, Asher, Zebulun, Dan, and Naphtali would meet in front of Mount Ebal and declare curses to those who violated God's law. The physical setting lent itself well to the messages: Ebal was barren and craggy, but Gerizim, just south of Ebal, was covered in trees and rich vegetation.

Between the tribes in the rich valley of Shechem below, Moses instructed the Levites, the priestly caretakers and spiritual leaders of the nation, to lead the people in this great act of remembrance: They were to recite a series of twelve curses intended for those who disobeyed, symbolic perhaps of the twelve tribes of Israel. Yet for those who followed the law, God promised blessing. The people would harvest abundant crops, keep enemies at bay, and remain prosperous. Their covenant would testify to the love of God, and the neighboring peoples would stand in awe of them (see Deuteronomy 28:10).

After Moses finished his instructions, he presented Joshua as Israel's new leader. A short time later Moses died, having glimpsed from a mountain peak the land he would never enter. But would the people of Israel take to heart his parting words?

In fact, they did. After the Israelites had defeated the Canaanite strongholds of Jericho and Ai, Joshua called for a great assembly of Israel in the place Moses had specified. The great stones of the altar were piled up, and Joshua copied the law onto the stones. Then, in what must have been an awe-inspiring sight, six tribes assembled before Mount Gerizim, and the others in front of Ebal.

Between them marched the Levites, holding the ark of the covenant. Joshua read the blessings and curses to the entire assembly, and they affirmed each word with a ringing "Amen!" So the dying words of Moses were fulfilled.

Spectacular as it must have been, the ceremony of the blessings and curses had one simple objective: to impress upon the Israelites the importance of their covenant with God. As the people would discover in the lawless period of the judges that followed Joshua's death, curses did follow in the wake of sin: only when they remembered God and turned to him were they saved from their plight.

To read more about the ceremony of blessings and curses, read Deuteronomy 27–28. To learn how Joshua fulfilled Moses' command, read Joshua 8:30–35.

The Valley of Fire

What unspeakable crimes were committed in a ravine near Jerusalem?

DESECRATION AND DEATH were the rites performed to pagan gods in the valley of Ben-Hinnom. The repulsive acts conducted at this notorious site included fire walking and the much more horrific practice of child sacrifice. The latter deed—killing the firstborn child in a fiery offering—was thought to pacify the cruel pagan deities Chemosh and Molech.

Gehenna is a Hellenized form of the name for the valley of Ben-Hinnom, a ravine south of Jerusalem where deadly pagan rites were conducted. A shrine for Moabite and Ammonite gods once existed in this valley, which was the border between Judah and Benjamin.

Biblical archaeologists have painstakingly pieced together evidence to learn what happened in Gehenna. How did a peaceful valley so close to the religious center of Israel become the scene for some of the worst excesses of paganism? Why did so few resist deeds that were blatantly evil? How widespread was the cult? How many people lost their lives in this horrible era? Answers remain unclear.

The memory of Gehenna's evil lived on in the minds of later generations. They made the word synonymous with a place of fiery torment, a prefiguring of the doctrine of hell. Eventually, King Josiah destroyed the altars and relics of idol worship. But the prophet Jeremiah warned that in the last days, the valley of Ben-

Hinnom would become a Valley of Slaughter, a trench in which scavengers would feed on the carcasses of countless people. This place of unspeakable evil would become a valley of judgment. What some people do in the name of religious fervor has always baffled the modern mind. At the time, of course, those engaged in offering human sacrifices must have somehow believed their action would appease an angry god. But lest we get too self-righteous and look down on the primitive behavior of ancient peoples, we might pause to remember that our own century also has seen its share of pointless suffering wrought by the hands of civilized peoples. Gehenna's cries of misery resonate with the agony of twentieth-century holocausts carried out in the name of righteous causes.

The story of Gehenna appears throughout the Bible. Start the tour with Joshua 15:8; 18:16; 2 Kings 23:10; 2 Chronicles 28:3; 33:6; Jeremiah 7:31; 32:35.

DID YOU KNOW?

Why did the ancient Israelites sacrifice their children to Molech in the valley of Ben-Hinnom?

Although the valley of Ben-Hinnom would eventually become the garbage dump of Jerusalem and a symbol of the corruption of hell, it was first the site of the worship of Molech, the god of the Ammonites. One of the rites associated with the worship of this "detestable god" (1 Kings 11:5) was the sacrifice of live children on a ceremonial fire. Precisely how these innocent children were sacrificed continues to be a fact buried in the distant past. Jewish rabbinic writers give us a clue, however. They describe a series of horrific rites revolving around a hollow bronze statue of a man with an ox's head. Inside this statue was a furious fire that burned to death those innocent victims who were shoved into this death trap. In clear and forceful language, Mosaic law condemned such hideous rites (see Leviticus 18:21).

Gideon's Army

Three hundred men overwhelm a huge Midianite force.

THE SUN SET and the land grew dark. Suddenly, in the pitch
black of the hill area surrounding their valley, a thousand lights
appeared—as if floating fire had been sent down from the heavens
in a perfect halo. Then, as the Midianites stared in increasing mys-
tification, trumpets blasted with a ferocity that shook the ground!
Having an army as numerous as the sands of the sea, the Midianites
never expected the terrible onslaught that was coming.

With a mighty roar, the Midianites heard the unified cry "A
sword for the LORD and for Gideon!" It was the sound of a million
warriors. Convinced that they were surrounded, the Midianites
began to flee in fear and panic. As their confusion mounted, they
turned on one another with swords, destroying one another with
their own hands.

Gideon had started out with thirty-two thousand men. However, the God of Israel wanted the Israelites to depend on him for
victory, not on their own strength. Most were dismissed because
they trembled with fear. The remaining ten thousand were tested
by the way in which they drank water! All the men who kneeled
down to drink with their mouths from the stream were dismissed.
But the few who cupped the water in their hands and lapped it with
their tongues were kept for the army—and only three hundred men
did so.

It was these Israelites who watched in fascination as the enemy
self-destructed in the valley below. Their God, the God of Israel,

had given them victory that day through Gideon. Contrary to what the people in the valley thought, only three hundred Hebrew soldiers stood on the hills. Gideon gave them each a trumpet and an empty jar with a torch inside. He then split the army into three sections of one hundred each. At his command, the soldiers blew their trumpets, broke their jars, held their torches above their heads, and with a mighty roar, cried out in unison. Gideon's masterful planning startled and terrified the Midianites and won a great victory for his people.

Read Judges 6–7 for a complete wrap-up of the victory.

A Curse for the Tyrant

A survivor of a massacre predicts the downfall of a murderous ruler.

THROUGH THE SMOKY HAZE, the woman in the tower kept her eyes on Abimelech below. He and his men had just besieged and captured the city, so all the people of the city had fled into the tower, locked themselves in, and climbed onto the roof. But as Abimelech and his men approached the tall tower in order to storm it, he was stopped dead in his tracks. His servant, inches beside him, could not believe what had just happened. The woman from the tower above had dropped a millstone, a round stone used for grinding grain. The falling stone fell in the right place at the right time. It struck Abimelech directly, crushing his skull.

With his last gasps of breath, Abimelech whispered to his servant to kill him with his sword, so that he would die honorably—not by a woman, but a soldier. Abimelech, king of Israel, ruler of the citizens of Shechem, was dead! "It's Jotham's curse!" one Israelite yelled out when he heard the citizens talking about the horrific and sudden death of Abimelech. All the people of the region had been wondering whether or not Jotham's curse, made three years earlier, would actually come true. Abimelech was their king! Yet, within the course of three days, he had torn apart his nation with battle upon battle. Now he was dead, the victim of a freak incident.

Three years earlier, Jotham had pronounced a curse on his older half brother Abimelech because Abimelech had murdered his sixty-nine half brothers—only Jotham had escaped. Fresh blood was still drying on the rocks of the murder scene, when miles away the citizens of Shechem and Beth-millo gathered to crown Abimelech king!

News of Abimelech's victory over the sons of Gideon had spread throughout Shechem. The people gathered to acknowledge his strength and cleverness. Everyone thought he would be a great king for Israel. No one could match his power. But on that fateful day, a voice rang out from Mount Gerizim. It was Jotham, the last of Gideon's sons. With anger and bitterness, Jotham placed a curse on Abimelech and the citizens of Shechem: "If you have acted honorably and in good faith toward Gideon and his descendants today, then may you find joy in Abimelech, and may he find joy in you. But if you have not acted in good faith, then may fire come out from Abimelech and devour the leading citizens of Shechem and Beth-millo; and may fire come out from the citizens of Shechem and Beth-millo and devour Abimelech!" (Judges 9:19–20).

Three years later, the city was destroyed by fire and Abimelech lay dead. Was this a mere coincidence, or divine justice? Was this a tragic set of unrelated events, or a fulfillment of a curse that was placed on Abimelech's head? The last statement about Abimelech in the book of Judges seems to leave no room for debate. "So the curse of Jotham son of Gideon was fulfilled" (Judges 9:57).

For more information on Jotham's curse and the violent life of Abimelech, read Judges 9.

Jephthah's Vow

Would an Israelite kill his only daughter?

A S THE DOOR of his house opened, Jephthah's face froze in horror. His only daughter was rushing out to greet him, dancing with a tambourine in her hand. At that moment, he realized what a terrible thing he had done—he was going to have to kill his only daughter. Jephthah cried out in anguish, "You have completely destroyed me! You've brought disaster on me! For I have made a vow to the LORD, and I cannot take it back." What kind of vow did he make?

Early that morning, Jephthah, a great warrior and a judge for the Israelites, made a vow to the God of Israel. He was about to lead his army against the Ammonite nation and asked God to give him victory that day. Jephthah promised that he would give God the first thing coming out of his house to greet him when he returned in triumph. He vowed to sacrifice whatever it was as a burnt offering. The God of Israel commanded the Israelites that when a man makes a vow he must not break his word. Consequently, it seems obvious that Jephthah sacrificed his only daughter as a burnt offering to God. But ambiguity remains.

Sacrificing children to pagan gods is part of the ugly record of some ancient religions. In fact, the Ammonites sacrificed their children to the god Molech to appease their vengeful deity. The God of the Israelites, on the other hand, abhorred human sacrifice. He explicitly forbade the practice of human sacrifice in his list of instructions for the Israelite nation (see Leviticus 18:21). In Genesis, God used the concept of human sacrifice to test Abraham. God asked Abraham to sacrifice his only and long-awaited son, Isaac. However, God was testing Abraham's faith and obedience. He stopped Abraham from carrying through with the sacrifice (see Genesis 22).

So why would the God of Israel, a God of love and mercy, accept Jephthah's vow? Did Jephthah really sacrifice his only daughter as a burnt offering? Surprisingly, his daughter's reaction to the vow was not anger or fear. She replied, "Father, if you have made a vow to the LORD, you must do to me what you have vowed, for the LORD has given you a great victory over your enemies, the Ammonites. But first let me do this one thing: Let me go up and roam in the hills and weep with my friends for two months, because I will die a virgin" (Judges 11:36–37).

The Bible says Jephthah did to her as he had vowed. She died a virgin. However, even scholars are divided over whether or not his daughter was sacrificed. The God of Israel could not possibly have honored a vow based on a wicked practice. Perhaps she was set aside as a virgin for the rest of her life, which in essence meant death for the family because there would be no children to carry on Jephthah's name. And why would she leave for two months if the whole point behind the sacrifice was immediate rejoicing and thanksgiving for Jephthah's victory?

For more Jephthah and his daughter, read Judges 11.

Ghost Town

Why was a curse placed on a thriving ancient city?

IN RECENT TIMES, we have seen cities and towns evacuated and leveled because of toxic contamination of the soil. Yet an ancient city was once leveled and abandoned because of its spiritual contamination.

Jericho fell (literally) into Israelite hands when Joshua obeyed the command of the Lord to do his famous seven-day march around the city walls. The walls fell at the blast of trumpets, and the city itself was destroyed. Joshua then promised that anyone who attempted to rebuild the ruins would experience a curse. "At the cost of his firstborn son, he will lay its foundation. At the cost of his youngest son, he will set up its gates" (Joshua 6:26).

Such words did not bother Hiel of Bethel, who, during the debauched reign of King Ahab, attempted to rebuild the great Canaanite city. Yet Joshua's curse struck Hiel's family with deadly accuracy—his firstborn son, Abiram, and youngest son, Segub, died during his reconstruction of the city.

Why would such an unusual curse be applied to a conquered city that had lots of economic potential and was now in Israelite hands? Surely the people could make good use of prime real estate. Why the clench-fisted rule outlawing any development?

Some have suggested that the curse pointed to the irrevocable difference between God's blessing on people who obey him and his judgment against those who do not. Jericho would remain a pile of rocks (though Israelites did populate the immediate region) as a symbol that the God who blesses also curses—fair warning to people who take God for granted.

So if you travel today to the Jordan River basin and walk down from sea level to the place of old Jericho, you'll still see a heap, though now it's an earthen mound, not a rock pile.

To read more about Jericho and its curse, see Joshua 6. For the fate of Hiel's sons, see 1 Kings 16:34.

Samson's
Amazing Strength

What was the secret of his astonishing power?

I F YOU EVER NEEDED an escort, a bodyguard, or a friend to walk with you down a dark alley, Samson was the guy. Possessed of legendary strength, he fought lions barehanded, mangled unsuspecting enemies, and laid to rest a contingent of one thousand troops, using only a donkey's jawbone. His last act of brute force was to pull down a stone temple using the power of his upper torso. Samson was not immortal; the stone that crushed a party of Philistines crushed him to death, too. But no one before or since has matched his raw fury. According to Scripture, the source of that peerless power was God himself.

Men who make a profession of bodybuilding can develop an extensive and well-defined muscle system, but still they seem to be minor leaguers compared to Samson. Certainly he had something inside that was most unusual—perhaps a rare genetic makeup combined with intense willpower and unsurpassed self-confidence. But does that explain his extraordinary feats? Consider, too, that his parents, after an amazing encounter with an angel, had dedicated Samson's life to God's service. They raised him according to the vows of the Nazirite sect, which meant, among other things, that he could not cut his hair.

Samson's physical prowess, though, was not always put to good use. He could be vengeful and impulsive, and his choice of partners ill-advised and naive. His trust in a treacherous woman, Delilah, led to his demise. Something about his uncut hair related directly to his strength; a barber was to Samson as kryptonite to Superman. Samson could not explain it (who can?), but he knew that a haircut would strip his strength. And that's exactly what Delilah arranged. She lured him to his enemies and conspired to have him bound and blinded. He remained a prisoner until he ended his life—and that of hundreds of Philistines—by destroying the temple of Dagon with his own hands.

So the mystery remains. How can one man possess such overwhelming strength? And what's the connection between the protein of a person's hair and the power of his deltoids? In the end, we may conclude with the author of Judges that God gave Samson such incredible strength to use in his service.

To find out more about Samson's adventurous life, read Judges 13–16.

Hemmed In

How could a man cut off a piece of a king's garment unnoticed?

IN A DARK and deserted cave somewhere in the hardscrabble of Israel's wastelands, David and Saul were in the same place at the same time, with only one of them realizing it.

Let's set the stage for this odd encounter. As David's popularity grew after killing Goliath, King Saul's jealousy accelerated until his Royal Highness could no longer hear David's name without flying into a rage. Saul set out with three thousand soldiers to catch David and finish him off. Meanwhile, David, now a hunted fugitive, gathered about four hundred other outcasts around him.

With tensions mounting, David fled to the wilderness and Saul pursued. One day, the hunter came close to his prey but didn't know it. To escape Saul's approaching scouts, David and his men hid in a cave. Then, as luck and physical necessity would have it, Saul rode right up to the mouth of that cave and went inside to go to the bathroom. While he was there, David got close enough to slice off the edging on Saul's royal robe—a sign that David had been close enough to have killed Saul, but didn't do it.

But why didn't David just do away with the tyrant who was making his life so awful? Hadn't the great prophet Samuel already anointed David to be Israel's next king? His men urged him to act decisively. Kill Saul and seize the throne! David refused. He knew that an assassination would set off a cycle of murder and revenge so typical of the godless nations. He also had great respect for Saul's office, if not for the man himself. David believed that God had placed Saul on the throne and that to resist God's will was a serious matter.

After Saul left the cave, David felt awkward and regretful. He knew he could have killed the man who wanted to kill him, and he was glad he chose to restrain himself. But still, he had shamed the king. So while Saul was still within earshot, David called an apology from across the valley, and Saul replied with his own apology. A chance meeting seems to have been the foundation of a tentative truce.

But we still might wonder how these enemies came within inches of each other in the same dark cave in the middle of the En-gedi wilderness. Even more puzzling—why didn't Saul ever notice?

To learn more about this strange meeting, read 1 Samuel 24.

The Prophet's Parable

A moving story brings a haughty king to repentance.

"YOU ARE THAT MAN!" The prophet underscored each of the four words with equal emphasis while pointing his index finger toward the king's chest. David's face blanched with fear as he swallowed hard. His heart pounded. Full of guilt, he fell on his face in abject repentance. It was a strange reaction indeed from a man who just minutes before had pronounced a self-righteous judgment on a fictitious villain.

David's day began like most. The king kissed his wife and new-born son good-bye as he left for the throne room to welcome guests. His secretary informed him that among those he would see that day was a fearless prophet. David had not seen Nathan for a long while, but then again, David had wanted it that way. His conscience had been bothering him since his affair with Bathsheba, a young married woman whose husband, Uriah, had subsequently died. David was not sure how many people knew the sordid details of his adulterous liaison and the cover-up that followed. He hoped Nathan was not among those who had heard the palace gossip.

As Nathan was announced, David was not prepared for the prophet to launch into a story. Nathan proceeded to tell the attentive king about two men. One was wealthy, the other extremely poor. The poor man and his family owned a pet lamb that was loved and treated as a member of the family. He even sat in the father's lap at mealtime to eat scraps from the table. The rich man owned herds of livestock, but when preparing for the visit of an out-of-town guest, he seized the poor man's lamb and slaughtered it for the evening meal.

The king, himself a shepherd, was incensed to hear of this purported injustice. He interrupted Nathan, calling for the wealthy man to be harshly judged. It was at that point that the steely-eyed prophet stared straight at the king and announced, "You are that man!"

At once David's attempt to rationalize his year-old sin collapsed like a house of cards. Nathan's story was no longer a curious tale. It was a parable with the reflective power of a mirror. The woman the king had viewed from his rooftop was indeed the wife of a man less wealthy and influential than he. David had many wives and concubines; Uriah claimed but one companion—his wife, Bathsheba. But David gave in to his lust and seduced Bathsheba. Upon hearing of her being pregnant with his child, David arranged for Uriah to be sent to the front lines of the battle, where he would surely die.

Uriah's death was not the only fatality in this strange episode. After Nathan confronted David, the child conceived in the king's tryst with Bathsheba died as well.

How is it that David could not have seen the parallel in the prophet's story without the tag line at the end? How could David have lived with himself for over a year knowing he had sinned against his God? Adultery was only one offense. Cover-up and first-degree murder were charges that rendered his moral credit overdrawn. Yet David prayed humbly for forgiveness, and his genuine repentance showed why God called him "a man after my own heart" (Acts 13:22).

Explore the issue for yourself in 2 Samuel 11–12. David's prayer of confession and restoration that resulted from his confrontation with Nathan appears as Psalm 51.

The Queen's Visit

Who was the royal visitor so taken with Solomon's power and wisdom?

EARLY IN HIS REIGN, Solomon, son and successor to King David, enjoyed one of the greatest reputations of any person in history: he was wise and charming! So evident was Solomon's wisdom that foreign delegations would travel to investigate the news they had heard on the trade routes and through international gossip columnists. One of those visitors was the mysterious queen of Sheba.

Of her real identity, science and archaeology know very little. She may have come from Yemen, where rule by royal queenships was common. She may have been a sage herself, eager to test her wisdom against Israel's king. To conclude that she was impressed understates the point. The queen was overwhelmed indeed, and Solomon likewise seems to have been delightfully shaken by the queen's aura.

Ethiopian tradition picks up where archaeology leaves off. According to traditional history, the first great king of that part of the world was Menelik I, Solomon's son, born as a result of the queen's state visit. Known as Queen Makeda, this amazing woman returned from her tour of Jerusalem with gifts in kind plus a pregnancy, which would not be so out of line with Solomon's royal privilege, as it turns out (see 1 Kings 11:1). Tradition also reports that Menelik returned to Jerusalem at age twenty-two to learn the Scriptures and to carry the faith back to his own emerging kingdom.

Royal tradition is both hard to prove and often hard to believe. But we do know that a woman of wealth, power, and curiosity once made a long journey to explore for herself the reputation of another young ruler and came away convinced that his dash and daring were more than equal to the rumors she had heard. We just don't know—exactly—who she was!

For more on the queen of Sheba, read 1 Kings 10.

The Prophet's Mistake

Lies and a lion spell doom for a man of God.

THE EVENING was eerily quiet. The setting sun cast unusual shadows on the path to Bethel. The villager wondered about the silence; as she rounded the corner, she stopped dead in her tracks. An intense, cold chill passed through her body. Directly in front of the villager was one of the biggest lions she had ever seen! More horrifying still, the lion was standing over a dead man, side by side with a donkey. The lion had neither devoured the donkey nor mauled the man! Carried away by fear, the villager ran as fast as she could back to town. Her cries were heard throughout Bethel as she recited the details of this bizarre event.

Nearby, an old prophet looked uneasily at his sons and asked them to saddle up his donkey. He was pretty sure he knew this dead stranger—a man of God who had eaten dinner at the old prophet's home that very day. The old prophet went to the spot the villager had told about and saw the lion, the donkey, and the corpse. What had happened?

Earlier that morning, the victim had entered the temple in Bethel. All eyes were on the great King Jeroboam, who was about to make a sacrifice to two golden calves—a profane one, offered to idols on the God of Israel's altar. Startling everyone around, the man of God cried out, condemning Jeroboam for his evil ways: "The LORD has promised to give this sign: This altar will split apart, and its ashes will be poured out on the ground" (1 Kings 13:3). Eyes blazing in self-righteous anger, Jeroboam roared, "Seize that man!"

But as he stretched his hand toward the man, it shriveled up; his fingers curved grotesquely inward, so that he could not pull the hand back. At that moment, the altar split apart and the ashes poured out. Relenting his anger, Jeroboam asked the man of God to intervene so that God would restore his hand. The man prayed for the king, and the king's hand became normal. Visibly relieved, Jeroboam beckoned the prophet to dine with him. But the man of God refused. He said, "Even if you gave me half of everything you own, I would not go with you. I would not eat or drink anything in this place. For the LORD gave me this command: 'You must not eat or drink anything while you are there, and do not return to Judah by the same way you came'" (1 Kings 13:8–10). And so he took another road home.

The sons of an old prophet living in Bethel were present at the temple that day. They ran home and told their father about the amazing feats of this man of God and what he had said to the king. The old prophet, perhaps skeptical of the younger men's integrity, saddled up his donkey and rode off to find him. Exhausted from lack of food and water, the man of God was resting under a tree. The old prophet said, "Come home with me and eat some food." But the man of God refused, repeating what he had told the king. So the old prophet replied, "I am a prophet, too." And then he lied. "An angel gave me this command from the LORD: 'Bring him home with you so he can have something to eat and drink.'" Convinced, the man of God went with him.

While they were sitting at the table, the old prophet cried out, "You have defied the word of the LORD and have disobeyed the command the LORD your God gave you. You came back to this place and ate and drank where he told you not to eat or drink. Because of this, your body will not be buried in the grave of your ancestors."

Soon after the man of God departed, a lion sprang on him on the road and killed him. But why? One explanation may be that the man did not take seriously the warning he had received and was too easily convinced of the old prophet's story. His lack of discernment became his downfall.

The old prophet later took the man of God's lifeless body and placed it in his own tomb. Showing his affection for the fallen prophet, he told his sons that at his death he wanted to be buried next to the man of God. *For more details of this puzzling death, read 1 Kings 13.*

ABUSED PROPHETS

Battered, beaten, and beheaded, being a messenger for God was no easy task, especially when your message was an unwelcome one. Here is what some of God's spokespersons endured.

SPOKESPERSON AND ABUSE	REFERENCE
Queen Jezebel wanted to kill all of God's prophets. One hundred of them hid in two caves.	1 Kings 18:3–4
After winning his contest with the evil prophets and destroying them, the prophet Elijah fled for his life from Queen Jezebel, who threatened to kill him.	1 Kings 19:1–3
The prophet Micaiah was slapped, arrested, put in jail, and fed only enough bread and water to keep him alive after he gave evil King Ahab unwanted news.	1 Kings 22:10–28; 2 Chronicles 18:12–27
The prophet Elisha was teased for having a bald head.	2 Kings 2:23–24
Hanani was jailed for rebuking King Asa's sin.	2 Chronicles 16:7–10
The prophet Zechariah was executed in the court of the temple after confronting the people of Judah for ignoring God.	2 Chronicles 24:20–22

Spokesperson and Abuse	Reference
The prophet Uriah was hacked to death with a sword and buried in an unmarked grave for speaking out against Judah's sin.	Jeremiah 26:20–23
The prophet Jeremiah was jailed and then thrown into a muddy hole in the ground for predicting the fall of Jerusalem.	Jeremiah 37:1–38:13
John the Baptist was beheaded after Herodias's daughter requested his head on a tray.	Matthew 14:6–12

Fire from the Sky

A bold prophet triumphs over a pagan cult.

THE LIFELESS BODIES of pagan priests were randomly piled at the base of Israel's famed Mount Carmel. A day of challenge was now complete. Baal's prophets had lost. A solitary prophet of God by the name of Elijah had been vindicated. But how had it happened? Only hours before on top of the mountain, thousands had gathered at the king's invitation to witness the duel of the century: Elijah against 450 prophets of Baal.

Elijah's challenge was simple. An offering would be presented to each deity—to Baal and then to the God of Israel. There was only one catch: flint starters and torches were prohibited. The fire to consume the sacrifice had to come from the respective deities. The scenario seemed impossible. Yet each side agreed to the terms of the challenge.

As the people gathered, there was excitement in the air. But watching the Baal prophets spend hour after hour imploring and pleading with Baal soon grew old. No matter how carefully they recited their ritual, no matter how passionately they shouted, no matter how fiercely they slashed themselves, nothing happened. Nothing. The sun passed high over their heads, and nothing happened. The only thrill of the entire afternoon was Elijah's loud taunt, "You'll have to shout louder." The afternoon sun began to fade on the horizon; still, nothing happened. The exhausted and embarrassed challengers gave up one by one.

It was Elijah's turn. His simple stone altar sat ready. At Elijah's command, the butchered animal was drenched with cool, sparkling water. After the entire altar was thoroughly soaked, Elijah called out to Israel's God. Suddenly, a deafening roar filled the air. Red-hot fire rained down from heaven. The sacrifice, the stone altar, and the ground around it were consumed in one breathtaking instant. All that was left was a blackened heap. The wide-eyed spectators stared at it in amazement.

What happened on that day? Was this a case of spontaneous combustion? Not likely. There would have been little chance that waterlogged lumber would spontaneously burst into flames. Could it have been a lightning strike? Lightning would surely have caused a fire, but it wouldn't have consumed the very stones of the altar. Moreover, there wasn't a cloud in the sky. The land had been suffering a drought for months.

The spectators of the incident were certainly convinced that only God could produce such a fiery feat.

To learn more about this spectacular event for yourself, read 1 Kings 18.

Elijah,
World-Class Runner

How did a prophet outrun a team of horses?

WHO CAN RUN faster than horses over a distance of seventeen miles after a hot day's work outside? This man's name connotes the image of a grizzled, tough-minded, sandpaper-voiced giant who tolerates no compromise with the truth. Indeed, of all the ancient prophets, Elijah faced the hardest challenges and addressed the most recalcitrant political leaders. One of those leaders was Ahab, supported and abetted (some might say controlled) by his cunning wife Jezebel.

At a showdown at Mount Carmel, Elijah challenged 450 pagan priests, Ahab's religious army, to call down fire on the carcass of a slain bull. The priests chanted and prayed, literally whipped themselves, and danced into a frenzy, but no cosmic fire appeared. Then Elijah prayed, but to make the occasion even more dramatic, he first doused the carcass with water. God answered the faithful prophet's prayer, and fire shot from heaven consuming the carcass and the wet altar it rested on. None of the priests survived the incident either.

Distressed beyond words, Ahab raced to his chariot and sped toward Jezreel, seventeen miles away. Not only were his priests gone, but a huge rainstorm was about to end the drought of the century and, of more immediate concern, bog down the wheels of his carriage in the same kind of mud that later stopped Hitler's army in Russia. Everyone was speeding home, in fact, except Elijah, who was left without a ride.

But wait. From his chariot Ahab could see the prophet up ahead, and on foot. Running. Racing. Striding. Galloping. What's this? Elijah would arrive at Jezreel before Ahab's speeding horses, and Jezebel would hear the bad news from him!

Athletic feats of strength and endurance always provoke our awe and wonder; for sometimes, it seems, mere people can outperform even our grandest human expectations. The limitations we place on human performance are broken to our amazement. People thought no one could ever run a four-minute mile—but some runners have!

Whatever powered Elijah that day came from the same energy source that ignited the burning altar. In both cases, it should not have happened. In both cases, it did.

To read more about Elijah's run, see 1 Kings 18.

The Flying Prophet

How did Elijah enter heaven?

L ONG BEFORE anyone imagined planes leaving the ground, a man was reported flying into heaven. Was this an alien abduction? Did Elijah know the physics of air travel thousands of years ago?

Here are the facts: When Elijah, one of the most famous of Israel's prophets, was nearing the end of his life, he gave his tattered old cloak to his follower and friend Elisha and said his goodbyes.

On a warm day sometime around 848 B.C., the prophet Elijah tested his understudy by suggesting that the younger prophet stay behind as Elijah headed to Bethel in accord with the Lord's instructions. But Elisha insisted on staying with Elijah. He knew something extraordinary was going to happen. But he did not know what.

Then Elijah turned to go. He dipped his cloak into the Jordan River, separating the waters. They crossed together. They shared a few words. Elisha, perhaps a bit nervous, waited for the sign of what was coming.

What came was a chariot of fire descending from the sky. In a rush of fierce, hot wind and a sharp thunderclap, the blinding chariot swooped Elijah up and away. With his cloak over his mouth and his hands shading his eyes, Elisha strained to keep his teacher in sight. But in seconds the scene was calm again—high clouds, blue sky, and hot summer sunshine, just like any other day.

What happened to Elijah? How could he have ascended into the heavens without the aid of modern aircraft? We know that air has weight and that the force called gravity causes objects heavier than air to stick close to earth. We also know that with proper fuel and propulsion, heavier-than-air objects like jumbo aircraft can defy gravity as long as the fuel keeps burning and the jet fans keep spinning. Did Elijah know something about aerodynamics that other people of his day could only dream about?

We can only guess at the physics explaining Elijah's unusual flight. The chariotlike object was obviously not bound by gravity's laws. Propelled by some force unknown at the time, it took Elijah into heaven. That is remarkable engineering. Not only did this open chariot travel at lightning speed, but the chariot traveled in a certain direction guided by some unseen intelligent force.

Elisha named that unseen force the God of Israel. God himself had gathered up the righteous prophet Elijah to his heavenly home. Elisha's response was to praise God. He went home a different man—a man empowered by God to continue in Elijah's footsteps as a prophet for God with power to accomplish extraordinary acts.

For more on Elijah's amazing ride, read 2 Kings 2.

The Queen of Heaven

What caused the prophet Jeremiah to denounce this goddess?

WHO WAS the Queen of Heaven? Sometimes she was called Ishtar, a goddess of love and fertility and identified in mythology with Venus, the brightest light in the heavens. Faithful worshipers hoped prayers to the queen would secure material welfare. Some of their prayers may have implored the goddess to help them with love and romantic interests.

Although the Bible deplores the cult that surrounded this goddess, we really know little about it. This much we know: the Queen of Heaven was widely revered in many Near Eastern societies. (Some scholars feel that the worship of Ishtar prefigures the cult of the goddess of Ephesus, Diana, which Paul encountered.) The cult had apparently flourished in Judah during the time of the prophet Jeremiah, a person who was clearly interested in neither finance nor romance.

People of all times have invented deities to meet their basic needs. Ancient people worried a lot about food, so their gods addressed those conditions beyond human control like rain, sun, pests, and sickness. Successful childbearing was crucial to the survival of any tribe; hence, fertility gods and goddesses were fashioned as a way of coping with those needs. In many cultures, syncretism—the mixing of religious traditions—became a common practice as conquered and conqueror shared belief systems. But such practices were forbidden to Israel, which from the time of Moses had been instructed to "not make for yourself an idol of any kind or an image

of anything in the heavens or on the earth or in the sea . . . for I, the
LORD your God, am a jealous God" (Exodus 20:4–5).

The worship of the Queen of Heaven symbolized the falling
darkness that would soon cover Judah. While the cult thrived, the
nation was slipping into slavery at the hands of more powerful
neighbors—first Egypt, then Babylon. When Jeremiah wrote his
message, the end was near. King Jehoiakim rebelled against Babylon and, for a time, managed to keep the enemy at bay. His successor, Zedekiah, would not be as fortunate. During his reign,
Nebuchadnezzar conquered and pillaged Jerusalem, and most of its
people were sent into exile. According to Jeremiah, the worship of
this mysterious goddess contributed directly to the invasion of Israel
by the ferocious and bloodthirsty Babylonians.

*For a glimpse of the worship of the Queen of Heaven, see Jeremiah 7:18; 44:17–19,
25.*

Babylon,
Then and Now

What happened to the great international hub of world power and commerce?

FEW ANCIENT CITIES have shared such a blackened reputation or been associated with so much corruption and evil as Babylon. It was one of the greatest cities of the ancient world, the capital of Mesopotamia, southwest of modern Baghdad, but it became a symbol of satanic deception and worldly power.

Babylon's origin will likely remain a mystery. The Bible mentions that Nimrod built a kingdom in the land of Babylonia (Genesis 10:8–10), and that same plain is the traditional location for the Tower of Babel (Genesis 11:1–9). Its rise to power begins to appear in recorded history around the time of the great Hammurabi, best-known king of the Third Dynasty of ancient Ur. The Hittites occupied it next, then the Assyrians. The brutal Assyrian king Sennacherib destroyed the city in 689 B.C., but his obstinate son rebuilt it. It begins to figure prominently in Bible history around the time of Nebuchadnezzar (605–562 B.C.) and later during the rule of the Persian king Cyrus.

Babylon's greatness began to wane after Nebuchadnezzar's death. After a series of ineffective kings, Babylon was occupied by the Medes and Persians. Decades later, Alexander the Great built Seleucia nearby, and the city slipped into obscurity. By A.D. 200, Babylon was largely a ghost town.

So what is Babylon today?

Once the seat of wealth and lavish splendor, Babylon is now a mound of dirt, a place where archaeologists gather to salvage what they can, given the region's high water table. It is a ruin, a tel, or a pile of junk, depending on your professional point of view. But its meaning in the Bible continues to tell the sad story of this city's relentless wickedness: when the New Testament writers try to describe the despicable mess the world will find itself in just before the return of Jesus Christ, they use the name "Babylon"—a city of corruption, treachery, and murder—as an example.

For more on Babylon, read Jeremiah 25, the book of Daniel, and Revelation 18.

DID YOU KNOW?

What is the strange land whose identity still eludes scholars and laypeople alike?

In the book of Genesis (see 10:2), the land of Magog is grouped with Meshech and Tubal, regions near present-day Turkey. Magog looms large in the prophetic visions of both Ezekiel and John, but the exact location of Magog remains shrouded in mystery. Ezekiel seems to use the names Gog and Magog as a metaphor for vast armies who will invade Israel from the north in the end-times (see Ezekiel 38:8). They are bloodthirsty enemies of God (see Ezekiel 38:14–23). These geographic references led a number of popular authors and speakers during the Cold War to equate Gog and Magog with the Soviet Union. The book of Revelation, while less specific than Ezekiel, uses Gog and Magog to describe people deceived by Satan who willingly do his bidding (see Revelation 20:8).

The Fourth Man

*What mysterious figure joined three condemned prisoners in
a blazing furnace?*

SOARING FLAMES licked the air surrounding the furnace, awaiting three prisoners destined for an agonizing death. The king,
already enraged by the insolence of the men, had commanded it.
Despite the fact that the furnace was already hot enough to kill any
living thing put inside, King Nebuchadnezzar ordered that the furnace be heated seven times hotter than usual. Then he ordered his
strongest soldiers to tie up Shadrach, Meshach, and Abednego, the
three men standing before him. Bound in heavy rope, they were
pushed toward the inferno.

The furnace was so blazing hot that the flames incinerated the
soldiers who had thrown the three in. Then King Nebuchadnezzar
was on his feet! Frantically he asked his advisers, "Didn't we tie up
three men and throw them into the furnace? . . . I see four men,
unbound, walking around in the fire unharmed! And the fourth
looks like a god!" (Daniel 3:24–25). All of his advisers, shocked with
amazement, stared into the fire. Sure enough, not only were the
three men walking around in the furnace, but there was a fourth
man with them.

Earlier that day, King Nebuchadnezzar had commanded thousands of people to gather in Babylon for the dedication of the
golden image. Ninety feet high and nine feet wide, the gigantic idol
towered over the people. King Nebuchadnezzar commanded all the
peoples and nations of every language to fall down and worship the

image of gold. Whoever did not fall down and worship would immediately be thrown into the furnace. Everyone worshiped the idol, except for three men who remained standing amidst the thousands of people gathered in that plain. These three men—Shadrach, Meshach, and Abednego—were Jews whom Nebuchadnezzar had recently appointed as administrators over the entire province of Babylon.

Angry and taken aback, Nebuchadnezzar thought their refusal was simply a misunderstanding. He gave the men a second chance to change their ways, but still they refused. They accepted the likely punishment of death gracefully and added, "If we are thrown into the blazing furnace, the God whom we serve is able to save us. He will rescue us from your power, Your Majesty. But even if he doesn't, we want to make it clear to you, Your Majesty, that we will never serve your gods or worship the gold statue you have set up" (Daniel 3:17–18). And so Nebuchadnezzar hurled the renegades into the furnace. Yet they not only survived, they escaped unharmed. When Nebuchadnezzar saw all this and witnessed the fourth man walking in the furnace with the other three, he ordered everyone to worship the God of Shadrach, Meshach, and Abednego.

Yet the question remains: who was the fourth man? Some Bible scholars say he was probably an angel sent to protect Shadrach, Meshach, and Abednego. Other Bible scholars say he might have been a human manifestation of God himself. In any case, Shadrach, Meshach, and Abednego became lifelong witnesses to the power of the God of Israel.

For more information, read Daniel 3.

GREAT ESCAPES

The Bible is full of stories of people who were rescued or who escaped from dangerous circumstances in the nick of time. How did they do it?

ESCAPEES	REFERENCE
Noah and his family escaped the flood that destroyed the entire earth because they were on a giant boat.	Genesis 6:1–8:22
Thanks to a warning from a couple of angels, Lot's family escaped Sodom just before the entire city was destroyed.	Genesis 19:1–29
Isaac narrowly escaped death when an angel stopped his father from offering him as a human sacrifice.	Genesis 22:1–19
Joseph escaped death when his brothers decided to sell him as a slave rather than kill him.	Genesis 37:12–36
Joseph's family escaped a great famine when Joseph provided a home and food for them in Egypt.	Genesis 42–47
Moses escaped the Egyptian death sentence for all Hebrew baby boys when his mother put him in a basket and sent him down the Nile River.	Exodus 1:1–2:10
The Israelites escaped the pursuing Egyptian army when the Lord miraculously parted the Red Sea for his people.	Exodus 13:17–14:31
Balaam escaped execution at the hands of an angel because of the quick thinking of his donkey.	Numbers 22:21–38
David got away from King Saul's men by having his wife pretend he was sick in bed while he was really on the run.	1 Samuel 19:11–18
King Saul escaped death at the hands of David when David chose merely to cut off a piece of the king's robe.	1 Samuel 24:1–22

ESCAPEES	REFERENCE
Four hundred Amalekite young men escaped on camels when David and his men came to destroy their land.	1 Samuel 30:1–31
Haman's plot to kill Mordecai backfired when the king discovered that Mordecai had earlier prevented his assassination.	Esther 2–7
Shadrach, Meshach, and Abednego escaped death in a fiery furnace because the Lord protected them from the flames.	Daniel 3:1–30
Daniel escaped from a den of lions unharmed because God closed the lions' mouths.	Daniel 6:1–28
Jonah escaped from the belly of a fish when God caused the fish to vomit Jonah onto the shore.	Jonah 1:1–2:10
Jesus miraculously escaped from a crowd that was planning to kill him by simply walking right through the crowd.	Luke 4:14–30
The apostles escaped from jail when an angel of the Lord opened the doors to the cell in the middle of the night.	Acts 5:17–32
Paul escaped the city of Damascus by being put in a large basket and let down through an opening in the city wall.	Acts 9:21–25
An angel helped the apostle Peter escape from a prison cell in which he was chained to two guards.	Acts 12:1–19
The apostle Paul escaped an attempt on his life when his nephew learned of the plot to kill the apostle.	Acts 23:12–35

How the Mighty
Have Fallen

What accounts for the mental breakdown of King Nebuchadnezzar?

H E ROAMED aimlessly through the fields, sleeping under the stars. He ate grass like a cow, and his hair grew as long as eagles' feathers, and his nails as long as birds' claws. What would cause a man to resort to such actions?

One brilliant day, the powerful and mighty King Nebuchadnezzar stood on the roof of his expansive palace and surveyed his empire—his beautiful gardens, his magnificent temples, his luxurious palaces. His heart swelled with pride. This was the kingdom he built; this was the city he had constructed. It was the crown of his life, full of his great achievements.

As he strolled on the palace roof, a prediction that had been pronounced by a Jewish advisor a year earlier came to pass. His sanity escaped him; his mind became confused. Nebuchadnezzar went stark raving mad, rushing to and fro. His lifestyle quickly deteriorated. Instead of eating the best food and drinking the best wine of the empire, Nebuchadnezzar began gobbling down whatever he could get his hands on. He began living like an animal, even eating grass. His own servants couldn't stand to wait on him or take care of him—he was uncontrollable. And eventually Nebuchadnezzar, the great king of Babylon, was driven from his own people to live in the fields, just as a common beast. No one took care of him. No one trimmed his hair or even his fingernails. He had gone completely insane.

What was the cause of his sudden calamity? Why such a complete reversal of fortunes? The entire kingdom of Babylon marveled at their king who was now wallowing in the fields. But a quiet Jew named Daniel knew the cause of the king's sudden bout of insanity.

A year earlier, the king had been troubled by a very disturbing dream about an enormous tree. The tree was so large that all creatures found shelter beneath it; its fruit was so abundant that all creatures were fed by it. Suddenly an angel appeared in the dream and ordered that the tree be cut down and its branches and fruit stripped. The angel then announced that an unidentified person would live like an animal for seven years.

The dream unsettled Nebuchadnezzar. He called for his advisors, including the quiet and pensive Daniel. The meaning of the dream became clear to Daniel. Both the tree and the unidentified "him" the angel referred to were Nebuchadnezzar himself. Like the tree, the king had become great and powerful. His kingdom encompassed most of the known world. Yet because the king refused to acknowledge the divine source of his power, Nebuchadnezzar would be "cut down to size." His kingdom would be taken away from him for seven years. During that time, the great King Nebuchadnezzar would become like an animal, eating grass and living in the fields. A year later, Daniel's prediction came true with startling accuracy.

But Nebuchadnezzar's disturbance had a happy ending. Eventually, he came to realize the cause of his madness and humbled himself before God. As his sanity returned, the king reassumed his responsibilities. He offered a prayer of thanks to God, whom he acknowledged as "the King of heaven" whose "rule is everlasting, and his kingdom is eternal."

For more information on Nebuchadnezzar's bout with insanity and his eventual recovery, read Daniel 4.

The Handwriting
on the Wall

Mysterious fingers spell doom for a Babylonian king.

A HUMAN HAND suddenly appeared from nowhere! The eerie fingers started writing on the palace wall, and the king was paralyzed with fear. He turned pale as a ghost, his knees knocked together, and his legs became like rubber and gave way beneath him.

King Belshazzar and his royal guests stared in disbelief. He couldn't understand the strange words, but the powerful king of ancient Babylon shuddered with a sense of impending doom.

Earlier that evening, those same walls rang with riotous laughter and music as King Belshazzar hosted a great feast for a thousand nobles, his court, and his family. As the party got louder and the wine flowed more freely, he ordered his servants to bring in the gold and silver cups that his predecessor, King Nebuchadnezzar, had taken from the temple in Jerusalem. Filled with wine and a sense of his own importance, King Belshazzar led his guests as they filled the cups with wine and drank toasts from them while they praised their idols of bronze, iron, wood, and stone.

But the party came to an abrupt halt when a hand appeared and wrote these puzzling words on the wall: MENE, MENE, TEKEL, PARSIN. The king called for his fortune-tellers and astrologers, but none of them could explain the strange words or the mysterious hand that wrote them. They were as mystified as everyone else.

Then someone remembered a young man named Daniel, who was known for his ability to interpret dreams and visions. King Belshazzar had Daniel brought in and asked him to interpret the writing on the palace wall. Daniel agreed and told the king the meaning of the words.

Where did the hand come from? What did the words mean, and who caused them to be written on the wall? Was the king's death that very evening connected in any way to the handwriting, or to his drinking wine from the cups from the temple?

Of course, everyone had an opinion about what happened. Most people thought the hand wasn't real but was just blurred vision and an overactive imagination caused from drinking too much wine. As for King Belshazzar's death that same night? Well, that was just a coincidence, they said. Just bad luck! But was it?

Daniel's own explanation was just as amazing: because the king had defiled the sacred cups and had praised the idols, the hand brought a message of judgment from God.

Daniel told the king, "*Mene* means 'numbered'—God has numbered the days of your reign and has brought it to an end. *Tekel* means 'weighed'—you have been weighed on the balances and have not measured up. *Parsin* means 'divided'—your kingdom has been divided and given to the Medes and Persians." With those words, Daniel predicted the downfall of Belshazzar. Later that same night, King Belshazzar was assassinated and Darius the Mede occupied the once mighty city of Babylon.

For more on the handwriting on the wall and King Belshazzar's untimely death, read Daniel 5.

Dinner Bell at the Lion Pit

How did a prophet withstand the appetites of wild beasts?

ONE OF THE WORLD'S most famous restaurants is the Carnivore in Nairobi, Kenya. There, patrons enjoy an unusual buffet of zebra, python, wildebeest, warthog, goat, and gazelle. But the most coveted dish is lion. Perhaps because a hungry lion is indeed "king of the jungle," the offer of lion on a menu seems like such an odd reversal of nature: the man-eater grilled to order.

Daniel, under the rule of Darius the Mede, conqueror of Babylon, was himself served up to lions in a cruel reversal of the Carnivore's cuisine. Laws at the time forbade prayers to anyone but Darius himself. For praying to God, Daniel was to be food for hungry beasts in the king's special execution pits.

Whether Daniel was afraid, worried, nervous, or upset, we don't know. However, we do know that Daniel was a determined man. He wouldn't bow to just any wish—even if it came from the emperor himself. Daniel kept praying to the God of Israel, the God he believed in. He stood up for his convictions and would not redirect his prayers to a person he knew was as mortal as he.

So Daniel was sentenced to the lion pit, and the sentence was carried out. But the lions did not disturb Daniel. Although he sat right beside them, they didn't touch him. The lions' dinner, Daniel himself, walked out of the pit the next morning, alive and well. Why would lions suddenly go on a hunger strike?

Lions eat only when hungry, not for recreation. Perhaps Daniel was fortunate to arrive during one of their siestas when they were not hungry. But the whole point of having a bunch of lions caged up was to keep them hungry. The ancients would typically starve lions so they could watch the ferocious lions tear up the ones convicted.

The fact that these lions were hungry is proven by how they savagely tore apart Daniel's false accusers. These were hungry lions.

Then what kept these lions from devouring Daniel? Daniel himself explained to the mystified king, "My God sent his angel to shut the lions' mouths so that they would not hurt me, for I have been found innocent in his sight" (Daniel 6:22).

Daniel lived for quite a few more years and never stopped praying to his God.

For more on Daniel among the lions, read Daniel 6.

UNDER THE INFLUENCE

Fermented beverages have contributed to bizarre behavior for centuries. From the first days of Bible history, humans have paid the price for imbibing too much. Here are some of the more notable episodes of public intoxication—with the tragic results.

IMBIBER	SITUATION	CONSEQUENCES	REFERENCE
Noah	He got drunk on the wine from his vineyard.	He foolishly cursed his son for uncovering his nakedness.	Genesis 9:20–23
Lot	Desperate to preserve their family line, his daughters got him drunk and then slept with him to get pregnant.	The sons these women bore became the ancestors of Israel's great enemies Moab and Ammon.	Genesis 19:30–38

IMBIBER	SITUATION	CONSEQUENCES	REFERENCE
Nabal	He had a stroke the morning after a night of drinking and died ten days later.	His opposition to King David and selfish living sealed his fate.	1 Samuel 25:1–38
Uriah	Though drunk, he refused to go home and sleep with his wife while his men were in battle.	Uriah had more honor than the king he served. Dismayed that Uriah acted so honorably (and thus didn't allow David to cover up his adultery with Bathsheba), David had Joab assign Uriah to the fiercest part of the battle, where Uriah was killed.	2 Samuel 11:1–27
Amnon	While drunk, he was killed by Absalom's men in retaliation for his rape of Tamar.	Amnon's careless life and heartless treatment of his half sister sowed the seeds of his disaster.	2 Samuel 13:1–39
Elah	This king of Israel was assassinated while he was drunk.	His death fulfilled a prophecy spoken by Jehu.	1 Kings 16:8–10
Ben-hadad	This king chose to get drunk even though hostilities with Israel were about to break out.	Ill-prepared for Ahab's attack, the Aramean army suffered heavy losses and fled.	1 Kings 20:1–22

Imbiber	Situation	Consequences	Reference
Xerxes	During a drunken party, this king ordered his wife Vashti to appear before the guests.	Vashti refused and was banished from the palace, setting the stage for Esther's rise.	Esther 1:1–22
Belshazzar	While drunk, this king used vessels from the temple in Jerusalem as wine cups.	Belshazzar's disrespect for the holy vessels of the temple led to his downfall.	Daniel 5:1–31

Mountaintop Encounter

Who stood with Jesus during the Transfiguration?

HAVE YOU EVER seen an apparition appear spontaneously in a halo of white light? Peter, James, and John saw what they could only suppose were ghosts, right before their eyes.

As the sun blazed down on them, Peter, James, and John followed Jesus up the rugged path to the very top of a mountain. From such heights, they could look far below on the few shepherds who gathered the flocks together in the barren valley. Jesus had come to this distant place to be alone with these three closest friends. He withdrew to a solitary rock to concentrate in prayer. The disciples, exhausted from the trip, fell down to rest.

Within seconds, Jesus' appearance seemed to get brighter and brighter. Soon, Jesus was dazzling white. His face was glowing; his appearance had completely changed. Suddenly two bright beings, as dazzling white as Jesus, appeared next to him. They were humans—but in some different, brilliant form. They conversed with Jesus for a while. And then a brilliant cloud shone over the entire mountaintop. From the cloud, a voice thundered, "This is my dearly loved Son. Listen to him." Then in an instant, the apparitions disappeared just as quickly as they had appeared. Jesus was left as he had been before—in a white but dusty robe.

Are ghosts for real? Do people from the past live in a different

Strange but True

dimension and return to earth for special visits, as in ghost stories?

At least in the case of these beings—identified as Elijah and Moses—it appears they do. This was no video replay in ancient times; the disciples witnessed this incident on an ordinary day about two thousand years ago. Such a phenomenon was not that much of a surprise to the disciples for they believed in a spiritual life that extends beyond physical death. That heavenly life which Moses and Elijah exhibited most certainly takes on a different form than the three-dimensional one we are accustomed to. Yet the similarities are striking. They looked like human beings to the stunned disciples. But the differences are even more striking. The disciples could not begin to understand or even describe the mechanics of life in other dimensions. It was beyond their comprehension, just as it is beyond ours. Peter, James, and John could only describe those heavenly life forms as wonderful. Even those words are too small to describe the event.

Do people from the past visit this earth often as Moses and Elijah did on that day? Scripture appears to indicate that this was a special manifestation of heavenly glories for the disciples' benefit. Yet the author of Hebrews reminds us that we sometimes entertain angels without recognizing them (see Hebrews 13:2). The mysterious apparitions on the mountaintop prove an interesting fact—life of another quality, pure and bright, in heaven forever.

To read about the disciples' encounter with heavenly beings, turn to Matthew 17, Mark 9, Luke 9.

The Shadows of the Crucifixion

What explains the phenomena that surrounded Jesus' death?

THE SKY was ominously dark. The radical rabbi from Nazareth hung from a Roman crossbeam between two common criminals. A crowd of the curious and a handful of Jesus' closest friends watched from a distance. As the controversial teacher slowly died, people in various parts of Jerusalem went about their pre-Sabbath rituals trying to make sense of what appeared to be a chain of seemingly unrelated circumstances.

From noon to three o'clock that dreadful Friday, the sky was indeed ominously dark. At first it was thought to be a total eclipse of the sun. But when it continued longer than an hour, other explanations were sought. At about three o'clock that afternoon, a light earthquake rumbled beneath the ground. Some of the more insecure buildings in Jerusalem and the surrounding villages toppled. Panicked children ran from their places of play to the safety of their parents. The priests who were gathered at the temple for afternoon prayers could be heard screaming. The thick woven veil that hung from the pillared heights of the temple and separated the Holy Place from the Most Holy Place ripped in two. What was especially curious was the fact that the veil tore from top to bottom.

Reports began to circulate around the city that a number of tombstones had rolled away from the entrances of above-ground burial caves. Individuals who had been long dead and buried were seen walking around the streets of Jerusalem. Something strange was going on. But no one could explain the cause of all the commotion.

Wouldn't it be realistic to think that the earthquake was the common thread of all the unusual activity that was being reported? The dark sky was probably some meteorological portent of the collision of intercontinental plates under the ground. And the earthquake could have caused the temple veil to tear. An earthquake would have the power to unseal gravestones. And the fear engendered by such a turbulent event would cause people to act hysterically and think they were seeing people they really weren't—like dead people walking.

But what if the events didn't hinge on an earthquake? What if the earthquake was simply a consequence of some greater cataclysmic occurrence? What if all the strange happenings of this unforgettable Friday were connected to the public execution going on outside the city limits? A centurion who stood at the base of the cross on which the rabbi Jesus hung wouldn't have been surprised if that were the case. He couldn't help but wonder about the person he stood watching. This was no ordinary criminal on this cross, and he knew it. And this was no ordinary afternoon.

But what if the seemingly insignificant rabbi was not insignificant? What if he was who he claimed to be? If, in fact, he was the Son of God, would not his death result in some supernatural consequence?

Draw your own conclusions about what happened that day. Read Matthew 27–28, Mark 15–16, Luke 22–24, John 19–20.

WEIRD WEATHER

Thunder, lightning, rushing wind—God used all of these signs to show his power to the world. Here is a summary of a few extraordinary weather events and a theological explanation of why they happened.

WEATHER OR ATMOSPHERIC CONDITION	WHAT HAPPENED	REFERENCE
Torrential rain	God sent torrential rain for forty days and forty nights, blotting out all life and covering the earth with water for 150 days. Only Noah and his family survived.	Genesis 7:10–24
Rainbow	God set a rainbow in the clouds for the first time to promise that he would never again destroy the earth with a flood.	Genesis 9:12–17
Hail, darkness	God visited plagues upon Egypt.	Exodus 9:13–35; 10:21–29
Wind	After the Lord miraculously parted the Red Sea, a strong wind blew all night to dry the sea floor so Moses and the people could cross on dry ground.	Exodus 14:21–22
Strange dew	In Israel's camp, dew covered the ground in the morning. When it dried, it turned into white flakes that tasted like honey bread. The people of Israel ate this food, called manna, for forty years!	Exodus 16:13–35
Raining quail	The Lord caused a huge wind that picked up thousands of quail from the sea and dropped them into the camp where Moses and the people were staying.	Numbers 11:31–33

WEATHER OR ATMOSPHERIC CONDITION	WHAT HAPPENED	REFERENCE
Earthquake	The earth split in two and swallowed up 250 people who were rebelling against God. They fell into the hole alive and the earth closed back over them.	Numbers 16:31–34
Hail	As the enemy was fleeing during one of Joshua's battles, God caused a hailstorm. The falling hailstones killed more men than had been killed in the entire battle.	Joshua 10:11
Fixed sun	Because of Joshua's prayer, the sun stood still in the sky, allowing Joshua to completely destroy a pagan army.	Joshua 10:12–14
Strange-shaped cloud	The prophet Elijah's servant saw a cloud about the size of a man's hand rising from the sea. A torrential rainstorm followed.	1 Kings 18:41–45
Mighty windstorm, earthquake, fire	God spoke to Elijah—not in these awesome events, but in a gentle whisper	1 Kings 19:11–12
Destructive wind	A powerful wind from the wilderness collapsed the roof of a house, killing all of Job's children.	Job 1:18–19
Whirlwind	God talked to Job from inside a great whirlwind.	Job 38:1
Bright star	A star guided the wise men thousands of miles to the place where Jesus was born in Bethlehem.	Matthew 2:2

WEATHER OR ATMOSPHERIC CONDITION	WHAT HAPPENED	REFERENCE
Terrible storm	High waves and a strong windstorm rocked the disciples' boat, making them afraid for their lives. But when Jesus rebuked the storm, it stopped and all was calm.	Matthew 8:23–27
Earthquake	The moment Jesus died on the cross, the whole earth was covered in darkness for three hours. A powerful earthquake rocked Jerusalem, and the curtain in the temple was split from top to bottom. Graves also opened.	Matthew 27:45–53
Earthquake	A massive earthquake caused a prison's doors to fly wide open and prisoners' chains to fall off, including those of Paul and Silas.	Acts 16:25–27

The Mysterious Death of Judas Iscariot

How did Jesus' betrayer end his days?

THE NAME JUDAS ISCARIOT will forever be linked with treachery and betrayal. Like Benedict Arnold's, Judas Iscariot's selfish deed earns him a place with the most notorious turncoats who ever lived. But the circumstances of his death have always puzzled scholars. The gospel of Matthew stipulates that Judas hanged himself (Matthew 27:5), but the book of Acts suggests that he plunged to his death (Acts 1:18). Which is correct?

Jesus himself chose Judas to be one of his twelve disciples, the close circle of men who traveled with Jesus and were taught by him. Yet his three years seeing the miracles and ministry of Jesus did little to change his heart. Apparently Jesus recognized this at one point, telling his disciples that one of them was "a devil" (John 6:70). The Bible does not suggest why Judas wanted to betray Jesus, saying only that "Satan entered into" him (Luke 22:3). Whatever the reason, Judas conspired with the religious leaders who were looking for allies in their plot against Jesus. In exchange for thirty pieces of silver, Judas agreed to lure Jesus to a place where the authorities could easily arrest him.

After Jesus was bound and sentenced to death, Judas seems to have had an attack of conscience. He returned the money to the chief priests and elders and said, "I have sinned . . . for I have betrayed an innocent man" (Matthew 27:4). The religious leaders were unmoved. Having achieved their goal, they had no concern that Judas was remorseful. In a final act of frustration, Judas threw the money into the temple and left.

What he did next remains a mystery. The book of Matthew says he "went out and hanged himself" (27:5). The book of Acts, however, provides a more gruesome and, some say, contradictory description of Judas's demise. "Falling headfirst there, his body split open, spilling out all his intestines" (1:18).

So which is it? Did Judas hang himself, or did he leap to his death? Actually, these two seemingly disparate descriptions can be fit together logically. One possibility is that after Judas hanged himself, his body was not discovered for some time. Therefore, when his body finally fell, either because of decay or because someone cut it down, it was so decomposed that it burst open. Another possibility is that the word "hanged" in Matthew actually means "impaled." If Judas chose to impale himself, as it were, on the rocks below, it would certainly explain the gruesome condition of the body described in Acts. Yet another explanation suggests that Judas strangled himself on a tree. As he lost consciousness, his body dropped and split open on the rocks below.

For more information on Judas's gruesome end, see Matthew 27 and Acts 1.

TRAITORS, TURNCOATS, AND TREACHEROUS TYPES

Judas is not the only traitor in the Bible. Many men and women betrayed friends and their own kin for money or power.

TRAITOR	ACTION	REFERENCE
Jacob	Betrayed his twin brother, Esau's, trust and his father's intentions by pretending to be Esau. He received his brother's birthright and blessing but had to flee for his life.	Genesis 27

Traitor	Action	Reference
Joseph's brothers (sons of Jacob)	Sick of their brother's special place with their father, nine brothers plotted to kill Joseph. They settled for selling him to Midianite slave traders for twenty pieces of silver.	Genesis 37:18–36
Miriam and Aaron	Out of jealousy, they challenged Moses' authority. This act of rebellion caused Miriam to suffer a short bout of leprosy.	Numbers 12
Achan	Jeopardized Israel's military campaign in Canaan by hoarding plunder. After a disastrous attack on Ai, Joshua discovered the crime and had Achan stoned.	Joshua 7
Delilah	Cooperated with the Philistines to betray Samson. She eventually coaxed the secret of Samson's strength out of him. This led to his capture.	Judges 16:4–22
Abner	Made an alliance with David after his king, Ishbosheth, confronted him for sleeping with his father's concubine.	2 Samuel 3:6–13
David	Betrayed Uriah by sleeping with his wife, then compounded the crime by having Uriah sent to his death in battle.	2 Samuel 11
Absalom	Led a rebellion against his father, David, but died in the struggle.	2 Samuel 15
Shimei	Cursed David when David was forced to flee from Absalom's invading army.	2 Samuel 16:5–13

TRAITOR	ACTION	REFERENCE
Ahithophel	Counselor to King David, he sided with Absalom's bid for power. When Absalom later rejected his advice, Ahithophel committed suicide.	2 Samuel 17:23
Zimri	Killed Baasha, king of Israel, then assumed power. When the army heard of Baasha's death, they chose a new king and turned on Zimri. After a seven-day reign, Zimri killed himself after the army took the capital of Tirzah.	1 Kings 16:8–20
Jezebel	Had some rogues proclaim that Naboth was a traitor to God and the king. This led to Naboth's being stoned to death. Her husband, King Ahab, then took Naboth's vineyard, which he had coveted.	1 Kings 21
Judas	Betrayed Jesus to the Jewish leaders for thirty pieces of silver. His kiss was the signal for Jesus' arrest.	Matthew 26:14–16, 47–50; Mark 14:10–11, 43–50; Luke 22:3–6, 47; John 18:1–6
Peter	Pretended not to know Jesus when Jesus was suffering through his trial. Jesus had predicted Peter's betrayal.	Mark 14:66–72; John 18:15–18, 25–27

Hog Wild

What caused thousands of pigs to go berserk?

TWO THOUSAND pigs driven off the edge of a cliff? One hot, dry day in ancient Palestine, livestock contentedly grazed near a hillside graveyard. Standing nearby were Jesus and another man, a disturbed vagrant who had terrorized the local populace for years. When Jesus motioned to the herd of swine, all two thousand of the prized pigs—to the amazement of the herdsmen—frantically ran off the side of a mountain and into a lake below, where they all drowned. Horrified and angry, the herdsmen realized they had suffered a catastrophic financial blow.

What in the world was going on? Was it a case of mass hypnosis? Could the rabbi from Nazareth throw his voice like a ventriloquist? If so, perhaps the pigs were responding to what they thought was a herdsmen's voice on the other side of the cliff. Maybe it had nothing to do with Jesus. It's possible that a wild animal in the brush had startled one of the herd, provoking hysteria.

The vagrant who had observed it all was beginning to draw his own conclusions. Homeless and deranged, he had lived among the tombstones of the graveyard. The herdsmen and townspeople kept their distance from this obviously crazed hermit. He wore no clothes! This wild man with matted, uncombed hair wondered if it was only coincidental that at the very moment the pigs ran off the side of the mountain, his unclothed body fell limp to the ground. The man felt a rush of peace wash over his mind and inner spirit.

For the first time in decades, his mouth formed a smile as he looked up at Jesus, who returned his smile.

Jesus had diagnosed the vagrant's problem as an extraordinary manifestation of demons. So many had inhabited the man that they called themselves Legion. The Roman term "legion" was a designation for the largest unit of the Roman army, consisting of three thousand to six thousand soldiers. Obviously an inner army had barricaded itself in this man's soul, holding him hostage.

Jesus had exorcised this man of demons, and those demons wanted to be sent somewhere else. Always looking to destroy, the demons entered the pigs and killed them.

For details on this puzzling occurrence, study the accounts in Matthew 8, Mark 5, and Luke 8.

Road to Recognition

Two travelers can't see the truth.

THEY SAY THAT MISERY loves company. On a country road long ago, one miserable pair got some very unexpected company.

Within a week after the death of Jesus, two of his followers were walking on the road to a village called Emmaus, just outside Jerusalem. Lost in grief and expressing to each other how much they missed Jesus, they were startled when a stranger joined them. He asked them what they were talking about.

"You must be the only person in Jerusalem who hasn't heard about all the things that have happened there the last few days," replied the one named Cleopas. When the stranger professed ignorance of the current events, the two followers described their teacher, Jesus. They told how they'd hoped he was the Savior that had been prophesied for centuries. But he had been arrested and violently killed on a cross—first-century capital punishment at its worst.

Cleopas and his companion were confused as well as sad. There had been talk of Jesus' rising from the dead, evidently rumors started by some women. Some of Jesus' followers had checked out the tomb, but they had found nothing. Not even a body!

The stranger couldn't take it anymore. He was actually the very man they were mourning, but somehow they couldn't see him for who he was. As they walked on toward Emmaus, Jesus proceeded to explain the prophecies in their Scriptures (our Old Testament) concerning his identity and work on earth. Still they didn't recognize him. They reached Cleopas's home and invited the stranger to at least stay for dinner.

Finally, as Jesus broke bread with them, the men recognized him. They realized that these same hands had broken bread with the disciples for the Passover meal the night before he had died. But just as their eyes were opened, Jesus vanished.

Why did these two distraught travelers not recognize Jesus from the start? Was their grief so great that they could hardly look into his face? Or was his appearance mysteriously changed, veiled to their eyes? What form did Jesus take?

Jesus' appearance to the two disciples marked the first of many appearances to his followers in the days following his crucifixion. Evidently liberated from a human body, Jesus could appear and disappear. Yet unlike a mere spirit, Jesus could eat and drink with them. He was alive. No one knows the exact nature of Jesus' resurrected body, but hundreds of disciples (including this pair that was walking on the Emmaus road) attested that Jesus was alive. They had seen him, touched him, and even heard him. It was the message that Jesus was alive that motivated the early disciples to travel around the world telling others the Good News.

For the full account of the journey on the Emmaus road, read Mark 16:12–13 and Luke 24:13–35.

POSTRESURRECTION APPEARANCES OF JESUS

The New Testament begins and ends with the salvation epic of Jesus of Nazareth. But the biblical record includes more than his birth, his ministry, and his death. Because he rose from the grave, his message continues to affect lives today. Here are the witnesses who saw Jesus after his death and proclaimed the news that he still lives today.

WITNESSES	REFERENCE
Two women saw him when they hurried away from his tomb.	Matthew 28:1–10

Strange but True

Witnesses	Reference
Eleven of his disciples saw him on a mountain in Galilee.	Matthew 28:16–20; Mark 16:15–18
Mary Magdalene saw him on Sunday morning.	Mark 16:9–11; John 20:11–18
Two people met him while walking in the country on the road to Emmaus.	Mark 16:12–13; Luke 24:13–32
He came personally to Peter in Jerusalem.	Luke 24:34; 1 Corinthians 15:5
Ten of his disciples saw him in the city of Jerusalem.	Luke 24:36–51; John 20:19–23
The disciple Thomas, who had not been with the rest when Jesus appeared to them in Jerusalem, finally saw him.	Mark 16:14; John 20:24–29; 1 Corinthians 15:5
His disciples saw him by the sea and had breakfast with him.	John 21:1–14
He was seen by a crowd of five hundred people.	1 Corinthians 15:6
He came personally to his brother James.	1 Corinthians 15:7
His disciples saw him before he rose to heaven.	Acts 1:3–9
Saul (later called Paul) encountered Jesus on the road to Damascus.	Acts 9:1–6
The elderly disciple John received a grand vision from Jesus on the island of Patmos.	Revelation 1

The Best for Last

What explains the unexpected presence of wine at a wedding?

SPARKLING RED WINE—at first glance, nothing seems peculiar, intriguing, or mysterious about a simple glass of wine. The natural processes of fermentation are widely known—even a small child knows when milk has been in the refrigerator for too long. But on one hot day in the little dusty town of Cana, simple jars of wine were not just a source of merriment; they were the source of wonder and bewilderment.

It was a normal wedding. The merry guests had gathered and celebrated the couple's new life together. However, the host of the wedding hadn't planned well for the festivities and the wine had run out—a serious social blunder. Throughout the day no one had suspected anything. Jesus accompanied his mother to the wedding, and she could tell that something was wrong. With a maternal concern for the host, she prompted Jesus to do something, anything. What could Jesus do? Why would his mother ask him for help?

After protesting to his mother that his "time had not yet come" (John 2:4), a mysterious statement in itself, Jesus calmly told the servants to fill six stone jars with fresh, cool water. By the time the servants brought a cup of water from these stone jars to the host, it had mysteriously changed molecular structure so that it was sparkling wine—the best the master of the banquet had ever tasted.

How did this occur? It is clear that we must dismiss notions of stretching a little leftover wine with water to appease the guests.

Ordinarily, the last wine bottle to be served was the newest wine and thus the least tasty. Diluting it would be pointless. Somehow the distillation process went into rapid overdrive and produced, almost instantaneously, what normally takes years. How did Jesus do that?

Well, maybe he didn't. Maybe the wine he made was really a grape juice that seemed to the already merry crowd like one of the cellar's best, but without the intoxicating quality.

Then again, maybe he did. The guests reported that Jesus had produced the very best wine. At face value, that eliminates the grape-juice explanation. These ancient wine connoisseurs would not rave about juice that didn't sparkle. This was choice wine, a delight to the host and his company.

How could water—not even grape juice—turn into wine within minutes? Some would say it is impossible. That was probably what the disciples thought. But when they couldn't disprove what they had seen right before their eyes and even savored in their mouths, their awe for Jesus grew. But how did Jesus do it? In short, it was a miracle, and the first of many. Jesus' public ministry began at that wedding in Cana, and the world would never be the same again.

For the full account of the wedding at Cana, read John 2.

The Prince of
Darkness

What does the Bible tell us about Satan?

How could a powerful, luminous angel spurn a perfect existence in God's presence? Universally known as the epitome of evil, Satan appears throughout the Bible in various guises—a cunning serpent, a fallen angel, a threatening demon. He is powerful (though the power he exerts is limited) and fearsome. He longs to destroy what is good, that is, anything God has brought forth. Job's prosperous life, for example, was torn asunder by disease, ferocious marauders, terrifying storms, earthquakes, and fire. Satan dragged Job down to the ash pit—literally. And throughout the Bible Satan appears as a relentless schemer who resorts to lies, fear, and temptations to lure others to a destiny they will share with him—a place of everlasting torment. In fact, his very name means "adversary."

Satan's very existence raises a lot of questions. Why would an all-powerful God allow such widespread rebellion? Why does an all-powerful God permit Satan to wield the considerable power he has? And on a purely practical level, what relevance does the devil have for modern humanity? Such questions have been debated endlessly and the answers remain elusive. But it would be a mistake, as the apologist C. S. Lewis has noted, to dismiss Satan as a quaint relic of a superstitious age. In Scripture, Satan stands at the center of the

08 *Strange but True*

world's troubles—corrupting people, sowing discord, prowling around, snaring unsuspecting victims, and masquerading as an angel of light. Jesus clearly declared that he was locked in a mortal struggle with the prince of darkness and that he would emerge victorious.

Satan's biography, if it were taken from the Bible, might begin with his preeminent place among God's creatures before the world began. Some scholars have suggested that Isaiah's description of a shining star thrown down to the earth gives us a glimpse of Satan's rise and fall (see Isaiah 14:12). He appears in the guise of a serpent in the Garden of Eden (see Genesis 3) and as Job's tormentor (see Job 1). The writer of Chronicles declares that Satan coaxed David into taking his ill-advised census (see 1 Chronicles 21:1).

In the New Testament, Satan's opposition becomes bolder. His demons oppress people and resist Jesus' works. He even tries to tempt Jesus (see Matthew 4) and enters into Judas Iscariot, who betrays Jesus (see John 13:27). He vigorously attacks the new church and spreads discord wherever he can. Small wonder that the writers of the New Testament epistles describe him as a formidable opponent (see Ephesians 6:11; 1 Peter 5:8).

Satan has wreaked havoc on the world and left a trail of broken lives behind. Yet God has already brought Satan down by the ultimate victory of good—the death and resurrection of the Son of God, the basis for the Easter celebration. The glimpse of the future presented in John's Revelation shows Satan's ultimate demise—everlasting torment in a lake of fire (see Revelation 20:7–10).

Many Bible passages deal with Satan. Start your investigation with Numbers 22:22; John 14:30; 1 Corinthians 7:5; Ephesians 2:2; 1 Peter 5:8; and 1 John 3:8.

DID YOU KNOW?

Why did the ancient Israelites use the obscure name "Beelzebub" to refer to Satan?

One of the most peculiar names for Satan, the prince of demons, is the name Beelzebub. The origins of this obscure word continue to puzzle many Bible scholars. The close association between Beelzebub and the name of the Ekron god, Baalzebub, seems obvious (2 Kings 1:2). Yet there remain persistent doubts whether Baal-zebub was actually a name for any ancient god. Baal-zebub literally means "lord of the flies," a phrase used by William Golding for the title of his nightmarish 1954 novel. Many scholars believe the real name of this god was Baal-zebul, meaning "lord of the heavenly dwelling." Since the Israelite prophets would not honor any god with such a distinguished title except the God of Israel, they seemed to have substituted a derogatory name meaning "lord of the flies" or "lord of dung" for this god. By Jesus' time, Beelzebub was a common epithet for Satan. At one point, the Pharisees said of Jesus, "It is only by Beelzebub, the prince of demons, that this fellow drives out demons" (Matthew 12:24 NIV).

Rushing Wind

Visitors to Jerusalem get an unexpected encounter with a new religious phenomenon.

THE SCENE was Jerusalem, several weeks after the death and supposed resurrection of the one called Jesus, the Christ. It was the day of Pentecost, fifty days after the Jewish Passover. Jews from every country in the first-century world were in the city. A small group of men who had followed Jesus the closest were in the city as well. About 120 counted themselves as believers at that time, led by the twelve disciples.

Gathered together in a house, the 120 believers heard and felt a violent wind. Amazingly, tongues of fire seemed to land on their heads. Neighbors and passersby came running. A crowd gathered, including scores of visitors gathered for the festival. The believers were all talking at once in the languages of the city's foreign visitors. How could these Galileans be speaking in the languages of Mesopotamia, of Judea and Cappadocia, of Egypt and Libya, of Asia and beyond?

They were not babbling; they were speaking recognizable languages, albeit languages they had never learned. They were describing the Good News of salvation through Jesus. "They're just drunk!" some jeered. But Peter—the same man who had turned his back on Jesus during his trial and crucifixion—raised his voice and gave his explanation. He connected what was happening with an Old Testament prophecy, that the wind and fire signified the coming of God's Spirit. The time had come, he declared, for all the world to know about God's redemption.

The wind, the fire, and the languages were indeed mystifying. Yet somehow they got the attention of about three thousand people who joined the tiny movement that day. Pentecost is often called the birthday of the Christian Church, which now claims over a billion members.

For the complete story, check out Acts 2.

Death Times Two

A real-estate transaction brings fatal consequences.

A SECOND BODY? The young men had barely returned from burying the first victim when they saw his wife's body on the floor. Was it a coincidence . . . or a double homicide?

Ananias and his wife, Sapphira, were members of the church in Jerusalem. The number of believers in the city had grown astronomically in the months following Jesus' death and resurrection. And the believers' commitment to one another had grown just as remarkably, to the point of sharing their possessions and money. To meet the needs of the poor church members, those who owned land—Ananias and Sapphira among them—began to sell their property and give the proceeds to the church leaders.

The day's transaction started well. The couple sold some property, and as they had agreed, Ananias brought the money to the leaders. Proudly he handed it over to a man named Peter. Yet a few moments later Ananias fell over—dead before he hit the floor. Was it a heart attack?

Unaware of her husband's death, Sapphira came before the committee a few hours later. Unbelievably, she met her end in the same way—falling down, not in a faint but in death. The young men who had buried Ananias had the sad task of burying her a short time later.

Great fear rippled through the fledgling church. What had Peter said or done to the couple? But those who had witnessed the double deaths verified that Peter was guilty of no wrongdoing. Sapphira and Ananias, however, had had their own agenda: they had decided to secretly keep some of the profits from the real estate transaction for themselves and donate the balance. While there was absolutely nothing wrong with that, the problem was that in order to look good, they professed that the money they were donating was the full amount of the sale. Who would be the wiser? When questioned by Peter, Sapphira had even calmly replied that they had given the full profits to the church.

But they hadn't reckoned on the experience and insight of Peter, one of Jesus' handpicked followers who had been credited with some startling deeds those first weeks after Easter (see Acts 1–3). The other church leaders reported that Peter seemed to immediately sense that Ananias was lying about the money. "You weren't lying to us but to God!" Peter said before Ananias collapsed to the floor and died. Nearly the identical scene was played out when Sapphira entered the room a few hours later. Her lifeless body was carried out to be buried with her husband's.

One sudden death could be tossed off as coincidence. But two? Their inexplicable demise forces us to take seriously the conclusion reached by Luke, the author of Acts: the two had been judged for lying and deceit.

To read the full story, read Acts 4:32–5:11.

Strange Lights and Mysterious Voices

What happened to Saul on the road to Damascus?

S AUL WAS ON A MISSION. He was determined to capture all the fanatical Christians from Damascus and bring them back to Jerusalem in chains.

The Christians were getting stronger and more numerous every day. To Saul, an orthodox Jew trained by the great religious teacher Gamaliel, the Christians' claim that a teacher named Jesus was the promised Messiah was heresy. To stop this upstart movement once and for all, Saul had determined to become a one-man police force, gathering up heretical Christians wherever he could find them— from the marketplace to their very own homes. Saul hated all Christians and everything they stood for. He vowed to stop them all if he could. According to Saul's thinking, there was no place in all of Israel that should tolerate this heretical sect.

But Saul never completed his mission. As he neared Damascus, a brilliant light suddenly blinded him, knocking him off his horse and sending him to his knees. A booming voice spoke out of the air. And then, as he picked himself up off the ground, he couldn't see! Completely blind, he had to be led by the hand to Damascus, where he spent three days without food and water. Later, after a visit with Ananias, he suddenly regained his sight.

After that fateful day, Saul was never the same. He began to use the Roman name Paul. To everyone's amazement, he became a great preacher and teacher and led several long, dangerous journeys that spread Christianity throughout the Roman Empire. Paul wrote many books of the New Testament, several of them from a prison cell while he was serving time for preaching about Jesus.

What really happened on the Damascus road? The eyewitnesses were just as mystified as those who heard about it later. They saw the blinding light and heard the voice but saw no one. At a loss to explain the event, they could only stand with their mouths open in stunned silence.

What was the bright light that stopped Saul in his tracks and knocked him to the ground? Where did it come from? Whose mysterious voice spoke to him, and what did it say?

Many thought the sun reflecting off a shiny object created a beam of light that struck Saul in the eyes and caused temporary blindness. Some said the voice was only the murmuring of the wind through the hills and valleys along the road. Others said Saul must have suffered heatstroke, which caused him to have hallucinations.

Saul's own explanation was just as strange and fascinating. He said when the light knocked him to the ground, he heard a voice saying, "Saul, Saul, why are you persecuting me?" When Saul asked who was speaking, the voice answered, "I am Jesus, the one you are persecuting! Now get up and go into the city, and you will be told what you must do."

The voice radically changed Saul's life forever. Once determined to wipe Christianity off the face of the earth, he now became a man on a new mission—to tell every person in the world about Jesus.

For more on Saul's transformation, see Acts 9 and 22.

HEARING VOICES

All of the people in the following chart claim they heard voices or divine messages. Skeptics still may discount these stories as hallucinations, but how does one explain voices heard by crowds? Read on to discover the circumstances behind these mysterious voices.

HEARER	CIRCUMSTANCES	REFERENCE
Balaam	Balaam's donkey spoke to him and rebuked him for his greediness and evildoing.	Numbers 22:21–31; 2 Peter 2:15–16
Young Samuel	Samuel was asleep in the temple when he heard a voice calling him three times. He thought it was Eli the priest, but Eli told him that it was God who was speaking.	1 Samuel 3:1–14
Elijah	After fleeing for his life from Queen Jezebel, Elijah heard God's voice telling him to go back to Damascus and anoint three people.	1 Kings 19:13–16
King Nebuchadnezzar	In a dream, he heard an angel's voice.	Daniel 4:14
Jesus, John the Baptist, and crowds	At Jesus' baptism, the crowd heard a voice from heaven say, "This is my dearly loved Son, who brings me great joy."	Matthew 3:16–17
Jesus, Peter, James, and John	The three disciples were with Jesus when his appearance changed and his face and clothes shone. Then a bright cloud appeared and a voice spoke to them.	Matthew 17:1–5
Paul	Paul was on his way to Damascus to persecute Christians when a dazzling light shone on him and he heard the voice of Jesus.	Acts 9:1–9

HEARER	CIRCUMSTANCES	REFERENCE
Peter	The apostle saw the sky open to reveal a sheet suspended by its four corners filled with animals, snakes, and birds (forbidden food for the Jews). He then heard a voice telling him it was all right to eat these things.	Acts 10:9–20
John	He heard a loud voice that sounded like a trumpet. It told him to write down everything he saw.	Revelation 1:10

Dungeons and Disciples

A prisoner disappears but leaves no evidence.

A JAILBREAK! Herod's royal guards were left in a panic early one April day. Peter, one of the most important prisoners left in their charge, had disappeared without a trace.

The facts were simple. The officer in charge had gone over and over them. He had left a total of sixteen soldiers (four squads of four soldiers) to guard Peter in the depths of the prison. Four soldiers were to guard Peter at all times—one chained to his left wrist and the other chained to his right. The other two were to stand watch outside. To make sure no one fell asleep, these guards were to rotate four times that night with another set of well-rested guards. Nothing could go wrong, or so the officer in charge thought.

But the next day, Peter was gone! The last shift of guards was still there, the chains remained, and the ground still showed the outline of where Peter had sat. But where Peter had gone or how he had freed himself from those heavy chains remained a puzzle. There was no sign of a forced exit—a broken latch or a hastily dug tunnel. Nothing! The guards officially denied seeing or hearing anything. But unofficially, some of them spoke of a mysterious bright light that had put them in a strange trance. How could Peter have escaped? Not even a seasoned escape artist could pull this off!

A careful investigation, headed by Herod himself, led nowhere. Herod could only conclude that it was an inside job. One of the guards had to have helped Peter escape. Such treachery deserved severe punishment, and all sixteen guards were led away to a swift execution.

Years later, Peter reemerged in Jerusalem. His version of what happened that night was extraordinary, explaining, in part, why Herod's investigation was so futile.

According to Peter, it was late at night and he was fast asleep when, suddenly, a bright light lit up his damp prison cell. A bright figure resembling a man ordered him to get up and get dressed. The man appeared to be so extraordinary—his face glowed and his long white robe shone—that Peter thought he was still asleep and seeing a vision (something that had happened to him before—see Acts 10). But when he got up, he could feel the cold steel chains unlatch themselves, freeing his sore wrists. The angelic creature led Peter through the dark corridors and past two guards on watch, who, strangely, did not seem to notice that Peter and his guide were even there. Before Peter knew what was happening, he was walking through the heavy iron gates of the fortress, which seemed to open at the angel's touch. Peter was out on the main street leading to the middle of Jerusalem. He took a deep breath of the cool night air and turned to his companion. But the man was gone, and the adjacent streets were abandoned. He decided to return to his companions in the faith who were praying for him in a nearby home. So astonished was the girl who answered the door that she forgot to let Peter in! The whole church rejoiced in the deliverance of the supposedly doomed disciple.

For more on Peter's miraculous escape, read Acts 12.

The King's Last Boast

Herod Agrippa's death is plagued by more questions than answers.

DEATH COMES suddenly for some people. Even in Bible times, death could be both surprising and instantaneous.

It was daybreak in Caesarea. The first rays of the sun peeped over the horizon. Orange, amber, and red streaked across the dark blue skies. Everyone had gathered—from lesser-known officials to the important provincial governors of Tyre and Sidon. Supposedly, they had come to celebrate Caesar's birthday, but many were driven by an ulterior motive—the opportunity to flatter Herod Agrippa I. The provinces of Tyre and Sidon were dependent on Galilee and Judea for food, and Herod Agrippa was threatening that lifeline. He was a cruel and conniving man, indulging in an extravagant, careless lifestyle, not even shrinking from masterminding his own brother-in-law's downfall. The officials from Tyre and Sidon knew they had to massage Herod's considerable ego in order for their tiny provinces to survive.

Dramatically, Herod Agrippa made his appearance. He strutted onto the platform in his usual extravagant way. He made a speech and the people swooned: "It's the voice of a god, not of a man!"

With a self-satisfied grin, Herod drank in their praise. Suddenly, with the loud cries of the people still ringing in his ears, Herod doubled over in severe pain. He was quickly rushed away by his attendants. Five days later, he died.

What happened on that fateful day? Did the officials of Tyre poison Herod? Or was Herod's sudden death evidence of God's instant judgment?

The questions abound. And with each answer come more puzzling details. The ancient Jewish historian Josephus reported that at the moment Herod was struck by pain, he saw a strange-looking owl sitting on a rope above his head. Almost a decade earlier while Herod languished in prison for some foolish comments in front of the Roman emperor, a fellow prisoner had sternly warned that if Herod ever saw an owl again it would be an omen of his impending death.

Luke, the author of the book of Acts, connected Herod's death not to omens or owls but to the angel of the Lord. On that tragic morning, Herod had accepted praise that only God deserved. God responded by sending a mysterious messenger of doom to mete out immediate judgment, leaving Herod to spend his last remaining hours writhing in pain from "worms," what medical doctors today diagnose as tapeworm.

Herod's untimely death reminds us of the words of Solomon: "Pride goes before destruction, and haughtiness before a fall" (Proverbs 16:18). In this case, the fall was orchestrated by God himself.

For more on Herod's doom, read Acts 12.

Midnight Deliverance

Was there any connection between a tumultuous earthquake and the faith of two prisoners?

MIDNIGHT. Sitting in their dark and dreary cells, the prisoners of the dank Philippian jail listened with eyes closed to the strangely comforting songs floating through the prison. The new prisoners, Paul and Silas, were singing again. The old-timers, the ones who had been languishing in prison for years, couldn't quite figure out those new prisoners: they had been severely flogged and were in the well-guarded and bare inner cell with their feet in heavy iron stocks; yet they were singing and praying! The soft music didn't wake the jailer, though. He had had a rough day.

The quiet night was suddenly interrupted when the ground under the prison began to shake violently! At first, it seemed like a mere tremor; then the quake grew more violent and fierce. The stone walls of the prison began falling in. Even the foundations of the prison cracked. This was a quake that the Philippians hadn't experienced for a long time. With dust and chunks of rock flying around, the doors of the prison cells flew open.

The Philippian jailer was ready to kill himself, knowing that his superiors would kill him anyway for allowing prisoners to escape. Except, oddly enough, not one prisoner ran. Out of fear and wonder, he came to the two prisoners who, it seemed, had caused the cataclysm, and asked, "Sirs, what must I do to be saved?" Paul and Silas "shared the word of the Lord with him and with all who lived in his household. . . . Then he and everyone in his household were immediately baptized" (Acts 16:30, 32–33).

The mighty hand of God had shaken the prison. God had freed Paul and Silas to demonstrate his power and to bring the family of a jailer to salvation.

For more information about this bizarre earthquake, read Acts 16.

Shipwreck

A prisoner foresees a terrible shipwreck and the survival of all on board.

THE RAGING HURRICANE whipped the boat from side to side. As the ferocity of the winds increased, Julius glanced anxiously at the prisoners in the hull. If the winds got any worse, there was a real chance of shipwreck! How would he, the highest-ranking Roman officer on board, prevent any of the prisoners from swimming away and escaping? The sailors were scurrying around, frantically throwing cargo overboard, securing the lifeboat, and even passing ropes under the ship to hold it together.

As a last resort, the sailors threw the ship's tackle overboard with their own hands. Without seeing the sun or stars for days, everyone aboard gave up all hope of being saved.

But then a prisoner named Paul stood up and told the men on board about a strange dream he had. The centurion Julius could hardly believe what Paul said: "None of you will lose your lives, even though the ship will go down. For last night an angel of the God to whom I belong and whom I serve stood beside me, and he said, 'Don't be afraid, Paul, for you will surely stand trial before Caesar! What's more, God in his goodness has granted safety to everyone sailing with you.' So take courage! For I believe God. It will be just as he said" (Acts 27:22–25). Julius may have laughed to himself. How could the ship be destroyed and yet not one of them would die? But if this man was telling the truth, did he mean the prisoners as well? Surely they would try to escape.

After fourteen days, as the storm drove the tiny ship across the raging Adriatic Sea, the experienced sailors sensed that land was drawing near. Fearing they would be dashed against the rocks of an island or coral reef, some let down a lifeboat in a desperate attempt to escape. Paul stopped them, telling Julius that the men would certainly die if they left the ship. For some reason, Julius believed this awkward and visionary prisoner who was so different from the others. The centurion ordered the soldiers on board and cut the lifeboat free.

Just as Paul had predicted, the ship struck a sandbar. The stern was broken to pieces by the pounding surf. Before the soldiers made their way to the safety of the island shores, they determined that they would kill all the prisoners, including Paul, because they knew that if any prisoners got away, the soldiers would pay with their own lives. But Julius interceded. Paul, though a prisoner, had already proven himself useful.

Remarkably, everyone got to land, saved from the ferocious seas just as Paul had foretold. Who was this man? How could he foresee the future? These were only some of the questions that plagued the soldiers and sailors who accompanied Paul.

But the surprises didn't end with Paul's prediction. Once on shore, Paul was bitten by a poisonous snake. In ancient times, this was a sure sign of instant death. But for Paul it meant nothing. Unaffected by poisonous snakes, he continued to tell the people about his great message of Good News. The islanders were nothing less than astonished. Who was this man? What kind of prophet could he be?

Then, Paul even healed the father of the chief official on the island by praying for him and laying his hands on him. Then other sick people came to Paul, and he healed them all.

What do you think Julius thought? Don't you wonder what impact Paul made on this tough Roman soldier?

To read more about Paul's adventures, see Acts 27–28.

SECTION TWO

Curious Connections

Binding Curses

MANY PEOPLE today flippantly curse everything—from a passing motorist to even a close friend. Not many people think twice about it. But the ancients knew that words should not be spoken so lightly. Words are binding. Words cannot be taken back once they have been said. And a curse can have as much power as the awful deeds they invoke. The following stories relate the power of curses on the lives of Bible people.

The Curse of the Garden

Everything was perfect when Adam and Eve started their life together in Paradise. They lived in the beautiful Garden of Eden, but their idyllic existence was disrupted with one simple act: a bite of a piece of fruit from the tree of the knowledge of good and evil. Adam and Eve ate and took upon themselves a curse that would plague them and their descendants. God told them that the land would bear a curse of thorns; the man would have to sweat long hours to obtain food to eat. The woman was also cursed: she would suffer pain in childbirth. And both Adam and Eve would die. Their sinful act was irreversible; the curse was also irreversible. Women still suffer great pain in childbirth today, and every person born to this earth can expect to die. (See Genesis 3.)

And the Verdict Is . . .

The ancient Israelites had an elaborate procedure for jealous husbands who suspected their wives of adultery. A suspicious husband could bring his wife to a priest. After making a mixture of dirty water, the priest would speak an oath that acquitted the woman if innocent and condemned her if guilty. The woman was then required to say, "Yes, let it be so," and drink the water. If the water made her sick, she was presumed guilty. The liquid would render her childless for the rest of her life. Her name would become a curse among the people. (See Numbers 5:11–31.)

He Means Business

Jericho had been laid waste—the walls had fallen and the city had been burned. The Lord had promised Joshua, Israel's commander, "I have given you Jericho, its king, and all its strong warriors" (Joshua 6:2). Just as the Lord had told Joshua, the city would literally fall, for its mighty walls would collapse. That accomplished, Joshua placed a curse on the city, saying that whoever tried to rebuild it would do so at great personal sacrifice. If a builder put down the foundation, his firstborn son would die; if he set up the city's gates, his youngest son would die. That left the city vacant for many years—that is, until a man named Hiel rebuilt Jericho. True to Joshua's curse, Hiel lost his oldest and youngest sons. (See Joshua 6:24–26 and 1 Kings 16:34.)

Lies, All Lies!

The Israelites had been victorious everywhere they went. The cities of Jericho and Ai had fallen to Israel's triumphant army, and the news of this spread fast. The people of the city of Gibeon were terrified. They knew that they had no chance against the invading Israelites, so they sent a delegation to the Israelites disguised as travelers from a distant land. This deceitful delegation approached Joshua with a humble request for a peace treaty. Joshua, believing them to be from a region beyond what Israel had determined to conquer, fell for the trick. He signed a peace treaty with them. But when he learned the truth later, he vehemently cursed them. He could not go back on the word of the treaty, but he could condemn them to chopping wood and carrying water for the Israelites—a curse that came to pass. (See Joshua 9:3–27.)

Armed Angels

FROM COLORFUL coffee-table books to cards, angels are pictured as radiant, gracious creatures. People usually associate angels with compassion. They are rarely pictured as rigid and stern—armed with long sharp swords. Yet in a number of passages, the Bible does picture angels as armed and dangerous. In fact, most angelic encounters in the Bible leave people cowering in absolute fear.

The Angelic Guardians of Eden

The first mention of angelic beings in the Bible occurs after Adam and Eve had sinned against God. Because of their sin, God exiled Adam and Eve from Paradise. To make sure no person would ever enter the garden again, the Lord dispatched angelic beings called cherubim to guard the place. Cherubim are angelic beings who look like people but have four wings (see Ezekiel 1:5–10; 10:1–22). According to the Bible, these fearsome angels guarded the garden. To assist them in this task, God gave them a flaming sword that flashed back and forth across the entrance to Paradise. No person could re-enter the garden without facing certain death. (See Genesis 3:24.)

The Angelic Commander of God's Army

Sword-bearing angels may inspire awe, but the fear is diminished if they are fighting on your side! Joshua, the great military commander of the Israelites, experienced this. He had to conquer the great walled city of Jericho, but its ancient defenses were formidable. One day when Joshua was surveying Jericho, he looked up and saw an angel with his sword drawn. Joshua reacted as a military man. "Are you friend or foe?" he queried. "Neither one," the man answered. The angel explained that he was the commander of the Lord's army. Joshua immediately fell to the ground in deep reverence. Like Moses, he removed his sandals, for he stood on holy ground. After this encounter, Joshua led his army to victory against Jericho. (See Joshua 5:13–15.)

The Angel of Death

The angel of death (though not specifically called such) is mentioned a number of times in the Bible. All the firstborn sons of the Egyptians suffered his fatal stroke during the first Passover (see Exodus 12:11–13, 28–30). Balaam narrowly averted the angel's deadly sword (see Numbers 22:31–34). And seventy thousand Israelites were cut down by this angel during King David's reign. David had sinned by counting his fighting men and taking pride in his military might. With one lethal campaign of the angel of death, God showed how helpless David truly was (see 2 Samuel 24:10–25). The only defense David had against this mighty, sword-bearing angel was a prayer to God. David begged God for mercy, and God gave it. He stopped the armed angel on the threshing floor of Araunah. This spot became the site of Solomon's temple and, as such, a symbol for God's mercy.

THE ANGEL OF THE LORD

A mysterious messenger from God, the angel of the Lord, appears often in the Old Testament. Much debate has revolved around the exact identity of this mysterious messenger. Was this angel God himself, or perhaps a preincarnate form of Christ? No matter what this messenger's identity, it is clear that this being commanded considerable respect from humans.

ENCOUNTER	REFERENCE
The angel of the Lord encouraged Hagar to return to her home and bear Abraham's child.	Genesis 16:1–16

ENCOUNTER	REFERENCE
The angel of the Lord stopped Abraham just as he was about to sacrifice his son Isaac.	Genesis 22:1–19
The angel of the Lord appeared to Moses in a burning bush and instructed him to lead the Israelites out of Egypt.	Exodus 3:1–22
The angel of the Lord stood poised to kill Balaam, whose life was spared because of the actions of his donkey.	Numbers 22:21–38
The angel of the Lord went to Bokim and told the Israelites he wouldn't drive the pagan people out of the land of Canaan, because they had made treaties with the people.	Judges 2:1–5
The angel of the Lord instructed Gideon to lead an Israelite attack against the mighty Midianites.	Judges 6:11–40
The angel of the Lord revealed to Manoah and his wife that they would have a son.	Judges 13:1–25
The angel of the Lord was stopped from destroying Jerusalem. At that moment, he was by the threshing floor of Araunah, which became the site for the temple.	2 Samuel 24:10–17; 1 Chronicles 21:14–30
The angel of the Lord strengthened and encouraged Elijah.	1 Kings 19:1–9
The angel of the Lord spoke to Elijah about the need for Elijah to visit King Ahaziah.	2 Kings 1:1–15
The angel of the Lord killed 185,000 Assyrian soldiers in one night.	2 Kings 19:35–36; Isaiah 37:36
The angel of the Lord interpreted a series of visions for the prophet Zechariah.	Zechariah 1:7–6:15

Signs and Shadows

G OD GAVE SIGNS and miracles to his people to draw them to himself. The Bible tells of many mysterious events and phenomena far beyond the human capability to understand. Reading the signs required more than intellectual discernment; it demanded a love and respect for God.

The Rainbow

When Noah stepped off of the ark, he was entering a new world. All of life had been wiped out by the calamitous flood that had covered the earth for months and months. His first gesture was to offer a sacrifice of thanks to God. God responded to that offering by making his first covenant with humankind. He promised never to destroy the earth again by flood. To give an everlasting sign of that promise, he set the rainbow in the sky—a beautiful, heavenly, and intangible reminder of his love for all people and for all creatures on earth. (See Genesis 8:20–9:17.)

So Prove It . . . Again!

Gideon just couldn't take yes for an answer. The angel of the Lord had already done a miracle by barbecuing Gideon's offering—well, more like charring it. In any case, Gideon had asked for a sign and received it; there was no doubt in his mind that God was right there with him (see Judges 6:17–22). But then as Gideon got ready for battle, he asked the Lord for a sign. He would put a wool fleece on the floor, and if, the next morning, the fleece was wet with dew and the ground was dry, then he would know that God would be with him. Guess what? That's just what happened. But then Gideon got worried. Maybe the fleece would have been wet with dew anyway. Maybe he should try again, just to make sure. "Please don't be angry with me," he said to the Lord. This time he asked that God let the fleece be dry and the ground be wet. And guess what? That's just what happened. And Gideon finally accepted that God would help him. This is where we get the phrase "putting out a fleece" for asking God to act a certain way in order for us to know an answer or make a decision. Not always the best method, but at least God was patient with Gideon and did as he requested. (See Judges 6:33–40.)

The Day a Shadow Moved Backward

When the prophet Isaiah told King Hezekiah that God would heal him from his illness, the king was doubtful and asked for a sign from God. Isaiah agreed, and asked the king whether he wanted to see the shadow on the sundial go forward ten points or backward ten points. "The shadow always moves forward," Hezekiah said. "Make it go ten steps backward instead." So Isaiah asked God to make the shadow on the steps move backward ten steps . . . and it did! Hezekiah recovered from his near-fatal illness to live another fifteen years. (See 2 Kings 20:1–11.)

The Voice

Jesus always told his disciples and the crowds that the miracles he performed were for their benefit. These signs confirmed that Jesus came from God. They also reinforced the faith of those who believed or were struggling with their faith. (Consequently, Jesus did not perform signs for the hardhearted or the disbelieving—see Matthew 12:38–42; Mark 6:5–6.) As Jesus neared the time of his death, he spoke to a crowd about the trials he would suffer and concluded, "Father, bring glory to your name." A voice from heaven declared, "I have already brought glory to my name, and I will do so again." The crowd, astonished by what they heard, debated its source: some thought it was thunder, while others thought they had heard an angel. Jesus then told them the voice was for their benefit, not his. After admonishing them to walk in the light before the darkness came, Jesus left them. (See John 12:27–36.)

Urban Decay

CITIES, like the people who live in them, grow and decline. Some prosper while others pass away quietly. But some cities expire suddenly—carried away by war, famine, or disease. The Bible records the fate of immoral cities that ignored God's warnings and collapsed in ruin.

Babylon

The raucous celebration had begun! Rising to the heavens in a phenomenal feat of will and imagination, the great Tower of Babel filled the human hearts with pride and self-satisfaction. Because it struck such a defiant gesture toward God's sovereignty, he sought to confuse the language of this civilization so that such pride would be forever hindered. Much later, Babylon continued to defy God. The prophet Isaiah declared that Babylon's rise would be heady but short-lived, its destruction would be complete, and it would never be inhabited or lived in through all generations. Today, the ancient city lies in ruin, buried under mounds of dirt and sand in present-day Iraq. (See Genesis 11 and Isaiah 13–14.)

Sodom and Gomorrah

Lust, rape, perversion, obscene and vile addictions . . . Sodom and Gomorrah housed all that was evil. The God of Israel could not find even ten good people in the whole city! Before absolutely destroying the cities, God's angels had to drag Lot, his two daughters, and his wife out of the city. They were warned not to look back as the cities burned. Lot's wife disregarded this command and glanced at

137

Sodom. She turned instantly into a pillar of salt. The burning pitch and sulfur from the skies destroyed not only the cities but also the entire plain and all the vegetation of the land. Abraham, who was living nearby, could see the smoke rising from ruins. (See Genesis 18–19.)

Nineveh

Idolatry, prostitution, witchcraft, exploitation of the helpless, and cruelty in war were only some of the evils practiced in the ancient city of Nineveh. Jonah was sent by the God of Israel to condemn this great Assyrian city. He proclaimed that the city would be destroyed in forty days! Remarkably, the Ninevites believed Jonah's message! All of them—young and old, poor and rich—fasted and pleaded with the God of Israel. Even the king proclaimed that all the people should put aside their wickedness and call on God. Jonah's God heard their pleas and had mercy on the people. Nineveh's reform did not last long, however. One hundred years later, God sent the prophet Nahum to pronounce judgment again on the city. The people spurned God's message this time. Within a few decades, the mighty Assyrian empire was crushed by the Babylonians. (See Jonah 3 and the book of Nahum.)

The Race for Children

THE PRACTICE of taking more than one wife was common in many Middle Eastern cultures, but it often brought great strife to the families affected. To secure their husband's favor, wives would try to produce children—a sign of fertility and of God's blessing. The struggle for heirs often encouraged wives to compete with other wives and concubines to secure affection. Here are some of the more famous "children contests" found in Scripture.

Sarah and Hagar

Sarah, wife of the patriarch Abraham, could not bear children. As was the custom of the day, she gave her Egyptian servant Hagar to Abraham so that he could produce an heir through her. Hagar became pregnant, but the tension between Sarah and Hagar was so keen that Hagar ran away. She eventually went back to her mistress and gave birth to a son, Ishmael. But after Sarah unexpectedly gave birth to Isaac, she wanted her competition, so to speak, out of the picture and ordered Abraham to send Hagar and Ishmael away. With regret, Abraham did so, but he had God's assurance that the two would be taken care of. Ishmael grew up to be an expert archer and the father of the Ishmaelites, a nomadic people of the Middle East. (See Genesis 17; 21.)

Rachel and Leah

No contest between competing wives was as fierce or enduring as the rivalry between Rachel and Leah. Daughters of Laban, they both wed Jacob, though the circumstances of their marriage created a rift that would never heal. Jacob had not intended to marry Leah, but Laban tricked him into doing so because Leah was the elder daughter. Jacob was allowed to marry Rachel in exchange for seven more years of work for Laban. The sisters tried to prove their favor before God and Jacob by bearing children. Leah bore Jacob six sons and a daughter, but Rachel was barren for a long time. Eventually, however, she gave birth to Joseph and Benjamin. The wives' maids Bilhah and Zilpah also produced sons for Jacob. Altogether Jacob had twelve sons, who became the founders of the twelve tribes of Israel. (See Genesis 29:16–35.)

Hannah and Peninnah

Hannah was desperate to have children. Her husband, Elkanah, dearly loved her, but his other wife, Peninnah, taunted Hannah because of her childlessness. So Hannah prayed earnestly for a son, telling God that she would dedicate him to holy service if her request were granted. God heard those prayers, and Hannah bore a son named Samuel. After the boy was weaned, Hannah fulfilled her vow and took young Samuel to the tabernacle. He grew up assisting Eli, Israel's chief priest, and became a great prophet who anointed Israel's first two kings, Saul and David. (See 1 Samuel 1.)

Miraculous Births

THE BIRTH of a newborn boy or girl is a small miracle. Parents stare starry-eyed at the wonder of new life as the rest of the world bustles on, behaving as if nothing spectacular has happened. Babies are born every day—but not to a ninety-year-old woman, a barren woman, or a virgin. Such births are extraordinary—an occurrence that inspires wonder and awe.

Isaac

Abraham and his wife, Sarah, were well advanced in their years, and Sarah was way past the age of childbearing. Yet at the age of one hundred, Abraham fathered a son! One day, three strange visitors in shining white came to Abraham and Sarah's tent as they were resting during the heat of the day. After Abraham and Sarah prepared food for them, one of the visitors told Abraham an unbelievable thing. He said that within one year Sarah would have a son. "Ha!" thought Sarah, "at my age?" But as she laughed at the idea, the visitor said, "Is anything too hard for the LORD?" One year later, at the age of ninety, Sarah gave birth to Isaac. (See Genesis 18:1–15; 21:1–7.)

John the Baptist

Zechariah and his wife, Elizabeth, were childless. Not only were they well along in years, but Elizabeth was also barren. One day when Zechariah was serving in the temple, a stranger appeared by the altar. The stranger called himself Gabriel, an angel of the God of Israel. Gabriel told Zechariah that his wife would bear a son. Zechariah was to name the son John and dedicate the child's life to God.

This child was to follow in the footsteps of the great prophet Elijah. Zechariah could not believe his ears and questioned the angel. Because Zechariah doubted the news, Gabriel said he would be struck dumb until the baby was born. Immediately Zechariah lost his ability to speak. But when a son was born to the once-barren and quite old Elizabeth, Zechariah's voice returned. The child became known as John the Baptist, a great prophet who told of Jesus' coming. (See Luke 1:5–25, 57–80; 3:1–18.)

Jesus

Mary, a virgin, was startled by a bright light. When she turned around, a stranger who called himself Gabriel, an angel of the God of Israel, was standing before her. He told her that she was to give birth to a son. She was to name the son Jesus, and he would be known as the Son of God. "How can this happen? I am a virgin," Mary asked. Gabriel replied, "The Holy Spirit will come upon you. . . . Nothing is impossible with God." There was no union between Mary and any man, and yet she gave birth to a son nine months after Gabriel appeared. Her son was named Jesus. (See Luke 1:26–38; Matthew 1:18–25. Also see Isaiah 7:14.)

Brushes with Death

THE BIBLE is filled with stories of people who barely escape a situation with their lives—some because they were in the wrong place at the wrong time, others because of what they believed.

Call Me Ishmael

The elderly Sarah finally became pregnant and bore a son for her husband, Abraham. Abraham, however, according to the custom of his day, had already fathered a child by her maidservant, Hagar. Having borne a proper heir, Sarah wanted Hagar and Hagar's son, Ishmael, sent away. The two wandered the desert until their water ran out. Hagar wept because she knew her son would soon die. But God heard the boy's cries and revealed to Hagar a well, which saved their lives. Ishmael grew up to be the father of a great nation. (See Genesis 21:9–21.)

Room Service

A prophet never won popularity contests. He or she usually delivered God's word at the risk of rejection and confrontation. Elijah, for instance, always found himself at odds with Israel's wicked King Ahab. Once, after warning Ahab of an upcoming drought, God sent Elijah off to hide in a cave. But God did not let his prophet die there. He sent ravens with food to feed Elijah until the time was right for his return. (See 1 Kings 17:1–7.)

Genocide

Defeated people are often hated people. Haman, trusted minister to King Xerxes of Persia, hated the enslaved Jewish people so much that he convinced the king to sentence them to death. What the king and Haman did not realize, however, was that Esther, King Xerxes' favorite wife, was a Jew. Before the deadly action could be taken, Esther interceded before the king for her people, thus risking her own life. The king not only stopped the scheduled slaughter, but he had the treacherous Haman put to death. (See the book of Esther.)

A Basket Case

The Jews in Damascus were beside themselves. Their greatest ally—the fierce Pharisee Saul—had gone and gotten himself converted! Saul had gone to Damascus to arrest Christians, so passionate was he about nipping Christianity in the bud and stopping the spread of the message of their heretic leader, Jesus. But on the way to the city, something happened and Saul became one of *them*—a Christian! And he started preaching! Right there in Damascus! The Jews got so upset that they plotted to kill him. Saul (Paul) learned of the plot, and his new Christian friends helped him escape by putting him in a large basket and lowering him through an opening in the city wall to the ground below. (See Acts 9:1–25.)

It's All Relative

Paul just couldn't stay out of trouble. Once again people were plotting to kill him. This time a group of Jews in Jerusalem bound themselves with an oath that they would not eat or drink until they had killed Paul. They then went and told the Jewish leaders, who then conspired to make up an excuse that they needed to have Paul brought to them the next day for questioning. "We will kill him on the way," the conspirators said. But a young man heard of their plan—he just happened to be Paul's young nephew. The brave boy went and told the Roman officers, who, in turn, foiled the murderous plan by moving Paul to a different location that very night. Wonder what happened to the murderers' oath . . . how long did they go without food and water? (See Acts 23:12–24.)

Shipwrecked and Snakebit

Probably few people in the Bible cheated death as much as the apostle Paul. He was beaten with whips and rods, stoned, and robbed. In one series of events recounted in the book of Acts, his nephew learned of a plot to kill him, so he had to be rushed away. Then, when he was on board a ship to Rome, a great storm hit, forcing the ship aground and nearly drowning the entire crew. On the island of Malta, a poisonous snake bit Paul's hand. Much to everyone's amazement, he shook off the snake and walked away unharmed. God had promised to send Paul to Rome, and not even a deadly viper could stop those plans! Church tradition maintains that Paul, in fact, later died in Rome, beheaded by the emperor. (See Acts 23:12–35; 27:1–28:6.)

Left Standing at the Altar

THE ALTAR has been the cornerstone of worship for many civilizations. In ancient Israel, the altar received gifts of thanksgiving and offerings of atonement for sin. Even at these holy places, however, the unexpected could suddenly occur.

A Dreaded Sacrifice

Isaac was the son Abraham had been promised by God. According to the Lord, he was going to make a great nation from Abraham's descendants. So it must have seemed odd to Abraham when God commanded him to build an altar and offer Isaac as a sacrifice. Without even a hint of objection, Abraham obeyed. After preparing the necessary wood, Abraham tied up his son and placed him on the altar. Surprisingly, Isaac did not resist. As Abraham raised his knife to kill his son, an angel of the Lord stopped him. God was so pleased by Abraham's obedience that he provided a ram to complete the interrupted sacrifice. Abraham's descendants—by way of his son Isaac—became the Jewish nation. (See Genesis 22:1–19.)

You Can't Do That!

The building of an altar once nearly ignited a civil war between the tribes of Israel. The tribes that had settled on the east side of the Jordan—Reuben, Gad, and the half tribe of Manasseh—had built an altar as a memorial. But the other tribes, fearful that the easterners had plunged into idolatry, prepared for war to purge the menace from their people. At a formal summit, the eastern tribes argued persuasively that they had not intended to rebel; they merely wanted to remind their descendants that they, too, were people of the living God. Their words won the day and bloodshed was averted. The people of Gad and Reuben then named their altar "Witness" to show their unity with all Israel. (See Joshua 22:10–34.)

Baal Buster

Gideon, one of Israel's most famous judges, took a hard line against idolatry. The Lord had instructed him to tear down his father's altar to Baal and to cut down the Asherah pole beside it. He was then to build an altar to the Lord using the wood of the pole to make the sacrifice. Gideon did exactly as he was told, but the town was outraged by Gideon's deed. They demanded that Gideon's father hand over his son to be executed, but his father refused and challenged Baal to defend himself. From that moment on, Gideon was known as Jerub-baal, which meant, "Let Baal defend himself." (See Judges 6:24–32.)

DID YOU KNOW?

Who was the goddess Asherah? What were Asherah poles? Why did the prophets of Israel passionately denounce the worship of Asherah?

Although the worship of Asherah was denounced again and again by the prophets of the Old Testament, the specific rituals associated with the worship of Asherah remain unknown to the modern Bible student. The Canaanites, a people who lived among the Israelites, revered Asherah as a goddess of fertility, perhaps even the goddess of sexuality. She was considered the wife of El, the supreme god in Canaanite mythology. The mysterious Asherah poles associated with the worship rites of this goddess were apparently tree trunks stripped of all their branches. The exact function of these poles—often associated with male and female prostitution—is unclear. What is known is the Israelite prophets considered these poles repulsive and ordered the kings of Israel to cut them down wherever they had been placed.

Memorable Meals

IN ANCIENT TIMES meals were occasions of great importance. Business would be conducted over meals, and great feasts would celebrate ancient treaties. Many of these ancient feasts provided an occasion of great joy to those who attended. But other celebrants faced fates far worse than indigestion.

The Most Expensive Meal in the Bible

Esau and Jacob, twin sons born to Isaac and Rebekah, had little in common. Esau, the older boy, liked the outdoors and won a reputation as a fine hunter. Jacob was more domestic, preferring to stay at home. One day Esau came home hungry while Jacob was cooking a stew. Esau demanded some, but Jacob insisted that he would give it to him only if the elder brother agreed to sell his rights as the firstborn son. Esau agreed without thinking, thus giving up all the wealth and power due to him according to the custom of his day. That one expensive meal would eventually change the course of Middle Eastern history. Jacob's descendants became the people of Israel, while Esau's became the nation of Edom, a nation that eventually vanished. (See Genesis 25:27–34.)

A Bad Case of Indigestion

Haman was beside himself with glee! A second banquet! He must truly have impressed King Xerxes and Queen Esther with his witty conversation. He felt that it went well, and then the queen asked him and the king to come back to another banquet the very next day. Haman swelled with pride at his obviously favored position in the Persian court. However, the banquet the next day didn't turn out as he anticipated. At that banquet, the queen made a strange request—she asked that her life and the lives of her people be spared. "Who would do such a thing?" the king demanded to know. Why would the queen's life be in danger? And Esther pointed at Haman, who had developed a law that the king had signed—a law that would exterminate the Jews (all in an effort by Haman to take out his sworn enemy, a Jew named Mordecai). Needless to say, the banquet did not end well for Haman. (See Esther 3–7.)

Off with His Head!

Prophets can be annoying at times—especially when their condemnations are directed at you personally. Herod Antipas, a ruler over Galilee and Perea, felt this way about John the Baptist, who pointed out to all who would listen that Herod had taken for himself his brother's wife, Herodias. Because of this, Herod had the prophet locked up. On the night of Herod's birthday, the daughter of Herodias danced for him and his dinner guests; the dance pleased him so much that he promised to give her whatever she asked for. Prompted by her mother, she asked for the head of John the Baptist on a platter, which is what she got. (See Matthew 14:1–12; Mark 6:14–29.)

A Cosmic Caterer?

The wedding host had committed a significant faux pas—he had run out of wine. Even inferior wine would have placated his guests at that point, but there was none to be found. Jesus, an invited guest, sized up the situation (at his mother's request) and ordered six large stone jars to be filled with water. Then the servants dipped a sample and gave it to the host, who tasted it. Not only had the water turned into wine, but it surpassed anything that had been served at the ceremony. With that miracle, Jesus began his public ministry. (See John 2:3–11.)

Five Thousand Families for Dinner

The people were hungry. The five thousand men were grumbling a bit, the women wondered why they hadn't planned better and brought along at least some bread, and the children—well—the children were getting a bit whiny to say the least. Still, the things this man said were so interesting, so life-changing. So they had all followed Jesus out to a remote place. Now the sun was going down. How would that many people get enough food to sustain them through the night? Suddenly thousands of robes rustled as the people began sitting down. "What's going on?" someone asked. With a shrug, another said, "I don't know. We've just been told to sit." What's this? The men were handing out food—bread and fish to everyone. It seemed to those on one side that the disciples' baskets would be empty long before they reached them—but the disciples just kept coming, handing out bread and fish, bread and fish, more bread and fish. How had this happened? (See Matthew 14, Mark 6, Luke 9, John 6.) And if that wasn't enough, Jesus did it again a bit later—this time with about four thousand families in attendance. (See Matthew 15, Mark 8.)

A Last Supper

With his closest friends around him, Jesus had supper. *They* didn't know to call it the "last" supper; but *he* did. Jesus washed their feet to show his dusty disciples what it meant to be a leader in this new movement he was inaugurating. He talked to them about who he was, about the coming of the Holy Spirit, about staying close to him like branches to a vine, about prayer. With the eating of the bread and drinking of the cups, Jesus gave special instructions to his disciples—these men (minus Judas) who would carry on this message after he returned to heaven. This special meal continues to be celebrated in Christian churches today—called Communion or Eucharist or the Lord's Supper. Paul wrote to the church in Corinth: "Every time you eat this bread and drink this cup, you are announcing the Lord's death until he comes again" (1 Corinthians 11:26). Clearly, this is the most memorable meal of all. (See Matthew 26; Mark 14; Luke 22; John 13–17.)

What a Way to Go

THOUGH SOME PEOPLE might argue that there is no good way to die, everyone would probably agree that the following deaths recorded in the Bible are particularly distasteful.

Dowry of Death

Prince Shechem was used to getting what he wanted. When he saw Dinah, the only daughter of Jacob, he was enchanted with her beauty. He seized and raped her. Shechem then wanted to marry Dinah, and so he asked her brothers and father for permission. He promised to pay any dowry they demanded as the price for his bride. Dinah's brothers, furious with what had happened, deceived Shechem by appearing to approve of the request, provided that the men of Shechem's village undergo circumcision. While they were recovering from their wounds, two of the brothers entered the town and killed every man there, including Shechem. Their retaliation infuriated Jacob, who feared that his neighbors would avenge the massacre. (See Genesis 34:1–31.)

A Splitting Headache

Sisera thought he had found refuge. The commander of the Canaanite forces, he had fled on foot after losing his entire army to the Israelites. He found the tent of Heber, a member of the Kenite tribe. Because Heber's clan was on friendly terms with the Canaanite king, Sisera accepted the hospitality of Heber's wife, Jael, who led him into her tent. He fell asleep from exhaustion, and Jael then crept to his side. She took a hammer and drove a tent peg through his skull. Deborah, the prophetess and judge, would commemorate Sisera's unseemly death in song. (See Judges 4:1–24; 5:24–31.)

A Hair-Raising Demise

Absalom, son of King David, might have lived longer if not for a head of remarkable hair. Weighing five pounds, it was thick and heavy. He cut it but once a year. Yet Absalom was vain and ambitious as well. He led a rebellion against his father that ended in failure. As he was riding a mule to flee from David's men, Absalom's hair became entangled in the branches of an oak tree. As he twisted in the air, Joab, David's general, killed him, then buried his body in a forest. Absalom's death grieved David greatly, despite his son's treachery. (See 2 Samuel 18.)

Twisted Sisters

THESE WOMEN are chiefly remembered for their scheming and callousness—but their plans came to naught in the end.

The Jilted Wife

Joseph, a fine specimen of a man, had been taken to Egypt in chains and was soon bought by Potiphar, one of Pharaoh's officials. He performed his duties well, but since he was also attractive, he caught the eye of Potiphar's wife. She was very direct: "Come and sleep with me!" Joseph refused day after day. Finally, with no one home but her and Joseph, she made one final, desperate bid; Joseph again rebuffed her. As he ran away, she grabbed his cloak. When Potiphar came home, his wife played the distraught victim. She showed him the cloak as evidence that she had fought off Joseph's advances. The enraged Potiphar threw the innocent Joseph into prison, where he languished for years before eventually being called out to interpret Pharaoh's dream. (See Genesis 39:1–23.)

Kiss and Tell

Samson was a man consecrated to God, though he certainly had his struggles with pride and anger. He also could not resist an enticing woman, regardless of her upbringing or character. Delilah, a Philistine woman, lived in the Valley of Sorek and caught Samson's eye. The Philistine leaders, who had been humiliated by Samson on many occasions, learned of the romance and convinced her to find out the secret of Samson's strength. Three times she tried in vain to discover his secret, but her nagging eventually wore Samson down.

He told her the secret: his hair had to remain uncut because he had taken a vow before God. While he was sleeping, the Philistines cut his hair and tied him up. Delilah's betrayal of her lover was complete. (See Judges 16:1–21.)

Killer Queen I

Jezebel was a downright scary lady. She caused a mighty prophet of God to run for his life and ask to die. She caused the death of a neighbor who was doing no more than minding his family vineyard. When Jezebel's husband, Ahab, wanted that vineyard, Jezebel arranged for him to get it. Jezebel brought idol worship and witchcraft into Israel, and it seems that she had no conscience, no morals, nothing to commend her. In fact, when the Bible describes an evil woman, it uses the name "Jezebel" (Revelation 2:20). She came to a fitting end—flung from a window and left to die on the pavement, where the dogs came and licked up her blood. (See 1 Kings 16–21; 2 Kings 9:7–37.)

Killer Queen II

Athaliah was grieved when her son Ahaziah, king of Judah, was killed. But she was not too grief stricken to stage a coup d'état. She made herself the legitimate ruler by murdering anyone with a claim to the throne—and that included all of Ahaziah's children. But her daughter-in-law Jehosheba got wind of her plans and sent the youngest son, Joash, into hiding. There he stayed for six years. Jehoiada, the high priest, cared for the boy until he decided the moment was right to bring down Athaliah. In a sudden, surprise public ceremony, Joash was crowned king. Jehoiada then ordered soldiers loyal to him to execute Athaliah, which they did. She was the only woman to rule over the kingdom of Judah. (See 2 Kings 11:1–15.)

God's Mountain

ALTHOUGH NO ONE today is completely certain of its location, there is a place mentioned in both the Old and New Testaments of the Bible as Mount Sinai. Also sometimes called Mount Horeb, this site is so important that it is referred to in some translations as "God's mountain," and for good reason. This holy site figured time and again in Israel's spiritual history.

The Burning Bush That Did Not Burn

Moses, who later became the great prophet of the Israelite people, was tending sheep in the desert of Sinai. While he was there, he saw a bush that was on fire but did not burn up. Fascinated, he approached to investigate. Imagine his surprise and fright when he heard a voice coming from the bush. Not just any voice, but the voice of the living God! Moses obeyed God's command to remove his sandals, for the mountainside he stood on was God's holy ground. Moses discovered then that he had been chosen to lead God's people from Egypt. (See Exodus 3:1–22.)

In the Presence of God

After the prophet Moses led the Israelite people out of slavery in Egypt, he took them to Mount Sinai as God had instructed. Leaving the people camped at the base of the mountain, Moses scaled its heights to speak with and worship God. Yahweh descended to the mountain in a bright cloud and gave his law to Moses. Afterward, when Moses returned, the people noticed that his face was shining brightly because he had been in the presence of God. The tablets he carried with him contained a summary of the law for Israel, often called the Ten Commandments. (See Exodus 34:1–35.)

Sanctuary

Having just experienced a tremendous victory over the priests of Baal, the Israelite prophet Elijah found himself on the run for his life. Jezebel, queen of Israel, had demanded his death for his humiliation of her priests. An angel told him to journey hundreds of miles to Mount Sinai. At Sinai, we are told, God came to him and asked why he was there. Elijah told God his troubles, and God responded by telling the prophet to go stand out on the mountain so that Elijah could see him when God passed by. Then a strong wind shook the mountain and shattered the rocks. It was followed by an earthquake, then a fire. But God did not reveal his presence until he spoke in the whisper of a gentle breeze. Reassured, Elijah followed God's instructions and returned the way he came. (See 1 Kings 19:1–18.)

DID YOU KNOW?

Who survived forty days without food or water?

A courageous dieter might try to abstain from food for a week. But how does forty days without food—or even water—sound? Fasting has enjoyed a revival in popularity for its health and spiritual benefits. Yet prolonged fasts are unusual. Doctors would call such behavior suicidal. We learn that Moses did just that—he abstained from all nourishment for forty days (Exodus 34:28). A person can survive without eating any food for

twenty-eight days. But water is even more crucial to life. A person can go without water only for seven days. How did Moses survive without water for forty days? Perhaps angels ministered to his needs, as they did when Christ undertook a similar fast in the desert (see Matthew 4:2). Perhaps he was sustained by God himself as he waited on the holy slopes of Mount Sinai.

THE LONG AND AMAZING LIFE OF THE BIBLE

The Bible is one of the oldest books known to humankind. Below is a list of the twists and turns in the long history of this manuscript.

INCIDENT	REST OF THE STORY	REFERENCE
It's been broken.	When Moses returned the first time from Mount Sinai with the stone tablets upon which God had engraved the law, he discovered the people in a pagan orgy. In anger, he threw down the tablets and broke them. God then issued a "second printing" of the law.	Exodus 32:19–20; 34:1–35
It's been boxed and engraved.	Efforts to apply the commands in Deuteronomy 6:8–9 resulted in several traditions that still characterize the Jewish people. The phrase "tie them on your hands and wear them on your forehead as reminders" developed into the tefillin, black straps with small boxes attached to the end. Devout Jewish males wear two of these tefillin in worship: one wrapped around their head so that the box containing handwritten Scripture hangs between their eyes, and the other wrapped around an arm. The phrase "write them on the doorposts of your house" led to the creation of mezuzahs, hollow plaques that include inside a tiny scroll of Deuteronomy 6:4 and that are nailed to the door frames in homes.	Deuteronomy 6:8–9; Matthew 23:5

INCIDENT	REST OF THE STORY	REFERENCE
It's been lost and found.	During Josiah's reign, the temple in Jerusalem was cleaned out and restored. As debris was removed, a scroll copy of the law was discovered. Apparently, neglect had resulted in a loss or misplacing of the Scriptures. The warnings and promised judgments added fuel to a spiritual revival in the land.	2 Kings 22:8–13
It's been praised.	A talented worshiper wrote an encyclopedic psalm in which every one of the 176 verses expresses respect and honor for God's word. The psalm has twenty-two sections, each corresponding to a different letter of the Hebrew alphabet, and each verse begins with the letter of its section.	Psalm 119
It's been cut and burned.	King Jehoiakim sliced off sections of Jeremiah's scroll and burned them after hearing what God had instructed the prophet to write.	Jeremiah 36:21–25
It's been eaten.	After singling out the prophet Ezekiel for special service, God included in his vision a scroll that he had the prophet eat. Although the writings on the scroll were full of sorrow, Ezekiel reported that the taste of the scroll was sweet.	Ezekiel 2:9–3:3
It's been twisted.	Jesus pointed out with anger that some "applications" of Scripture actually resulted in twisting God's commands. For example, teachers in Jesus' day told people that the necessity for caring for their parents could be avoided if they merely "dedicated" all their belongings to God.	Mark 7:6–13

DID YOU KNOW?

Why would the Hebrews worship a calf? How could a golden statue inspire an orgy?

The story of the golden calf still evokes surprise in modern readers. Why would people want to worship an object they had made with their own hands? And how could they forget the law Moses had presented to them just days before? The first commandment, above all, warned the Israelites not to worship false gods. But Aaron, Moses' brother and future high priest, yielded to popular pressure and made a calf out of gold. The people responded with an unrestrained orgy of drinking and carousing (see Exodus 32).

Scholars have debated the appeal of this idol for centuries. Some have suggested that it wasn't actually a calf, but a bull. The writers of the Bible used the word *calf* to express their contempt for the object the Israelites worshiped. The bull was worshiped by many in the ancient Middle East. For instance, the Egyptians worshiped Hapi, a god represented by a bull. It's possible that, having just left Egypt, the Israelites fashioned a god that looked familiar. It's also possible that the Israelites were modeling their "calf" on the bulls that embodied the Canaanite god Baal. In ancient times, a bull was a common symbol of fertility. This explains why a "calf" might spark all kinds of debauchery.

Ordinary Objects

THE BIBLE relates many strange stories about common, ordinary objects like sticks, wooden rods, and shepherds' staffs that do uncommon and extraordinary things.

The Serpent Staff

God had chosen Moses to return to Egypt and lead God's people out of slavery. But Moses was unsure and hesitant and gave many excuses why he couldn't do it. God told Moses to throw his shepherd's staff on the ground. He did, and it became a snake. When he picked it up by the tail, it became a shepherd's staff again. Moses used that staff to perform many signs that convinced (albeit only temporarily) Egypts' Pharaoh to let God's people go. (See Exodus 4:1–5.)

Sticks and Stones

Moses and the people of Israel had escaped from Egyptian slavery but faced the new challenge of a hostile wilderness. When they reached a desert place that had no water, the thirsty people began complaining and grumbling against Moses. God told Moses to strike a rock with his shepherd's staff. When Moses obeyed, enough water came gushing out for all the people and their animals. Years later, they came to another desert place where there was no water. This time, God told Moses to speak to a rock and he would find water. But instead of speaking to the rock, Moses struck it twice with his staff. Water came out, but because he had not followed God's instructions, Moses was not allowed to enter the Promised Land with the people. (See Exodus 17:1–6; Numbers 20:1–12.)

A Wooden Staff that Budded

Moses told each of the twelve tribal chiefs of Israel to bring a wooden staff with his name written on it to be placed in the inner room of the tabernacle. The man whose staff was chosen by God would have authority to rule over Israel under Moses. They would know the man of God's choice because buds would grow on his staff. So each man, including Aaron, brought a staff with his name on it, and Moses put them in the tabernacle. The next morning, Moses and the tribal chiefs knew that God's choice was Aaron because Aaron's staff was blossoming, with ripe almonds hanging from it! (See Numbers 17:1–11.)

A Small Stone and a Big Headache

Two stunned armies watched as the giant man in the massive armor plunged to the ground. The match had looked like no more than a joke—a little Israeli shepherd boy coming center stage for one-on-one combat with a seasoned Philistine soldier who was over nine feet tall. Whoever won this contest would win the battle, and the Philistine army must have sat chuckling as Goliath put on his 125 pounds of armor. David tried to put on armor, but it was too heavy. Instead, he ran to the nearest stream and picked up five smooth stones. The Israeli army must have been taking off their armor, preparing to run for their lives. What was King Saul thinking when he allowed this to happen? But David wasn't worried. "I come to you in the name of the LORD of Heaven's Armies!" David shouted at Goliath. As the giant came toward him, David put a stone into his sling and sent it whizzing. The stone hit Goliath in the forehead, bringing him down. David used Goliath's own sword to kill him by cutting off his head. (See 1 Samuel 17.)

The Stick That Made an Ax Head Float

The prophet Elisha stood on the banks of the Jordan River helping students cut down trees to build a new dormitory. As they worked, one student's borrowed ax head fell off the handle and sank under the water. It was made of iron, a rare metal in those days, and quite valuable. Frantic, he asked Elisha to help him. Elisha inquired where the ax head had fallen, and the anxious student showed him the spot. Elisha cut a stick and threw it into the river. Miraculously, the ax head defied gravity and the rushing current, floating to the surface, where the man was able to retrieve it. (See 2 Kings 6:1–7.)

Instant Leprosy

GOD'S GREAT PATIENCE was sorely tested by those who angered him or defied his commands. Sometimes he used illness or affliction to change cold hearts or to end rebellion. In the case of Moses, he used an illness to demonstrate his mastery over all nature. Scripture relates a few episodes of instant illness that struck without warning.

A Sign from God

God had just revealed his plan of redemption to Moses. Fearful and confused, Moses blurted out his concern that no one would believe that God had chosen him. So God gave him two signs: his staff, which could turn into a serpent and back again, and his own hand. When Moses placed his hand under his robe and removed it again, it was leprous—as white as snow! But when he placed his hand in the robe a second time, the hand returned to normal. God told Moses to use these signs before the people of Israel so that they would know he had sent Moses to lead them. (See Exodus 4:1–8.)

A Jealous Sister

Moses was the leader of his people, and his sister, Miriam, enjoyed a great deal of status as a worship leader. Still, she expressed jealousy with Moses' unchallenged leadership and teamed with her brother Aaron to criticize Moses' marriage to a foreign woman. God heard her complaint and chastised her for her attitude. To punish Miriam, he inflicted her with leprosy for seven days—an affliction that forced her to remain outside the Israelite camp until she was pronounced clean. (See Numbers 12:1–15.)

Pride Goeth Before a Fall

Uzziah had been a good king, but he became proud of his power. One day he disobeyed God by going into the temple and burning an incense offering to God, which was the duty of the priests alone. Because of this, Uzziah was stricken with leprosy for the remainder of his life. That meant he could never again enter the temple or even his palace. His son had to rule in his place. And when Uzziah died because of his disease, he could not be buried in the royal tombs. (See 2 Chronicles 26.)

Circumstantial Circumcision

THE ANCIENTS practiced circumcision of male boys, just as many people do today. For the Israelites, this practice identified them with God as his people. It was an initiation rite. But sometimes the deed was carried out in threatening or bizarre circumstances.

The Forgotten Deed

Moses should have remembered. He had been entrusted with leading Israel out of bondage and bringing renewal to God's people. Yet he had neglected to circumcise his own son—a major blunder for the new leader of God's people! So God confronted Moses and was about to kill him when Zipporah, Moses' wife, grabbed a flint knife and circumcised the boy, then chastised Moses. (See Exodus 4:24–26.)

The Price for a Bride

David was getting lots of attention after his defeat of Goliath. In fact, more attention than the king himself, which didn't make King Saul happy at all. King Saul was going to give his daughter Michal as David's wife, but Saul demanded a rather unusual dowry for his daughter. The king ordered David to bring him the foreskins of one hundred Philistines. Saul secretly hoped that David would be killed by the Philistines while collecting the dowry. The king was unpleasantly surprised when David returned later with two hundred Philistine foreskins—twice the dowry Saul had asked for. (See 1 Samuel 18.)

A Source of Controversy

Timothy, the son of a Jewish mother and a Greek father, was an early convert to Christianity. This young man was so highly thought of in Lystra and Iconium that Paul decided to take Timothy with him on a missionary journey. Paul knew that he and Timothy would encounter Jewish converts on their journey. He also knew that these Jewish converts would be offended by an uncircumcised son of a Jewish mother. In order to avoid this potential problem, Paul circumcised Timothy before the journey. (See Acts 16:1–4.)

Sorcerers' Apprentices

S CRIPTURE HAS ALWAYS sternly warned God's people to stay away from sorcery and witchcraft. Those who practice these black arts rebel against God and place themselves and others in danger. Not surprisingly, the magicians and sorcerers we encounter in the Bible are usually up to no good. Here are three stories of sorcerers who found themselves on the wrong side of a spiritual battle.

Jannes and Jambres

Magicians—even ones that worked on the wrong side—could perform astonishing feats. The sorcerers who served in Pharaoh's court knew and practiced the ways of the occult. When Moses and Aaron came before Pharaoh, Aaron threw down his staff, which became a snake before the Pharaoh's eyes. Egypt's sorcerers were able to produce similar results, so Pharaoh remained stubbornly opposed to the warnings of Moses and Aaron. The magicians were also able to replicate some of the plagues that followed—the blood in the Nile River and the hordes of frogs that covered the landscape. They failed, however, to reproduce any of the other plagues. (Oddly enough, you might think that truly powerful sorcerers would attempt to stop the plagues instead of adding to them! But they couldn't—they could only replicate some of what Moses and Aaron did, and in turn, they made the plagues that much worse.) The sorcerers recognized a force greater than they could summon. "This is the finger of God!" they exclaimed (Exodus 8:19). Paul identified the magicians who opposed Moses as Jannes and Jambres, and referred to these men as an example of all who willfully oppose the truth. (See 2 Timothy 3:8–9.)

The Medium at Endor

The stranger came in the cover of darkness, for he had come to seek the counsel of a fortune-teller. Mediums had long been banned in Israel, and the penalty for practicing black arts was death. The man asked the medium, a fearful and suspicious woman, to bring up the spirit of the prophet Samuel, who had recently died. The woman screamed when she saw Samuel's ghostly form because she then realized that her night visitor was the king of Israel, Saul himself! Saul promised her that she would not be punished. Then he learned from the spirit that he would die in battle the next day. The prophecy proved all too true, as the very next day the Philistines killed Saul and his sons. (See 1 Samuel 28.)

Elymas

In the town of Paphos, Paul and Barnabas encountered a sorcerer named Bar-Jesus, also called (in Greek) Elymas. This man had become a kind of spiritual advisor to the governor of Cyprus. Fearful of losing his influence, Elymas urged the governor not to grant an audience to the missionaries. But Paul confronted Elymas for his stubborn resistance to God's ways and declared that the sorcerer would be struck with blindness. Instantly Elymas's sight failed, and he began groping in the darkness. The governor, who had witnessed this confrontation, was astonished and eagerly received Paul's words. (See Acts 13:4–12.)

Water,
Water Anywhere

H UMANS CANNOT live without water. In the arid regions of the Middle East, traveling without water invites great risk, even death. So what were God's people to do when water was nowhere in sight? Here are miraculous stories of water that came from the most unexpected places.

Dying of Thirst: Part I

Early on during their march in the wilderness, the Israelites began complaining to their leader Moses about the lack of water. They had just escaped from Egypt, but the Israelites had apparently lost their short-term memory; they whined as if God were no longer inter-ested in their welfare. The book of Exodus records that Moses asked God what to do, and God had him take the elders to a rock at Mount Sinai and strike it with his staff. From the rock came water for the people to drink. Even so, the place became known as Massah and Meribah—meaning "test" and "arguing"—because of the Israelites' lack of faith. (See Exodus 17:1–7.)

Dying of Thirst: Part II

Several years after the incident at Massah, the Israelites again tested God's patience. Arriving at Kadesh in the wilderness of Zin, they complained because of the lack of water. They challenged Moses and declared that they would be better off dead. God told Moses to simply speak to a nearby rock in the presence of the people, and water would gush out for them and their livestock. Moses instead struck the rock with his staff, adding, "Must we bring you water from this rock?" The water burst forth, and the people drank their fill. Because he had acted contrary to God's instruction, Moses was not allowed to enter the Promised Land. (See Numbers 20:1–13.)

A Spring for Samson

He sat on the ground, exhausted. Samson, the great hero of the Israelites, had struck down a thousand Philistines using only the jawbone of a donkey. The ordeal had drained him. Crying out, Samson complained to God that he was dying of thirst. Suddenly a spring of water gushed out of a hollow in the ground, and Samson drank until he was satisfied. In gratitude, Samson named the place "The Spring of the One Who Cried Out." (See Judges 15:18–19.)

Winning
Against All Odds

T HE BIBLE tells many stories of people achieving astounding victories against incredible odds. How these people escaped from certain death or defeat is a baffling puzzle that even the most dedicated inquirer cannot answer through the usual means.

Hands Up!

A short time after the miracle at the Red Sea, the Israelites encountered resistance again—this time from the Amalekites, a fierce people who inhabited the wilderness of Sinai. Moses summoned Joshua to assemble the Israelites for war. The ensuing battle turned into a seesaw event. As long as Moses held up his staff with his hands, the Israelites prevailed. But when he lowered his hands, the Amalekites would push back the Israelites. Finally, Aaron and Hur had Moses sit on a rock while they held up his hands. By sunset, Israel had crushed the invading tribes. A grateful Moses built an altar to the Lord at that site. (See Exodus 17:10–16.)

Daylight Savings

The resounding victory that Joshua gained over the Amorites witnessed a series of remarkable supernatural interventions. Joshua had traveled to the besieged city of Gibeon to rescue its inhabitants. Scripture declares that the Lord threw the Amorite armies, surprised by Joshua's rapid arrival, into a panic. Their ranks broke, and soldiers fled on foot, where they were pounded by a hailstorm that took more lives than had fallen in battle that day. More astounding was the answer of Joshua's prayer. Before the battle, he had earnestly asked God to make the sun stand still over Gibeon. And Scripture remarks that the sun indeed stopped its motion until the Amorites were defeated. The concluding statement of this passage sums up the amazing event: "There has never been a day like this one before or since, when the LORD answered such a prayer." (See Joshua 10:9–14.)

Outnumbered

Gideon couldn't believe it. Three hundred men? Only three hundred men? The Midianite army they had to fight had thousands of trained soldiers; how was he going to win a battle by sending home almost thirty-two thousand soldiers, leaving three hundred chosen by the way they drank from a stream? But God wanted Gideon to understand that the battle would not be won by him or his army; God would bring the victory. Sure enough, that night, when Gideon's men blew their horns, raised their lamps, and shouted at the tops of their voices, the Midianite army fell into confusion and began fighting against one another. Israel won the battle. (See Judges 7.)

The Army That Couldn't See Straight

The Arameans were at war with Israel. They tried frequently to set up ambushes, but the prophet Elisha would tell the king of Israel about it and the soldiers would have time to escape. So the king of Aram got angry with Elisha and decided to go after him. When he found out where Elisha was, he sent his troops to surround the city at night. The next morning the Aramean forces attacked, and as they did so, Elisha prayed and asked God to strike the men blind. Instantly, the Aramean soldiers all became sightless. Elisha went out and told them that they were on the wrong road and had attacked the wrong city. He then led them to Samaria, Israel's capital. As soon as they entered the city gates, he prayed for their sight to be restored. They were captured. The king of Israel then gave them a feast and sent them home, and the Arameans stopped their attacks on Israel. (See 2 Kings 6:8–23.)

Animal Tales

ANYONE who has toured a zoo knows that there are some strange animals. Here are some strange stories involving animals that appear in the Bible.

Zero Tolerance for Repeat Offenders

Oxen with nasty tempers probably did not last too long in Israel. According to the law of Moses, an ox that killed a man or woman could be stoned to death and its owner fined. If the ox had a history of harming people and the owner did not take steps to prevent such behavior, then the owner and the animal would both be stoned. (See Exodus 21:28–30.)

The Talking Donkey

It wasn't the donkey's fault—he just saw the massive angel with the sword standing across the road and didn't want to mess with him. Unfortunately, his master couldn't see the angel. So as the donkey bolted off the road, tried to squeeze by, and finally simply refused to move, the master beat him over and over. Finally, the donkey spoke up: "What have I done to you that deserves your beating me three times?" Oddly enough, his master answered. They talked about this until the Lord opened the master's eyes and he saw the angel with the sword. The master realized that the donkey had saved his life. (See Numbers 22:21–36.)

Don't Get That Bald Guy Mad

In Israel's culture, youth were expected to show deep respect for their elders. Moses' law, for instance, meted out severe penalties for children who failed to honor their parents. Perhaps that explains Elisha's angry reaction to a band of young men who confronted him on the road to Bethel. They began teasing and insulting him, chanting, "Go away, baldy!" Elisha looked at them and cursed them. At that moment, two bears charged out of the woods and mauled forty-two of Elisha's detractors. Thus avenged, Elisha continued on his way. (See 2 Kings 2:23–24.)

Just a Light Lunch?

The lions should have pounced on him. As the special executioners of the king, these lions were kept just hungry enough to maul, kill, and eat anyone who displeased the king and was unfortunate enough to be thrown into the lions' den. So when Daniel landed amongst them, he should have been nothing more than a quick lunch. Instead, Daniel landed, sat up, and looked around. One big lion looked at him, yawned, and then went back to sleep. A couple may have growled at him. In any case, they didn't pay any attention to Daniel, for God was watching over him. The next day, when Daniel was pulled out safely, the king decided to execute all those who had accused Daniel. The hungry lions killed them before they even hit the floor of the den. (See Daniel 6.)

DID YOU KNOW?

What ferocious beast mentioned in the Bible has defied scientific classification?

In the book of Job we meet the strange creature called the Leviathan (Job 3:8). With rows of shields on its back, scales as sharp as glass on its underside, and fearsome, sharp teeth, it struck fear in human hearts. This beast of the sea (the Hebrew word for Leviathan literally means "sea serpent") was also said to spurt fire and smoke from its mouth and nose (see Job 41:1–34).

Many Bible commentators have suggested that the Leviathan is an exaggerated description of the crocodile, emphasizing the strength of this reptile. Others have suggested that the Leviathan might be some kind of fierce dinosaur from the ancient past. Some scholars have noted the remarkable similarities between the descriptions of the Leviathan in the Bible and the Lotan, an evil, seven-headed sea monster prevalent in ancient Canaanite lore (see Psalm 74:14). These commentators have suggested that the multiheaded, fire-breathing Leviathan is a primitive symbol of chaos and depravity.

Whether these extraordinary descriptions of a multiheaded monster actually matched some huge serpent that roamed the ancient seas remains unknown. But what *is* known is that this beast became a powerful image of evil. The book of Revelation alludes to a seven-headed sea monster that will wreak havoc on the earth in the last days (see Revelation 13:1–9).

Sudden Death

O NE SECOND the person is alive, the next he or she inexplicably drops dead. The Bible is filled with accounts of people whose lives were snuffed out in an instant. What had they done? What brought about such retribution?

Flash in the Pan

Even having a famous father is not enough when you disobey God. Nadab and Abihu were the sons of Aaron, the brother of the great prophet Moses and the first high priest of the Israelites. While making offerings in the tabernacle, Aaron's sons burned incense to God in a pan in an improper manner. Seconds later, fiery flames shot down from heaven and incinerated them. It was not just that they made a mistake; their actions revealed deep disrespect for God and for the rules of worship he had given. This terrifying and sobering lesson was not lost on Aaron and his two remaining sons. (See Leviticus 10:1–3.)

No News Is Good News

Best known as the mentor of the prophet Samuel, Eli was the high priest of Israel during the time of the judges. Yet his own weakness as a father caused him to neglect the irreverent behavior of his sons Hophni and Phinehas. A prophet approached Eli with news that his failure would forever hound his family and that his sons would die on the same day. Soon afterward, his sons carried the ark of the covenant into battle with the Philistines. Both were killed, and the ark was captured. When Eli heard the report from the battlefield, he

fell backward from his seat and died instantly from a broken neck.
(See 1 Samuel 4:12–21.)

The Touch of Death

Uzzah should have known better. The law of Moses had made clear
that there were proper and improper ways to move the ark of the
covenant. Instead of carrying the ark on poles as the law required,
it was moved on an oxcart. When the oxen stumbled, Uzzah tried
to save the ark from falling and reached out to steady it. His gesture, though well intended, disregarded the holiness of the object
he touched. Uzzah died instantly, and that put an immediate end to
the festive procession. (See 2 Samuel 6.)

A Deadly Pair

Ananias and Sapphira had a plan. In order to look good to the Christians, they would sell a piece of property and bring the money to the
apostles (a guy named Barnabas had done that, and he was getting
all kinds of attention). However, they really intended to give only
part of the money and keep some for themselves. And that certainly
was acceptable; no one said they had to donate the entire sale price.
The problem was that they lied about how much they were bringing. Such dishonesty had to be punished, and these two received
the ultimate punishment. The minute Ananias realized he'd been
caught, he died instantly. His body was taken out and buried. About
three hours later Sapphira arrived, told the same lie, and died the
same way. She was taken out and buried beside her husband. And
the believers learned a powerful lesson about truthfulness. (See Acts
5:1–11.)

Stoned

THE PRACTICE of stoning a person to death has largely disappeared today. Yet in many ancient cultures, stoning was demanded for crimes against God and society. The Bible first mentions this practice in Exodus 8:26, where Moses voiced the fear that Hebrew worship would incite the Egyptians to stone his people. The law mandated death by stoning as punishment for human sacrifice, blasphemy, sorcery, and other crimes. Yet innocent people also became victims, as the record of Scripture shows.

The First Execution
The first record of a stoning occurs in Leviticus 24:23. Here we read that the unnamed son of an Israelite woman and Egyptian man was put to death for cursing the name of the Lord. The young man should have known the law—one of the Ten Commandments given by Moses said, "You must not misuse the name of the LORD your God. The LORD will not let you go unpunished if you misuse his name" (Exodus 20:7). Hence, the man had fair warning that his crime was punishable by death. Later, another Israelite was stoned for gathering wood on the Sabbath. (See Numbers 15:32–35.)

Collective Guilt
A beautiful robe imported from Babylon, hundreds of silver coins, a bar of gold—the young Israelite named Achan saw the rich plunder that had been seized from the Canaanites. Rather than destroy the loot as God had ordered, Achan decided to take a portion for himself and kept it buried under his tent. However, after a disastrous

battle and an episode of soul-searching, God told Joshua that Israel's misfortune had been caused by Achan's disobedience. Immediately, Achan, his family, his possessions, and the hidden plunder were taken to the valley of Achor. The community stoned them to death and buried everything under a great pile of rocks. (See Joshua 7:1–26.)

Greed Kills

King Ahab thought he had offered a fair deal to Naboth. In exchange for Naboth's vineyard, which was situated near his palace, Ahab offered a handsome price or the promise of better land. Naboth refused the offer, however. According to God's law, it was Naboth's duty to keep his ancestral land in his family. Ahab's wife, Jezebel, then cooked up a wicked scheme to seize the land. She coerced the elders of Naboth's town to hold a meeting at which two hired false witnesses would appear to accuse Naboth of cursing God. Everything transpired as Jezebel had ordered, and Naboth was stoned to death. Ahab then claimed the vineyard, but at a terrible price: the prophet Isaiah confronted him with the news that his kingdom would be destroyed. (See 1 Kings 21:1–22.)

Left for Dead

The apostle Paul endured many physical hardships in his years of ministry, but none perhaps as harrowing as his near-death experience in Lystra. Rounded up by an angry mob that Jewish opponents had stirred to action, Paul was dragged outside the city gates and stoned. Left for dead, Paul revived as fellow believers gathered around him. He went back into the city and resumed his travels the next day. (See Acts 14:19–20.)

Tall Tales

THROUGHOUT the Old Testament we find evidence of a mysterious race of giants. Where they came from remains cloaked in uncertainty; what eventually became of these people is likewise lost in the shadows of time. In any event, they almost certainly disappeared long before the birth of Jesus.

The Nephilites
Genesis 6 tells of an early race of giants that many translations say were the extraordinary beings known as the Nephilites (some Bible versions say "Nephilim"). These mammoth beings roamed the earth before the flood, and they may have been the offspring of supernatural beings who consorted with humans (see Genesis 6:4). So large were they and their descendants that, in a later account, the Israelites said that they seemed like grasshoppers in comparison to the Nephilites. (See Numbers 13:33.)

The Rephaites
Another race of giants appears in the Old Testament books. Known as the Rephaites (some Bible versions say "Rephaim"), they were noted for their physical might, but they did not survive the Israelites' invasion of Canaan. Reportedly the last survivor of this race, King Og of Bashan, slept in an iron bed thirteen feet long and six feet wide (Deuteronomy 3:11).

The Philistine Giants
The formidable Goliath, who stood nearly nine feet tall, was the best

known of a group of giants called the descendants of Rapha. (Their relation to the Rephaites is uncertain.) A few skirmishes with these warriors appear in 2 Samuel and again in 1 Chronicles. Ishbi-benob, a descendant of the Rapha, tried to kill King David but was himself killed. David's mighty men also killed other giants, including the brother of Goliath and a warrior with six fingers on each hand and six toes on each foot! (See 2 Samuel 21:15–22; 1 Chronicles 20:4–8.)

A Throw of the Dice

DICE THROWN, lots cast—decisions were often made by games of chance. The ancients believed that divine guidance, not luck, would determine the outcome. Besides the Urim and Thummin, the mysterious stones that the priest of Israel consulted, lots, and dice often shaped the destiny of ancient Israel and even the early church.

And the Winner Is . . .

After Israel had captured vast tracts of territory in Canaan, they had to divide the land among the twelve tribes. Five of the tribes had sections of land that became their inheritance, but the remaining land had to be divided by the other seven tribes. Their leader Joshua left that decision in God's hands. At Shiloh, the resting place of the tabernacle, Joshua ordered that the remaining land be surveyed, then divided by the casting of sacred lots. In this way each tribe gained its inheritance. (See Joshua 18:1–10.)

And the Guilty Party Is . . .

Saul, the first king of the Israelites, wanted to destroy the Philistine army by pursuing them in an all-night chase. At the suggestion of his priest, Saul cast lots to determine if this course was wise. But the lots gave him no answer, so Saul knew that something was wrong. He cast lots again to determine the source of the sin. The results pointed to his own son Jonathan, who had tasted honey despite Saul's order to the army that they fast until the enemy was defeated. Saul was prepared to execute Jonathan, but the people of Israel persuaded him not to because of Jonathan's heroism in battle. (See 1 Samuel 14:36–45.)

You Can Run But You Can't Hide

Jonah had received orders from God—orders that he did not want to follow. He tried to run by getting on a ship and sailing away. A great storm sprang up and threatened to destroy the ship. The sailors were frightened and wanted to know who was causing their misfortune. They cast lots and discovered that Jonah had angered the gods. So, at Jonah's bidding, they did what they thought best to calm the seas, and threw Jonah overboard. The storm stopped, and the sailors offered prayers and vows to the Lord that Jonah served. (See Jonah 1:3–16.)

Judas's Replacement

The twelve apostles lost one of their numbers when their former comrade Judas killed himself. They decided to choose a replacement in accordance with Scripture: "Let someone else take his position" (Psalm 109:8). Two men were nominated: Joseph called Barsabbas (also known as Justus) and Matthias. The apostles prayed to God to show them who should be chosen, and then they cast lots. The lot fell to Matthias, who took Judas's place. Ironically, Matthias's name does not appear in Scripture again. (See Acts 1:20–26.)

DID YOU KNOW?

What were the Urim and Thummim?

Did you know that the ancient high priests of Israel used Urim and Thummim to receive direct revelations from God? How the high priest received these revelations and what the Urim and Thummim actually were remains a mystery buried in the ancient past. All that is known for certain is that the Urim and Thummim were connected with the breastplate worn by the high priest (see Exodus 28:30) and that the Urim and Thummim were a means of casting sacred lots (see Numbers 27:21).

Some have suggested that the twelve stones on the breastplate of the high priest (one stone for each tribe of Israel) were in fact the Urim and Thummim, but many biblical commentators believe that the Urim and Thummim were gems kept in a pouch over the high priest's heart. Some believe these gems were engraved with some symbol that reflected yes, no, or divine silence (see 1 Samuel 28:6). Other commentators have suggested that the high priest received revelations by observing some type of mysterious light reflected by these gems. The details concerning Urim and Thummim remain a mystery because their use decreased after King David's reign. After that, Israel's prophets revealed God's will to the people.

One-Man
Wrecking Crews

Most people love to root for the underdog. Whether it's a college basketball game or the latest Hollywood action movie, the odds are stacked against the little guy. The Bible contains many stories of people who prevailed in the face of unbelievable odds. Take a look at some of these mismatched contests.

Shamgar vs. the Philistines

Chapter 3 of the book of Judges sums up the accomplishments of Shamgar in one verse. But the tale of that one verse is quite incredible. In a battle with the Philistines, Shamgar struck down hundreds of enemy soldiers with an ox goad, a long wooden rod with a metal tip used for prodding domesticated animals. Judges 3:31 records that Shamgar alone was responsible for six hundred Philistine deaths!

Jonathan vs. the Philistines

Once again the Philistines took it on the chin from a one-man vengeance squad. This time, Jonathan, the son of King Saul, administered the beating. Trusting in the power of God, Jonathan, accompanied only by his armor bearer, climbed up a cliff and attacked a Philistine military outpost. After Jonathan had killed at least twenty Philistine soldiers, the rest of the Philistine army began to panic. Israelite lookouts spotted the disturbance and informed King Saul. Seizing the opportunity presented by his son's attack,

Saul ordered his army to attack and soundly defeated the Philistines. (See 1 Samuel 14:1–23.)

One Small Shepherd Boy vs. One Big Bad Boy

He really shouldn't even have been there. David was too young to be in battle, but he had arrived at the Israelite encampment with provisions for his brothers. When he arrived, the giant Philistine was strutting his stuff in the valley between the two armies. Goliath issued a challenge: "Choose one man to come down here and fight me! If he kills me, then we will be your slaves. But if I kill him, you will be our slaves!" Problem was, the man was over nine feet tall, with heavy bronze armor and a huge javelin. No one in Israel wanted to take the chance against him—it would be certain defeat. No one, that is, until David arrived. He began asking, "Who is this pagan Philistine anyway, that he is allowed to defy the armies of the living God?" You see, David knew that Israel's God was way bigger than any armor-clad giant. And David was right. The small shepherd boy with the sling defeated the massive giant and won the battle. (See 1 Samuel 17.)

Mightiest of the Mighty

Many skilled warriors joined David before his days as king. The bravest of them became known as David's mighty men, or the Thirty, and among them were three who set themselves apart as the Three, the mightiest of the mighty. We might call Eleazar the One. On one occasion he and David challenged the Philistine army that had gathered for battle. David's forces engaged the Philistines, but the Israelites soon fell back in retreat. Eleazar, however, stood his ground. He fought the Philistines single-handedly until the entire Philistine militia had fallen to his sword, wrapped tightly in a hand so cramped he couldn't peel it off the hilt. The Israelite army returned later to plunder the bodies of the Philistine soldiers. (See 2 Samuel 23:9–10.)

Elijah vs. the Prophets of Baal

Compared with Shamgar, Eleazar, and Jonathan, Elijah was a decidedly nonviolent one-man wrecking crew. The Lord used Elijah to single-handedly destroy the credibility of Baal worship. Elijah challenged 450 prophets of Baal to a contest. Elijah would prepare a sacrifice to the Lord on one altar; the prophets of Baal would prepare a sacrifice to Baal on another altar. The deity who sent fire to accept his sacrifice would be declared the God of Israel. Despite their frantic efforts (which included slashing themselves), the prophets of Baal were unable to get their god to respond. The God of Israel, on the other hand, sent a fire that consumed not just Elijah's sacrifice, but also the altar itself! As a result of Elijah's victory, all 450 prophets were slaughtered in Kishon Valley. (See 1 Kings 18:16–40.)

MIGHTY WARRIORS

Ancient warriors of the Bible defeated thousands—even tens of thousands. Below is a list of many of the Bible's mighty warriors.

PERSON	EXPERIENCE	REFERENCE
Nimrod	A mighty warrior/hunter who was considered the standard by which great hunters were measured. He built cities like Nineveh, Rehoboth Ir, and Calah in Assyria. He was a descendant of Ham, son of Noah.	Genesis 10:8–12
Abram	Led 318 trained men to battle against four kings who plundered Sodom and Gomorrah, where his nephew Lot had settled. Abram won the battle and got back Lot, his families, and all of their possessions.	Genesis 14:11–17
Joshua	Selected to lead the Israelites into the Promised Land after Moses. Led the Israelites in several battles with various Canaanite groups to gain control of the land. Defeated the armies of thirty-one kings.	Joshua 1–11

Person	Experience	Reference
Barak	Defeated the Canaanites who were led by Sisera. His reluctance to go to battle without the prophetess Deborah resulted in his loss of the ultimate victory, the death of Sisera. The honor went to a woman instead.	Judges 4
Sisera	Canaanite general who had nine hundred iron chariots and was greatly feared until his defeat by Barak and the Israelite army and his murder by Jael.	Judges 4:2–24
Gideon	Sent to fight against the Midianites, although he was reluctant to do so at first. Went to battle with a ragtag group of three hundred men against thousands of Midianites—and won.	Judges 6–8
Jephthah	This Gileadite went to war against Israel's enemies, the Ammonites, and defeated them. Later became a leader of Israel.	Judges 11:1–33
Samson	A judge of Israel known for having incredible physical strength, he killed one thousand Philistines with the jawbone of a donkey, killed a lion with his bare hands, and knocked down the pillars of a Philistine temple, which killed three thousand men and women and also led to his own death.	Judges 14:6; 15:15–17; 16:23–30
Saul	Picked as Israel's first king and chosen to deliver Israel from the Philistines. He won many battles.	1 Samuel 9:16; 11:8–11; 31:2–3
Jonathan	Son of Saul. With his armor bearer, attacked a Philistine outpost single-handedly.	1 Samuel 14:1–14; 31:2–3; 2 Samuel 1:22–25
Abner	King Saul's army commander who later became a victim of a vengeful Joab.	1 Samuel 14:50; 17:55

PERSON	EXPERIENCE	REFERENCE
David	A skilled shepherd and fearless warrior who became king. Defeated the giant Goliath, champion of the Philistines, with a sling and five rocks. God did not want him to build the temple because he was "a warrior" and had "shed much blood."	1 Samuel 16:18; 17; 2 Samuel 8; 10; 1 Chronicles 28:3
Goliath	Champion of the Philistines. A man over nine feet tall. His armor alone weighed over 125 pounds. Taunted the Israelites and their God, which lead to his death.	1 Samuel 17
Abishai	A member of David's cadre of thirty warriors—a group of elite fighting men.	1 Samuel 26:6–9
Uriah	A Hittite warrior in David's army. David exposed Uriah to certain death so that he could take Uriah's wife.	2 Samuel 11
Zadok	Described as "a brave young warrior."	1 Chronicles 12:28
Pekah	This son of Remaliah once killed 120,000 soldiers in Judah when Judah turned away from God.	2 Chronicles 28:6
Zicri	An Ephraimite warrior who killed Maaseiah, the king's son; Azrikam, the officer in charge of the palace; and Elkanah, second to the king.	2 Chronicles 28:7

"Idol" Hands Are the Devil's Workshop

SOMETIMES the most appalling cults sprang from casual indifference and financial greed rather than blatant idolatry. These three stories share that common thread. And in all three cases, tragedy followed. Read about how these "idol" hands fashioned disaster for God's people.

Gideon's Ephod

Gideon had triumphed decisively over two Midianite kings, and his followers wanted to reward him. They offered to let him rule over them. Gideon declined, but asked instead for a small portion of gold from each man, which they gladly gave. From this Gideon made an ephod of gold and placed it in his hometown of Ophrah. The ephod—most likely a breastplate—was probably displayed for public viewing. Perhaps influenced by the customs of pagan neighbors, who often venerated such objects as they would idols, the Israelites soon began to worship the ephod itself. The author of Judges comments that the ephod "became a trap for Gideon and his family" (Judges 8:27). Soon after Gideon's death, Israel slid back into idolatry. (See Judges 8:22–28.)

Micah's Idols

During the time of the judges, the Israelites were religiously confused, to say the least. The story of Micah, a well-meaning but misguided man, exemplifies the spiritual poverty of the era. Micah owned a shrine in which he kept an ephod and household idols. He hired a Levite—a member of Israel's priestly line—to serve as his personal priest, believing he would receive a blessing for such piety. Instead, the priest was lured away by a band of warriors from the tribe of Dan, who used the priest as a sort of good luck charm as they plundered a nearby village. Not only did they take the Levite, but they grabbed the idols too. When Micah protested, the Danites threatened to kill him. So Micah was left with nothing. The warriors then leveled the town of Laish and set up their own shrine to worship the idols. They appointed a descendant of Moses to serve as their priest and maintained the shrine for many years. (See Judges 17:1–18:31.)

The Jealous Silversmith

Demetrius had a bad feeling about the new religion that was winning converts in his city of Ephesus. A silversmith who made a good living making and selling shrines of the goddess Artemis, Demetrius saw big losses and red ink in his future. Gathering a number of fellow craftsmen, he stirred them to a fury, blaming the Christians for all their troubles. The rage spread to other parts of town, and soon a great riot began. Dragging the apostle Paul's companions to an outdoor theater, the craftsmen began shouting and protesting. Soon the scene broke down into utter chaos. Finally, the mayor of Ephesus was able to restore calm, and Paul and his fellow missionaries were able to leave the city unharmed. (See Acts 19:21–41.)

Unlucky Seventies

THE BIBLE records a few incidents in which scores of people are killed by war, plague, or murder. Curiously three of these stories have the same number of victims—seventy. The following connections highlight the tragic histories of these people, who were in the wrong place at the wrong time.

The Murderous Heir
Abimelech (the offspring of the judge Gideon and a concubine) aspired to rule over Shechem. Upon his father's death, Abimelech approached the leaders of Shechem and won their support for his plan. Not satisfied with their approval, Abimelech took it upon himself to murder his seventy half brothers in order to eliminate any future threat. But one brother, Jotham, got away and called down a curse on Abimelech as he was being crowned. Jotham's curse came to pass when Abimelech was killed during the siege of Thebez. (See Judges 9.)

A View to Die For
The ark of the covenant—the sacred container of God's covenant with Israel—had been seized in battle by the Philistines. Naturally, Israel was overjoyed by the ark's return sometime later to the village of Beth-shemesh. Out of curiosity or carelessness, the men of the village looked inside the ark, a brazen gesture God equated with entering the Most Holy Place unworthily. Seventy died, causing fear and mourning throughout Israel. (See 1 Samuel 6:19–20.)

Seventy Heads

Jehu, king of Israel during the time of the prophet Elisha, was commanded by the prophet to destroy the house of the former king Ahab. Ahab had seventy sons and numerous close relatives. Jehu sent the guardians of Ahab's children a letter that told them to pick the best son, set him on his father's throne, and prepare to defend themselves. The guardians, administrators, and chief men of the palace were frightened. They replied that they would do whatever Jehu said. So Jehu sent a second letter that told them to take the heads of the seventy sons, put them in baskets, and stack them in two piles on either side of the entrance to the city gate. They obeyed the letter but were then killed themselves. Jehu continued his bloodbath until all remaining relatives and close acquaintances of Ahab were wiped from the face of the earth. (See 2 Kings 10:1–17.)

MURDERERS' ROW: KILLERS IN THE BIBLE

The Bible does not shrink from recording the sordid details of perverse and wicked people—from gory murders to persistent family jealousies. The Bible reader finds a whole list of real-life people with real-life problems. Just as modern society has its murderers, so did ancient Israel. Here is murderers' row.

MURDERER	CIRCUMSTANCE	RESULT	REFERENCE
Cain	Out of jealousy, killed his brother, Abel.	Became a fugitive who wandered the earth.	Genesis 4:1–16
Lamech	Killed a youth who supposedly tried to harm him.	Challenged any who dared to avenge the death.	Genesis 4:23
Simeon and Levi	Killed the entire population of Shechem to avenge their sister's rape.	Jacob feared the Perizzites and Canaanites would despise him.	Genesis 34:1–31

MURDERER	CIRCUMSTANCE	RESULT	REFERENCE
Moses	Killed an Egyptian taskmaster.	Fled to the wilderness of Midian, where he stayed for many years.	Exodus 2:11–12
Ehud	Assassinated Eglon, king of Moab.	Israel defeated Moab and lived in peace for eighty years.	Judges 3:12–30
Jael	Struck down Sisera, the Canaanite army commander.	Fulfilled Deborah's prophecy that the honor of killing Sisera would go to a woman.	Judges 4:1–21
Abimelech	Slew his seventy half brothers.	Was critically wounded by a woman, and so asked his armor bearer to kill him so that it wouldn't be said that a woman had killed him.	Judges 9:50–56
Gibeonites	Murdered a Levite's concubine.	Sparked a civil war with the rest of Israel.	Judges 20:1–13
Doeg	Murdered eighty-five priests of Nob.	Confirmed Saul's deterioration and David's favor with God.	1 Samuel 22:18
Unnamed Amalekite	Hoping to earn David's favor, claimed to have killed Saul.	David ordered his execution for killing the Lord's anointed king.	2 Samuel 1:15–16

MURDERER	CIRCUMSTANCE	RESULT	REFERENCE
Joab	Murdered Abner in retaliation for his brother Asahel's death.	Joab became the unquestioned commander of David's army.	2 Samuel 3:22–39
Recab and Baanah	Beheaded Ishbosheth as a prize for David.	David condemned their murder of an innocent man and had them executed.	2 Samuel 4:1–12
Absalom	Murdered Amnon for raping his sister Tamar.	Absalom was estranged from David for many years, but they were reconciled for a short time.	2 Samuel 13:28–29
Joab	Killed Absalom as he dangled from a tree.	Joab earned David's displeasure and was demoted.	2 Samuel 18:1–18
Joab	Treacherously struck down Amasa, David's general.	Joab's bloody deeds would result in his own death (1 Kings 2).	2 Samuel 20:10
Baasha	Killed Nadab, king of Israel.	Became king, but his evil deeds brought judgment.	1 Kings 15:27–29
Zimri	Killed Elah, son of Baasha.	He ruled as king for a week, then committed suicide.	1 Kings 16:8–12
Jezebel	Conspired to have Naboth stoned to death.	Jehu would have her killed for her crimes.	1 Kings 21:7–16

MURDERER	CIRCUMSTANCE	RESULT	REFERENCE
Hazael	Suffocated Ben-hadad, king of Aram.	Became king and oppressor of Israel.	2 Kings 8:7–15
Athaliah	Murdered the children of her dead son Ahaziah so she rule in his place.	The priest Jehoiada hid Ahaziah's son Joash and revolted against her six years later.	2 Kings 11:1
Jozacar and Jehozabad	Trusted officers and advisers who assassinated King Joash.	Amaziah became king of Judah.	2 Kings 12:20–21
Menahem	Killed Shallum, king of Israel.	He became king, but his reign was overshadowed by the Assyrian invasion.	2 Kings 15:13–14
Pekah	Assassinated Pekahiah, king of Israel.	Became king but was himself assassinated.	2 Kings 15:25
Hoshea	Killed Pekah, king of Israel.	Became king but was soon imprisoned by the Assyrians.	2 Kings 15:30
Adrammelech and Sharezer	Murdered their father, Sennacherib, king of Assyria.	Their brother Esarhaddon became king.	2 Kings 19:37
Ishmael	Killed Gedaliah, puppet ruler of Judah who had been appointed by Nebuchadnezzar.	Babylon exacted retribution, and the Judeans fled.	2 Kings 25:22–26
Herod	Murdered the infants of Judea.	His attempt to kill Jesus failed.	Matthew 2:13–18

MURDERER	CIRCUMSTANCE	RESULT	REFERENCE
Barabbas	Was arrested for murder during an insurrection.	Was released during Passover instead of Jesus.	Luke 23:19
Herod Agrippa I	Put James to death.	Died of a sudden illness.	Acts 12:1–2

Temples of Doom

A HOUSE OF WORSHIP, a sanctuary of quiet, a monument of beauty—such are the images we associate with a temple. But several episodes in the Bible remind us that conflict, strife, and violence can enter even those holy places.

Pillar of the Community

Samson was feared for his great strength. His mortal enemies, the Philistines, eventually discovered that his hair was the source of his power. With the help of a deceptive mistress, they cut off his hair then bound, blinded, and enslaved him. Over time, however, his hair grew back, and with it his strength. At a great celebration in the temple of the Philistine god Dagon, Samson was paraded before a jeering audience. Yet he would get his revenge when he pushed on the supporting columns of the great building, collapsing the structure and killing thousands of his enemies as well as himself. (See Judges 16:4–30.)

A Subtle Hint

The Philistines rejoiced when they captured the ark of the covenant. An ornate container overlaid with gold, the ark housed sacred items belonging to the Israelites. The celebration turned to horror, however, once they placed the ark in the temple of their god Dagon. The book of 1 Samuel records that the next morning the Philistines discovered the statue of their god facedown on the floor in front of the sacred chest. They righted it, but the following morning they found it facedown again; its head and hands had broken off and were lying on the floor in the doorway. The Philistines were also afflicted with sores and tumors and, in a panic, sent the ark back to Israel on an oxcart. (See 1 Samuel 5:1–6:18.)

Horns of a Dilemma

Holy places could become an island of refuge for those escaping persecution. Yet they did not guarantee safety for those guilty of crime. Joab fled from King Solomon for his act of treason; he entered the tabernacle and grabbed the horns of the altar so he would not be killed. But Joab did not receive even a reprieve; he was struck down beside the altar after he refused to leave the tabernacle. (See 1 Kings 2.)

Trust Me

Jehu, a king of Israel, had little use for the priests who worshiped the pagan god Baal, but he didn't let them know that. In fact, he told them that he was their biggest supporter and wanted to personally offer a sacrifice in their temple. After he lured them and their followers there, he had them killed and the temple destroyed, turning it into a public toilet, thus ending for a time the worship of Baal in Israel. (See 2 Kings 10:18–29.)

Pernicious Priests

E VIL, CORRUPT, AND CONNIVING. No, these aren't descriptions of criminals; they describe some of God's priests! Priests were charged with the care of the tabernacle and with leading the people in worship. Most served honorably, but a few hardened souls surrendered their honor for power and greed. Here are the sorry tales of some renegade religious leaders.

Brothers Grim

Hophni and Phineas had everything they needed to be successful leaders. They came from a line of distinguished priests, and their father, Eli, was a trusted and devout caretaker of the tabernacle at Shiloh and a priest himself. But such heritage mattered little to these young men. They violated the rules for burnt offerings so they could have their fill of food, and they seduced women who assisted them in front of the tabernacle. Their continued sin brought a message of judgment from a prophet who predicted their approaching deaths. Soon afterward, the Philistines killed Hophni and Phinehas as the two men carried the ark into battle. Their family's priestly line ended. (See 1 Samuel 2:12–26; 4:1–22.)

I Don't Want to Hear It

The prophet Jeremiah drew enemies as if they were magnets. His habit of blunt talk and fearless preaching to the rich and powerful made many a hearer uncomfortable. One day Jeremiah stopped outside of the temple and proclaimed a message of doom to those present. Pashhur, the priest in charge of the temple, heard Jeremiah and had him arrested. Pashhur added to Jeremiah's humiliation by having him flogged and put in stocks. When Jeremiah was released the next day, he told Pashhur that he and his entourage would be sent into exile for their refusal to heed the prophet's warnings. (See Jeremiah 20.)

The High Priest Before the High Priest

In Hebrews 7, Jesus is described as a great high priest who intercedes for sinners in God's presence. How ironic, then, that Jesus was condemned to death by an unworthy high priest, Caiaphas. Matthew tells us that Caiaphas presided over the trial that brought forth several false witnesses to accuse Jesus of wrongdoing. His melodramatic reaction to Jesus' alleged blasphemy led the religious leaders to vote for death. Later Caiaphas orchestrated the events that convinced Pontius Pilate to release Barabbas and carry out Jesus' sentence as the priests demanded. (See Matthew 26:1–27:26.)

Slapped

"Brothers, I have always lived before God with a clear conscience!" With those words Paul began his address to the high council. But he didn't see the punch coming. Ananias, the high priest who heard those words, ordered the men standing next to Paul to slap him on the mouth. Infuriated by such ill treatment—after all, he had not even been charged with a crime—Paul retorted, "God will slap you, you corrupt hypocrite!" But after learning that Ananias was the high priest, Paul offered a quick apology. Ironically, Paul's heated remark proved to be prophetic. Ananias, widely despised by Jews for his corruption and favoritism toward Rome, was later hunted down and murdered by his own people. (See Acts 23:1–5.)

Demonic Possession

WHAT EXACTLY constitutes demonic possession? Is it possible for evil spirits to inhabit a person? The New Testament, in particular, records several episodes that describe a spiritual force of some sort that invades the human body. The possession can appear in many forms, including seizures, violent behavior, self-mutilation, and illness. In these accounts, the torment is relieved when the demons are cast out by a greater spiritual presence.

The Demonic Despot

A psychiatrist who examined the life of King Saul might conclude that he suffered from manic depression or another mental illness. His erratic behavior and sharp mood swings surely indicated a disturbed personality. Over time, the king became obsessed with the rise of David, the talented shepherd whose earnestness and purity outshone his mediocrity. We learn in 1 Samuel 19:9–10 that David was in Saul's house playing the harp for him when an evil spirit entered into Saul and he hurled a spear at David, narrowly missing him. Saul later attempted to kill his own son Jonathan. (See 1 Samuel 16:14–23; 19:1–20:42. The rest of the book of 1 Samuel describes Saul's continuous pursuit of David until Saul's death on the battlefield.)

When Legion Moved Out

Everyone was afraid of him. He ran around naked, cut himself with stones, and was so violent everyone avoided the area where he lived. When Jesus and his disciples arrived in his neighborhood (a cemetery away from the town and not far from the lake), the man met him at the boat, screaming to be left alone. The ensuing conversation revealed that the man was inhabited by a legion of demons (a legion was the largest unit of the Roman army, comprising thousands of soldiers). But Jesus sent them out, and the man was immediately sane, whole, and at peace. (Matthew 8:28–34; Mark 5:1–20; Luke 8:26–29.)

Not for the Fainthearted

One of the more puzzling encounters with demons occurred after Jesus came down from the Mount of Transfiguration. Jesus met a man whose son exhibited disturbing behavior—speechlessness, foaming at the mouth, and seizures. The man claimed that Jesus' disciples had tried but failed to expel the demon that had been causing the affliction. After rebuking the crowd for their lack of faith, Jesus ordered the demon to leave the boy. The boy shuddered and collapsed, but soon recovered. Later, Jesus told the disciples that the demon they encountered could only be exorcised through prayer. (See Matthew 17:14–21; Mark 9:14–29; Luke 9:37–43.)

Enough Already!

Some demons apparently were not dangerous but were annoying. A humorous account in the book of Acts tells of Paul and Silas in the city of Philippi being followed by a girl who had a spirit of divination in her, which meant that she had the power to tell the future. The girl followed the men for days shouting that they were servants of the Most High God and that they were telling how to be saved. Paul finally had enough and turned around and sent the demon out of the girl. The girl's owners were not amused. They had used the girl for making money, and so they had Paul and Silas dragged into court. (See Acts 16:16–19.)

Tragic Ends
to Twisted Tyrants

L IFE IS NOT ALWAYS FAIR, but some people in the Bible clearly reaped what they sowed. At times it seemed as if the more despotic a leader was, the more horrible his fate.

He Who Lives by the Sword

Saul, the first king of the Israelites, began his reign with God's blessing but wound up a paranoid despot. His brutal end came as he fought the Philistines, the Israelites' most hated enemy. The battle had not gone well. His sons had been killed, and he had been mortally wounded. Like Abimelech, Saul ordered his armor bearer to kill him so that the Philistines would not capture and torture him. But Saul's attendant refused, so the king fell on his own sword. (See 1 Samuel 31, 1 Chronicles 10.)

A Chink in His Armor

Ahab, the weak and often treacherous king of Israel, could not escape the death the prophet Elijah had predicted for him. As he engaged the army of Aram, he disguised himself so he would not draw fire from enemy archers. But a warrior drew his bow and unwittingly struck Ahab in a vulnerable spot in his armor. He died a slow, painful death. Later, his chariot was washed at a pool where prostitutes bathed. As Elijah had foretold (1 Kings 21:17–19), dogs then came and licked up his blood. (See 1 Kings 22:29–40.)

Dog Food

If Ahab was the most despicable king in a long line of godless monarchs, Jezebel, his wife, was a most fitting companion. Her crimes included the murder of Naboth and the theft of his vineyard, and persecution of God's prophets, including Elijah. Jezebel also suffered a gruesome demise. Jehu marched to Jezreel and ordered the queen's eunuchs to throw her out of a high window, where she fell to her death. Hours later, Jehu's men went out to bury Jezebel's body, but all they could find was her skull, her feet, and her hands. Dogs had consumed most of her remains. (See 2 Kings 9:30–37.)

Scripture Streakers

NUDITY AND NAKEDNESS, in the buff and in the raw—we use many different words for being in the state of undress. Nakedness is a cause for awkwardness, embarrassment, and some bright red blushing. Many Bible readers are surprised by the amount of nudity described in Scripture. Of course, the classic biblical occurrence of nudity is Adam and Eve (see Genesis 2:25), but other incidents, such as Samson stripping thirty men of their clothes (see Judges 14:19), are a bit more bizarre.

Exposed Emissaries

Typically, ambassadors to other countries are treated with respect and honor. When King David sent a delegation to the Ammonites to express sympathy over their king's death, he expected his party to be treated respectfully. Instead, Hanun, the new king, ordered them to be shaved and their clothing sheared at the waist. Ancient prisoners of war were often denigrated in this fashion, but this wasn't acceptable protocol for entertaining dignified delegates. Such humiliation angered King David greatly; he considered it an act of war. Over forty thousand Ammonite soldiers perished in the war that resulted from this incident. (See 2 Samuel 10:1–5.)

The Naked Biographer

Only the gospel of Mark contains a curious fact about the details of Jesus' arrest and trial. After Jesus was seized and led away, some of the soldiers evidently noticed a young man "clothed only in a long linen shirt" following Jesus. They grabbed him but he managed to wriggle away. In the struggle, he lost his garment and had to flee naked. How did Mark know about this streaker? Perhaps because he was that naked young man! Many scholars believe that this odd incident was Mark's way of placing himself in the drama. (See Mark 14:51–52.)

Seven Shamed Sons of Sceva

Exorcising demons isn't a game. The seven sons of a Jewish priest named Sceva learned that lesson one fateful day. They were attempting to exorcise an evil spirit by invoking Jesus' name, although they really had no expressed belief in the Christian faith. They were not prepared for the challenge that greeted them, however. Instead of obediently leaving the possessed individual, the evil spirit cried out, "I know Jesus, and I know Paul, but who are you?" The demon proceeded to savagely attack the faithless sons of Sceva, leaving them stripped naked and bleeding. (See Acts 19:13–16.)

Liars' Club

Y OU MUST NOT TESTIFY falsely against your neighbor," proclaims the ninth commandment (Exodus 20:16). But some people never learn. These liars told some whoppers to improve their standing or to cover up embarrassment. But as they discovered, the truth wins out!

Ziba

Ziba profited greatly from the kindness of King David, but he wanted more. He was the servant of Saul and became the overseer of the lands David gave to Mephibosheth, Saul's grandson. When Absalom rebelled against his father, Ziba sided with David but claimed that Mephibosheth had welcomed the uprising as a chance to reclaim the throne for his family. Upon hearing that, David gave all Mephibosheth's land to Ziba. David confronted Mephibosheth after he returned to Jerusalem; this time he heard a different story: Mephibosheth had wanted to accompany the king, but Ziba had prevented him. His humble actions told David plainly that Ziba had lied; but put in a difficult spot, David chose a weak compromise—he divided the land between the two men. (See 2 Samuel 16:1–4; 19:24–30.)

Hananiah

Like it or not, prophets often had to deliver news that was gloomy or highly critical of the status quo. Jeremiah fell into that category. His messages brought him complaints, persecution, and imprisonment. No wonder that the public embraced the glad tidings of Hananiah, another prophet who promised Judah that its slavery to Babylon would soon be over. In a public confrontation with Jeremiah, Hananiah smashed to bits the yoke Jeremiah was wearing and predicted the release of Israel's captives. Encouraging as that news was, Hananiah's words were false. Jeremiah returned to announce that Judah's destruction was imminent—and that Hananiah would soon die. Two months later, the false prophet died, and within a few years Jerusalem lay in ruins. (See Jeremiah 28.)

The Roman Guards

The embarrassment and shame must have crushed the proud soldiers. They had been sent to guard the tomb of Jesus at the request of the Pharisees, to keep the disciples from stealing the body. At dawn they awoke to an earthquake and the presence of an angel. They fell into a dead faint, and when they recovered, the tomb was empty! Hurriedly they met with the religious leaders, who helped them devise the only excuse anyone might believe—that the disciples had indeed stolen the body. The guards were no doubt grateful for the religious leaders' cooperation, for such seeming ineptitude on the guards' part could have resulted in their execution. Matthew remarks that the religious leaders eagerly spread the tale, and that many continued to believe it years later. (See Matthew 27:62–28:15.)

The Rise and Fall
of the Temple

THE LONG and dramatic history of the temple in Jerusalem continues to intrigue scholars and laypeople alike. In Israel's history, three temples were built, each of them eventually destroyed. Only a portion of the western wall (the famous Wailing Wall where orthodox Jews gather to pray) remains today.

Solomon's Temple

Solomon, the third king of Israel, earned renown as the wisest and wealthiest man of his day. To him came the honor of building the first temple for the Israelite people. (David, who purchased the site for the temple, was not allowed to build it because he had shed so much blood in the warfare that had solidified the nation—see 1 Chronicles 28:2–3). The magnificent structure took thirteen years to build. It was adorned with precious stones throughout. Gold covered the ceiling beams, doors, frames, and walls. Solomon dedicated the temple in a magnificent ceremony that culminated when the ark of the covenant was brought into the Most Holy Place and the glory of the Lord filled the temple (1 Kings 8:6–11). The temple survived several raids but was completely destroyed by the Babylonians in 586 B.C. (See 1 Kings 5–8; 2 Chronicles 3–7.)

The Second Temple

Standing for nearly five hundred years, the second temple survived longer than either Solomon's or Herod's temple. Built by the Jewish exiles after their return to Jerusalem from captivity in Babylon, this house of worship was not as grand as the house of worship that Solomon had built. Many of the expensive furnishings could not be replaced, and the sacred chest, the ark of the covenant, had disappeared. This temple's completion was nonetheless a moving moment for the exiles, who wept for joy—and for sorrow over the loss of what had been the glory of the first temple. The Roman general Pompey besieged it in 63 B.C. (See Ezra 1–6.)

Ezekiel's Temple

The Jewish prophet Ezekiel, who wrote in exile in Babylon, had a vision in which he saw a glorious temple. Some insist he was merely recalling the majesty of Solomon's temple, but his description is at odds with what we know about Solomon's temple. So, other possible scenarios have arisen. Some have suggested that Ezekiel was in effect proposing plans for a new temple to be built by the returning exiles. Others believe that his temple is an allegorical description that predicts the blessings God would give his people. Another interpretation posits that Ezekiel's prophecy describes Jesus' return and the setting up of his messianic kingdom. But the questions remain—the meaning of Ezekiel's temple is still a mystery. (See Ezekiel 40–43.)

Herod's Temple

Herod, ruler of Judea, was a foreigner despised by the Jewish people. In an attempt to win their good will, he began rebuilding the temple in Jerusalem around 19 B.C. The main structure took about ten years to complete, but it would not be entirely finished until A.D. 64. Just six years later, the Roman army leveled Herod's temple to complete its suppression of a Jewish revolt. (See Matthew 24:1–2.)

DID YOU KNOW?

How did a prophet know the name of the man who would order the exiles to return to Jerusalem and rebuild their temple?

Isaiah was an extraordinary prophet—a man who had commanded a shadow to move backward, who had seen the throne room of heaven, and who had paraded for three years stripped of clothing as a prophetic sign (see 2 Kings 20:8–11; Isaiah 6:1–13; 20:1–5). Isaiah prophesied from around 740–681 B.C., but his predictions encompassed all of human history. He predicted Jerusalem's destruction one hundred years before it happened, and the rebuilding of the temple two hundred years before it occurred. The most intriguing prophecy is the one involving Cyrus. One hundred fifty years before Cyrus reigned as king of Persia (559–530 B.C.), Isaiah predicted that a man named Cyrus would rule many kings and would order the Israelites to rebuild Jerusalem and the temple, which actually happened in March of 538 B.C. (Compare Isaiah 44:28 with Ezra 1:1–4.) Jewish tradition claims that Cyrus read Isaiah's prophecy and was astonished with the resemblance to his life.

Kings and Jokers

COURT JESTERS were a common sight in medieval royal courts. Their humor kept kings, princes, and lords in good spirits. Surprising as it may seem, the prophets of God sometimes employed puzzles and disguises to dramatize their messages to the kings of Israel. These puzzles, however, were not jokes. On the contrary, they exposed the truth in sharp light.

Nathan's Tale

It wasn't going to be easy to go to the king with this bad news, but Nathan knew he had to do it. David had committed a grievous sin in stealing a man's wife, getting her pregnant, and then making sure that her husband was killed in battle. It appeared to David that his cover-up had worked, but the Lord sent the prophet Nathan to confront David. To make his point, Nathan used a story about a poor man who had one lamb. He loved the lamb dearly, like a pet. One day, a rich man who had many sheep wanted to entertain a guest. Instead of the rich man using one of his own sheep, he stole the poor man's lamb and killed it for the meal. David was furious that someone would do such a thing until Nathan pointed a finger at him and said, "You are that man!" (See 2 Samuel 11–12.)

Ahijah's Riddle

A high official of Solomon's court by the name of Jeroboam was walking on the road that led out of Jerusalem. He met a strange-looking man in a bright new cloak. The man stopped right in front of Jeroboam. With one sweeping gesture, he pulled off his cloak with one hand and pulled out a dagger in the other hand. He stared down Jeroboam and proceeded to slice up his new cloak. Needless to say, Jeroboam was quite startled. He didn't know if he had run into a bandit or a madman. Then the man spoke: "Take ten of these pieces, for this is what the LORD, the God of Israel, says: 'I am about to tear the kingdom from the hand of Solomon, and I will give ten of the tribes to you.'" Jeroboam quickly gathered up the ten scraps of clothing. As the prophet predicted, the kingdom of Israel soon split into warring factions. (See 1 Kings 11:26–40; for the prophecy's fulfillment, see 1 Kings 12:20.)

A Prophet in Disguise

No one could understand the wandering prophet's strange command, "Hit me." A soldier refused the bizarre request. The prophet rewarded his refusal with a dire prediction of the soldier's death: a lion would maul him. A second man, who was posed the same question, didn't hesitate. He promptly struck the prophet. The prophet bandaged his wound with a large handkerchief that covered his face. Disguised in this fashion, he waited on the side of a dusty road. When King Ahab approached, the prophet yelled out a disjointed tale. He claimed he had inadvertently allowed a prisoner to slip away. Because of his negligence, he was being required to pay with his own life. What was the king's verdict? Ahab's judgment was severe: the prophet would have to die for his mistake. At this point, the prophet ripped off his disguise and announced God's judgment on Ahab. The king's verdict would fall on his own head, for he had let a prisoner—the king of Syria, the one who God had condemned—go free. (See 1 Kings 20:23–43.)

Elisha's Puzzle

When King Jehoash heard that the prophet Elisha was on his deathbed, the king immediately came to seek out his advice. Instead of getting straightforward answers, Elisha prophesied to him in strange riddles. First he had Jehoash shoot an arrow out of an open window. As the arrow soared toward the distant horizon, Elisha shouted,

"This is the LORD's arrow, an arrow of victory over Aram." That was a clear enough prediction of success. But then Elisha commanded Jehoash to do something strange indeed—he was to strike the ground with the remaining arrows. Jehoash did so—one, two, and three times. Then he stopped and looked up at Elisha. What next? Elisha grew red hot with anger. "You should have struck the ground five or six times. Then you would have beaten Aram until it was entirely destroyed. Now you will be victorious only three times." Elisha then died, leaving the king puzzling over the strange ritual he had just witnessed. (See 2 Kings 13:14–20.)

MASTERS OF DISGUISE

The following people tried to cloak their identities from other people. In some cases, they had a good cause for doing so. But others had selfish reasons for hiding themselves and paid dearly for their deception.

NAME	DISGUISE	REASON	REFERENCE
Adam and Eve	Fig leaves sewn together	To hide their sin from God.	Genesis 3:7
Jacob	Goat skins	To deceive his father, Isaac, so that he would receive Esau's blessing.	Genesis 27:15–16
Tamar	Veil	To protest Judah's broken promise that he would give his son to her in marriage.	Genesis 38:14
Michal	Goat skins and stone idol	To deceive Saul into thinking David was ill while he made his escape.	1 Samuel 19:11–13

NAME	DISGUISE	REASON	REFERENCE
Saul	Common clothing	Since mediums had been forbidden in Israel, Saul wore a disguise to consult with a spiritualist.	1 Samuel 28:8
Jeroboam's wife	Clothing	Not wishing to be known as the wife of Israel's wicked king, she disguised herself to consult with the prophet Ahijah.	1 Kings 14:2
Unnamed prophet	Bandage over his eyes	He disguised himself so that he could expose the folly of King Ahab's treaty with Aram.	1 Kings 20:38
Ahab	Clothing of a common soldier	To avoid attack from the warriors of Aram—he was killed anyway.	1 Kings 22:30
Josiah	Clothing of a common soldier	Ignoring the warning of Neco, king of Egypt, Josiah went disguised into battle and was killed.	2 Chronicles 35:22

Fabulous Food

EATING FOOD is a common, everyday activity. But in times of famine or in desolate deserts, obtaining food can be a gargantuan task. The Bible describes a number of occasions in which obtaining food to eat was truly a stupendous feat. Sometimes the food came from a mysterious, heavenly source. Sometimes ordinary food lasted an extraordinarily long time. Yet, in all of these cases, the people marveled over the food that kept them alive.

Banquets in the Wilderness

As the Hebrews headed out of Egypt guided by the miraculous hand of God, they should have realized that God would not let them go hungry. But growling stomachs have a way of causing even the most trusting people to get a bit testy. As the people began to complain, God promised that he would rain down food from heaven. And he did. First, God sent vast numbers of quail, which flew into the camp. Next, God began to provide special food that appeared every morning, like dew on the ground. The people could gather as much as their families would need for each day. (See Exodus 16.)

A Meal That Kept on Going . . . and Going . . . and Going

During the bleak days of a severe famine, the prophet Elijah went to a widow to ask for some food and water. The widow told him that all she had was a handful of flour and a little cooking oil. It was just enough for one last meal. Afterward she and her son were going to sit down and wait to die. But Elijah promised that she would live through the famine if she used her flour and oil to bake him a loaf of bread. Each day after that, the woman was amazed to find enough flour and oil to feed herself, her son, and Elijah. No matter how much she used, there was always a little left in the containers for another day. (See 1 Kings 17:8–16.)

Angel Food?

Elijah was tired, hungry, and thirsty. He was fleeing for his life from the evil Queen Jezebel. But in the middle of the desert, he collapsed in utter exhaustion. He didn't have an ounce of energy left. Under a scrawny bush, he fell fast asleep. Suddenly, an angel touched him, awakening him from his deep sleep. "Get up and eat!" the angel said. When Elijah opened his eyes, he saw a jar of water and bread baking on hot stones. He drank and ate until he was full and then went back to sleep. Again, the angel shook him awake. "Get up and eat some more, or the journey ahead will be too much for you," he told Elijah. Elijah obeyed. Once again he ate all the food that was before him. (See 1 Kings 19:1–8.)

Death in the Pot

Elisha was entertaining a group of prophets, when he ordered his servant to start making a stew for his guests. The servant obeyed, gathering all kinds of wild herbs, squash, and vines in the fields nearby. He diced these and threw them into a pot of boiling water. After he had finished the stew, he served it to the prophets. But as the prophets began to taste it, they cried out, "Man of God, there's poison in this stew!" Poisonous plants had mistakenly been added to the ingredients. Elisha remained calm. He sprinkled some flour into the pot and ordered his servants to serve the stew to his guests again. The hungry guests ate the stew, but mysteriously no one died or was even sickened by the deadly ingredients. (See 2 Kings 4:38–41.)

FAMINE AND HUNGER

Famine is not a modern-day phenomenon; the harshness of hunger existed during Bible times, too. Sometimes a coming famine was prophesied; at other times, the famines were the result of war and siege.

PROPHET	AFFECTED AREA	CIRCUMSTANCES	REFERENCE
None	Canaan	Abram went to Egypt because of famine.	Genesis 12:10
Isaac	Canaan	Had to go to Abimelech because of a famine in the land.	Genesis 26:1
Joseph	Egypt and surrounding lands	Pharaoh had a dream of a seven-year famine after seven years of plenty. Because there was food in Egypt, people in other countries traveled there to buy grain.	Genesis 40–41
None	Judah	Naomi, Elimelech, and their two sons moved to Moab because of a famine in the land of Judah.	Ruth 1:1
David	Israel	Israel suffered a three-year famine. It was a divine judgment because Saul, the previous king, had persecuted the Gibeonites.	2 Samuel 21:1

PROPHET	AFFECTED AREA	CIRCUMSTANCES	REFERENCE
Elijah	Israel	Sent to King Ahab to predict that there would be no rain on the earth for three years. Consequently, there was a famine in Samaria.	1 Kings 18:2
Elisha	Israel	This prophet ran into famine more than once. During one famine in the land of Samaria, the Aramean army surrounded the city to starve the people. The city's inhabitants cooked and ate their own children.	2 Kings 4:38; 6:24–8:2
Jeremiah	Jerusalem	King Zedekiah watched Judah endure a severe famine in Jerusalem because of the encircling Babylonian army.	2 Kings 25:1–7
None	Postexilic Judah	Famine hit the land, and poor families had to sell themselves into slavery to keep alive.	Nehemiah 5:1–4

PROPHET	AFFECTED AREA	CIRCUMSTANCES	REFERENCE
Isaiah	City-states of Philistia	The prophet Isaiah predicted that a famine was coming to destroy the Philistines.	Isaiah 14:28–30
Jeremiah	Judah	Judah had been disobedient to God, and God sent drought and famine.	Jeremiah 14–16
Ezekiel	Israel	The Lord revealed plans to allow the Israelites to experience the destruction of famine and wild beasts because of their disobedience.	Ezekiel 5:8–17
Agabus	Roman world	Predicted a severe famine that would happen throughout the world.	Acts 11:28

Fantastic Healings

THE BIBLE IS FILLED with wondrous and mysterious healings. What is fascinating about them—besides the fact that they were miraculous—is that they often were so different. How these healings happened remains a baffling mystery.

A Healing Bath

The commander of the invading army of Aram, Naaman, suffered from leprosy. Now, in most cases the Israelites would be glad. After all, the Arameans had raided Israel and taken captives. Among their captives was a young girl who was given to Naaman's wife as a maid. She felt bad for her mistress's husband and told her that Naaman should go see the prophet in Samaria and he would be healed of his leprosy. So Naaman went. The prophet just told him to wash himself seven times in the Jordan River. At first Naaman was angry and refused, but his officers encouraged him to just do it. He did so, and his leprosy went away! (See 2 Kings 5.)

Simply Simplicity

Some miraculous healings in the Bible amaze us because they seem to take place without drama. One such healing is recorded in three of the Gospels. We are told of a crippled man lying on a mat who was brought before Jesus, who was speaking to a crowd. Jesus told the man to get up, pick up his mat, and go home. Without so much as a wave of his hand, a magic incantation, or the use of a magic wand, he restored the man to health. The formerly paralyzed man picked up his mat and went home rejoicing. (See Matthew 9:1–8; Mark 2:3–12; Luke 5:18–26.)

The Clothes Make the Miracle

Jesus once performed a miracle without deliberately doing anything. The story went as follows: A woman had been bleeding for twelve years. Doctors had been powerless to stop it. The woman came up behind Jesus and barely touched his clothes, believing it would make her well, which it did. But Jesus actually felt the power go out from him and turned to see who had touched him. He comforted the woman, who was frightened by being discovered, and declared that her faith had made her well. (See Matthew 9:19–22; Mark 5:24–34; Luke 8:43–50.)

The Shadow Knows

The leaders of the early church ministered to others through miraculous healings. The book of Acts records that the sick and crippled were brought out to the road and placed on cots and mats in hopes that the apostle known as Peter would walk by and cast his shadow on them, thus healing them. (See Acts 5:12–16.)

People Raised
from the Dead

DEATH REMAINS an enduring mystery. Our technology can tell us nothing about what awaits the person who dies. Yet tales of near-death experiences abound. The Bible has a number of intriguing stories not only about people surviving near-death experiences, but also about people actually coming back from the dead. These are people whose stories continue to amaze us.

Sneezing from the Dead
Elisha was widely known for his miracles. So it was no surprise when a distraught mother came to him after her son died. Elisha went to the dead boy's room, where he shut the door and prayed to God. He then got on the bed and stretched out over the dead boy. He placed his mouth over the boy's mouth, his eyes over the boy's eyes, and his hands over the boy's hands. The boy's body became warm, and then the boy sneezed seven times and opened his eyes. It was not, however, the actions of Elisha that brought the boy back from the dead; rather, it was his prayer to God. (See 2 Kings 4:32–37.)

The Man Who Touched Elisha's Bones
In the years that followed the death of Elisha the prophet, the people of Israel were plagued by Moabite raiders who invaded their land every spring. One such raid occurred during an Israelite burial ceremony. Fearing the marauding Moabites, members of the burial

party hurriedly threw the corpse into the tomb of Elisha. The Bible reports that as soon as the corpse touched the bones of Elisha, the dead man revived. (See 2 Kings 13:20–21.)

A Widow's Only Son

As Jesus and his disciples were on their way into the village of Nain, they came upon a funeral procession coming out of the village. A widow's only son had died—in that culture, this left the woman virtually without help or hope. She would be destitute. The Bible says that when Jesus saw her, "his heart overflowed with compassion." He walked over to the coffin and told the dead boy to get up—and he did! (See Luke 7:11–17.)

A Touch of the Hand

Among the many miraculous healings recorded in the Gospels, rarely do any have a flair of showmanship or self-congratulation. The healing itself was enough, as with the case of the Jewish leader Jairus and his daughter. While Jairus was bringing Jesus home, messengers announced that she had died. Jesus calmly told them to have faith and continued on to the house. When he arrived, he told everyone that she was merely asleep. They laughed, but Jesus then took her by the hand and told her to get up. When she did, the laughing stopped. The girl had been raised from the dead. (See Matthew 9:18–26; Mark 5:21–43; Luke 8:40–56.)

Lazarus

Mary and Martha were two of Jesus' most faithful followers. When their brother, Lazarus, became ill, the two women sent immediately for Jesus. Yet when Jesus heard the news of Lazarus's illness, He chose to stay where he was for two days before going to visit the sick man. By the time Jesus got to Bethany, Lazarus was dead. In fact, he had been buried for four days. Jesus ordered that the stone be removed from in front of Lazarus's tomb. When the stone was rolled away, Jesus prayed and then called in a loud voice, "Lazarus, come out!" To the astonishment of the crowd, Lazarus did just that—still wrapped in his grave clothes. (See John 11.)

The Kind Woman

Peter was traveling and preaching, and he was also healing people. When he arrived in Lydda, he healed Aeneas, who had been paralyzed for eight years. The news spread all around that region, so when a believer in the nearby town of Joppa died, the believers went to get Peter and bring him back. Tabitha (also called Dorcas) had been well loved by the believers for all the kind things she did for them. Peter went into the room where her body lay, prayed, and then commanded that she "get up." She opened her eyes, sat up, and was returned to her friends and family. (See Acts 9:36–43.)

Eutychus

On the last day of the apostle Paul's visit to Troas, he and some Christians of the city talked late into the night in an upstairs meeting room. A young man named Eutychus was present at the meeting. Apparently Eutychus was sitting on a window ledge listening to the apostle. As the hour grew later, Eutychus began to nod off. Somehow he lost his balance and fell to his death three stories below. Paul rushed downstairs, threw himself on the young man's corpse, and then announced, "He's alive!" And so he was. After a late meal, the people of the city took the presumably now-wide-awake young man home. (See Acts 20:7–12.)

Firestorms
from Heaven

SEEING FIRE pouring down from heaven would be a terrifying
sight for any human. Yet such storms happen several times in
the pages of Scripture! Where did these firestorms come from? Why
did they occur? Here are a few lesser-known cases of this startling—
and often deadly—phenomenon.

The Temple's Fiery Dedication
The magnificent new temple atop Mount Moriah towered over the
city of Jerusalem. King Solomon had dedicated much time, energy,
and care to making certain that this building, with all its shining gold,
bronze, and silver, was worthy of the almighty God. Upon its completion, the people of Israel gathered to dedicate the newly constructed
house of worship. Lavish feasts and joyful songs accompanied the
occasion. When the first sacrifice was offered, King Solomon stood
up and led the people in prayer. When he finished, the entire sky
brightened, and a column of fire shot down from heaven and licked
up the animal sacrifice that lay on the large golden altar. In holy fear,
the people bowed in worship. (See 2 Chronicles 7:1–4.)

A Fiery Grave
The fire that burned up Solomon's sacrifice was one of those rare
events in which heavenly fire expressed God's pleasure with his
servants. Fire from the skies most often destroyed life. Job knew

such sorrow firsthand. On one fateful day, he lost most of his family, servants, and livestock to incredible calamities. Some were killed by marauders. His family was killed when the roof of their house caved in. Job also received the tragic news that fire from heaven had burned up his flocks and the servants who tended them. We may conclude from the context of God and Satan's earlier exchange that Satan himself had called forth the fire. Through it all, Job refused to blame God for the tragedy. (See Job 1.)

Satan's Fiery End

According to the book of Revelation, firestorms from heaven will mark the end-times. Revelation describes a final battle between Satan and God. The wicked will gather around Satan to form a terrifying army. Satan's evil hordes will surround God's people, preparing themselves for the final, deadly assault. But at the last moment, Satan's entire army will be wiped out with a hot, fiery blast from heaven. The defeat leads to Satan's everlasting torment in the lake of fire and to the victory of God's people. (See Revelation 20:9–10.)

Poison-Pen Letters

THE PEOPLE who received these messages were not likely hanging around their mailboxes waiting for them. The recipients learned they would suffer punishment, persecution, or death. Read how these grim letters predicted the end of kingdoms and rulers— or boomeranged on their senders.

Right in the Guts

Jehoram, king of Judah during the time of the prophet Elijah, was an evil man. He received a letter from Elijah condemning him for marrying a woman who worshiped idols, for murdering his six brothers, and for encouraging prostitution and idol worship among his people. The letter predicted that his possessions, sons, and wives would be taken away. The letter also said that Jehoram would die from a lingering disease of the bowels. Shortly after the letter arrived, the Philistines attacked Judah and took away everything Jehoram owned, including his sons and wives. Within two years he died of the debilitating illness Elijah wrote of. He passed away, to no one's regret. (See 2 Chronicles 21.)

The Letter that Backfired

Sennacherib had brought Assyria to unrivaled power and glory. Naturally, he expected little opposition from tiny Judah, for he had subdued much larger kingdoms. He sent a daunting letter to Hezekiah, king of Judah, telling him that resistance was futile. Sennacherib even declared that the Lord had told him to destroy Judah! Hezekiah tore his clothing and prayed earnestly for deliverance. Isaiah then comforted Hezekiah with a prophecy of victory. That night, almost two hundred thousand Assyrian soldiers perished in a mysterious plague. Sennacherib returned to his land in disgrace and was later murdered by two of his sons. (See Isaiah 36:1–37:28.)

The Burnt Scroll

King Jehoiakim and the people of Judah had reveled in idol worship and persistent immorality. The prophet Jeremiah composed a scroll warning Judah of the disasters that awaited them. Incensed by what he had heard, Jehoiakim burned the scroll in sections. So Jeremiah penned a second scroll, this time condemning Jehoiakim and predicting a disgraceful death for him and his attendants. Jeremiah's words came to pass—Jerusalem was sacked by Babylon's King Nebuchadnezzar, and Jehoakim died in captivity as he was being transported to Babylon. His son was killed as well. (See Jeremiah 22; 36.)

Vanishing Books

At times, the Bible speaks of books or quotes from books that are not known today. Here is a list of these phantom books.

Phantom Books Mentioned in the Old Testament	Reference
The Book of the Wars of the Lord	Numbers 21:14
The Book of Jashar	Joshua 10:13; 2 Samuel 1:18
The Book of the Kings of Israel and Judah	1 Chronicles 9:1; 2 Chronicles 16:11; 20:34
The Record of Samuel the Seer	1 Chronicles 29:29
The Record of Nathan the Prophet	1 Chronicles 29:29; 2 Chronicles 9:29
The Record of Gad the Seer	1 Chronicles 29:29
The Prophecy of Ahijah from Shiloh	2 Chronicles 9:29
The Visions of Iddo the Seer	2 Chronicles 9:29
The Record of Jehu Son of Hanani	2 Chronicles 20:34

PHANTOM BOOKS MENTIONED IN THE OLD TESTAMENT	REFERENCE
The Commentary on the Book of the Kings	2 Chronicles 24:27

BOOKS QUOTED IN THE NEW TESTAMENT	REFERENCE
The Assumption of Moses	Jude 1:9
The Book of Enoch	Jude 1:14

AUTHORS QUOTED IN THE NEW TESTAMENT	REFERENCE
Aratus	Acts 17:28
Cleanthes	Acts 17:28
Menander	1 Corinthians 15:33
Epimenides	Titus 1:12

A LOST NEW TESTAMENT LETTER	REFERENCE
The lost Letter to the Corinthians	1 Corinthians 5:9

BOOKS OF END-TIMES	REFERENCE
The Book of Life	Psalm 69:28; Philippians 4:3; Revelation 3:5; 13:8; 17:8; 20:12, 15; 21:27
The Scroll of Seven Seals	Revelation 5:1–5
The Book of Judgment	Revelation 20:12

Listen Up!

GOD PROCLAIMED the seriousness of his judgments in remarkable ways. His prophets relied on dramatic and memorable gestures to make sure they were getting God's message across to the people. Some people listened; others refused and suffered the consequences.

The Naked Truth
In the book of Isaiah, God accuses Egypt and Ethiopia of serious crimes. He announces that their people would be led away naked, slaves of the king of Assyria. To emphasize his point, he had his prophet Isaiah remain naked for three years. In Middle Eastern culture, nakedness invited terrible humiliation—the kind of shame God's enemies would endure. (See Isaiah 20.)

Grunge Clothing
God told the prophet Jeremiah to buy a linen loincloth and put it around his waist. That was unremarkable, but then God told him to take the loincloth and hide it in a rocky crevice. Several days later Jeremiah dug it up, and it was rotted and ruined. Thus, the people of Judah and Jerusalem would see how God would use Babylon to destroy their pride, which they wore like the worthless loincloth. (See Jeremiah 13:1–11.)

Yoke of Oppression
A yoke is a heavy, cumbersome object put on the shoulders of oxen to control and steer them. The prophet Jeremiah couldn't have been

thrilled when God told him to put a yoke on his own shoulders. The yoke served as a message to God's people and the neighboring peoples that they must serve their conqueror, King Nebuchadnezzar, and follow his direction, just as a beast obeys the turn of its yoke. This was not a popular message. (See Jeremiah 27–28.)

The Sunken Scroll

The last message Jeremiah gave was about the nation of Babylon. He recorded on a scroll all the terrible disasters that would come upon Babylon because of its great evil. Jeremiah instructed Seraiah to read the scroll aloud and then to tie a stone to the scroll and throw it into the Euphrates River. This would symbolize that Babylon and her people would sink, never to rise again. Quite a message when Babylon was at the peak of its power. (Jeremiah 51:59–64.)

Get the Picture?

Ezekiel had the unenviable task of prophesying in exile to many of his countrymen who were in exile with him. At one point, he was instructed to warn the exiles that the remaining people in Jerusalem would face a horrible siege. His unusual actions pictured the length of time and the horror of the coming siege. At another time, he packed his bags and left his home—a picture of more people coming into exile. Perhaps worst of all, Ezekiel's wife died, and he was not allowed to mourn her in public. This was to show the people that so much death and destruction were coming that no one would be able to mourn all who would die. (See Ezekiel 4–5; 12:3–7; 24:16–17.)

Ego Trip

Nebuchadnezzar, the king of Babylon, had become quite impressed with himself. So much did he bask in his accomplishments that he came to believe that he alone had been responsible for his greatness. As Daniel tells us, Nebuchadnezzar was suddenly forced from his palace. His kingdom was taken away from him for seven years, and he was forced to eat grass and live like the wild animals. Only after he realized that God was in control of all earthly kingdoms and rulers did God listen to Nebuchadnezzar's prayer and restore his mind. (See Daniel 4.)

Radical Commitment

The scanty details of Hosea's marriage to the prostitute Gomer in chapters 1 and 3 of the book of Hosea has alarmed many theologians. Why would a holy God order his prophet to join himself with a thoroughly base woman? To resolve this theological conundrum, some commentators have suggested these chapters are allegorical, merely a picture of Israel's spiritual adultery. These commentators still have to explain away the clear and straightforward message from God to his prophet: "Go and marry a prostitute" (Hosea 1:2). Nevertheless, the imagery is poignant and unforgettable, showing Israel how God loved his people in spite of their sins. (See Hosea 1–3.)

Fishy Stories

EVERYONE has heard about a fisherman catching what he thought was a fish, only to find out it was a rubber boot. The Bible has its own fish stories, but the evidence surrounding them suggests that they had the ring of truth.

Reluctant Prophet

Jonah didn't want to go to Nineveh. That evil city was the capital of Assyria, a ruthless enemy of Israel. God called, and Jonah ran—the other direction. He got on a boat heading west (when God wanted him to go east). But the boat ended up in a horrible storm, and when a throw of the dice pinpointed Jonah as the problem, Jonah admitted that he was running from God. He told the sailors to toss him overboard and the storm would stop. At first they didn't want to do that, but when they ran out of options, they threw Jonah overboard. Immediately the storm stopped. But that wasn't the end of Jonah's story. God needed to transport his reluctant prophet back to land, so he arranged for a great fish to swallow Jonah and eventually vomit him back on the shore. (See Jonah 1–2.)

Better Than a Tax Refund

When Jesus and his disciples arrived in Capernaum, tax collectors from the temple asked Peter if Jesus was going to pay the tax required of adult males. Peter said yes, but met with Jesus to discuss the matter. Jesus implied it was unnecessary to pay the tax, but he did not want to offend the tax collectors. He told Peter to go down to the sea and throw in a fishing line and hook. He was to open the mouth of the first fish he caught and pay the taxes with what he found inside. Peter, himself a fisherman, obeyed and went to the seashore with a fishing line. When he caught the first fish, he opened its mouth and found a coin inside, just the right amount to pay the taxes for himself and Jesus. (See Matthew 17:24–27.)

Food for All

On two occasions, Jesus astonished his followers and detractors alike by making do with a few fish and producing a tremendous meal. Having taught great crowds for hours, Jesus felt pity for the men, women, and children who would have to trudge many miles home to eat. Finding a few small baskets of fish and bread, he ordered his disciples to pass them out to the thousands gathered. Not only did all eat until they were satisfied, but the disciples gathered many baskets of leftover food! (See Matthew 14:13–21; 15:32–39; Mark 6:30–44; 8:1–10; Luke 9:10–17; John 6:1–15.)

The Catch of the Day

One day Jesus was preaching beside a lake, and a mob of people crowded around to hear him. He stepped into an empty fishing boat and asked the owner, Simon Peter, to take him out into the water so he could speak to the people. After he finished speaking, Jesus told Peter to go out into deeper water and he would catch a lot of fish. Peter said he and his crew had fished all night and hadn't caught a thing. But he said, "If you say so, I'll let the nets down again." They rowed out to the spot where they had caught nothing all night and let down their nets. Incredibly, their nets were suddenly so full of fish they started to tear apart. Peter called to his partners, who rushed out in the other boat to help. Together, they hauled in so many fish that both boats were about to sink. Peter, amazed, fell at Jesus' feet. Jesus told Peter, "From now on you'll be fishing for people!" When they reached shore, Peter and his partners left their boats and nets, and followed Jesus. After his resurrection, Jesus did a similar miracle for his disciples. (See Luke 5:1–11; John 21:1–10.)

LAKES, OCEANS, RIVERS, AND WATERS

Oceans, rivers, and lakes were mysterious, foreboding, and daunting in Bible times. Their power and danger were respected, and they often became the scene for miracles and other unusual occurrences.

EVENT OR MIRACLE	REFERENCE
God once punished the Egyptians by causing all the fish in the Nile River to die, making it smell so foul that they could not drink its water.	Exodus 7:21
God allowed the Red Sea to part so that the Egyptians could cross, but closed it over Pharaoh and his armies when they followed behind. Pharaoh and his armies were drowned.	Exodus 14:21–31
The Israelites needed water—they'd been traveling for three days in the desert without finding any. When they got to an oasis, the water was bitter. The Lord told Moses to throw a piece of wood into the water and it would be good to drink.	Exodus 15:22–27
God commanded Moses to strike a rock twice with a stick. When he did, water gushed out—enough for all the people and animals to drink.	Numbers 20:11
The Levites carried the ark of the covenant into the Jordan River and the water parted, allowing the people to cross to the other side.	Joshua 3:14–17
God provided a spring to refresh the exhausted Samson.	Judges 15:19
Elijah struck the Jordan River with his cloak, and the water parted.	2 Kings 2:8
Elisha healed the waters of a polluted spring.	2 Kings 2:19–22

Event or Miracle	Reference
Elisha told Jehoshaphat he would be able to water his flocks in the midst of drought. The next day, the valley was filled with water.	2 Kings 3:17–20
When Naaman washed in the Jordan River seven times, he was completely healed of his leprosy.	2 Kings 5:9–14
The prophet Daniel once had a dream where he saw a river of fire.	Daniel 7:10
During a fierce storm, the prophet Jonah told his shipmates to throw him into the sea. When they did, the storm stopped immediately.	Jonah 1:12–15
Jesus was baptized in the Jordan, and the Holy Spirit descended on him in the form of a dove.	Matthew 3:13–17; Mark 1:9–11; Luke 3:21–22
When Jesus' disciples saw him walking on the water, they were terrified and thought he was a ghost. Then Peter got out of the boat and walked on the water as well.	Matthew 14:22–33; Mark 6:45–52; John 6:16–21
Possessed by demons, a herd of two thousand pigs rushed down a steep bank and into a lake, where they drowned.	Matthew 8:32; Mark 5:13; Luke 8:33
The apostle Paul's ship was tossed about in a great storm and then ship-wrecked on the island of Malta.	Acts 27
The apostle Paul listed flooded rivers and stormy seas among the gravest dangers he had faced.	2 Corinthians 11:26
The book of Revelation tells of a sea that looks like crystal-clear glass in front of God's throne.	Revelation 4:6

Event or Miracle	Reference
In Revelation, the dragon's mouth gushed a flood of water like a river, which swept a woman away. But the earth swallowed the flood, saving her.	Revelation 12:15–16
In Revelation, an angel pours out a bowl into the oceans, turning them into blood and killing everything in them.	Revelation 16:3
The lake of fire mentioned in the Bible is composed of burning sulfur.	Revelation 19:20
After the present earth is destroyed, there will be a new earth, and it will have no sea.	Revelation 21:1

Puzzling Parables

MANY OF THE PARABLES found in the Gospels are straight-forward; the meaning and example of the good Samaritan of Jesus' story have even made their way into common expressions of the English language. Not all of Jesus' parables, however, lend themselves to easy interpretation.

The Workers in the Vineyard

Jesus' listeners, most of whom came from the laboring classes, would have understood the background of this parable. A landowner, eager to harvest his crop, went out to hire workers at several points during the day. Much to the surprise of those who were hired at sunrise, all of the workers got the same wage—even those who had worked only an hour in the cool of the twilight. It seemed unfair to Jesus' audience as well. Is this how God rewards people? Those who jumped to a hasty conclusion likely missed the point the parable really teaches us: God's generosity extends even to those who find him at the last hour. It masterfully points out that God is just (he pays all workers fairly) as well as merciful. (See Matthew 20:1–16.)

The Shrewd Manager

One parable that Jesus told only to his disciples concerned a rich man and his business manager. The manager had been wasteful and was in danger of losing his job. After receiving a warning and being called to give an account of himself, the manager cut some shady deals with the rich man's debtors, hoping for their favor when he found himself out of a job. Strangely, Jesus did not tell the parable to condemn the manager's unethical behavior. Quite the contrary! The owner commended the servant, and Jesus told his disciples, "Use your worldly resources to benefit others and make friends. Then, when your earthly possessions are gone, they will welcome you to an eternal home." Although the point of the parable is still debated, we can infer that we should make wise use of our financial resources and whatever opportunities they give us. When we use money to help others find Christ, our earthly investment will reap eternal rewards. (See Luke 16:1–12.)

The Persistent Widow

Jesus had many intriguing things to say about prayer, but one parable that he told his disciples had an interesting twist. A widow tormented a judge time after time, asking for justice against her adversaries. Time after time she went away frustrated. Finally, he grew so sick of the annoyance that—not from his sense of godliness or righteousness, but simply to be rid of her—he granted her request. "This woman is driving me crazy. I'm going to see that she gets justice, because she is wearing me out with her constant requests!" Jesus makes an immediate correlation to God's answering of his people's prayers. So was he suggesting that God regarded repeated petitions as annoyances to be answered so he could get some peace of mind? Actually, the point of this parable is the necessity of faithfulness in prayer. If repeated requests could wear down a heartless judge, how much more would a loving God respond to our fervent pleas? (See Luke 18:1–8.)

Church Creeps

THE WORLD is full of impostors, swindlers, and charlatans—those creeps your mother warned you about long ago. They lurk everywhere—including churches, unfortunately. The New Testament mentions the disgraceful deeds of a few infamous characters who spread dissension, told lies, and in general set bad examples. Here are their stories.

Simon the Sorcerer

Simon knew that the new faith he had witnessed was powerful—more powerful than any he had ever seen. He was also one of the first to recognize that this power could make him healthy and wealthy. Before he had joined the church, Simon had been a magician. His tricks would not only amaze onlookers but also would motivate gullible people to dig deep into their purses. Simon became envious of Peter's supernatural gifts of healing, so he offered Peter money to learn how to give people the Holy Spirit by laying his hands on them. Peter responded with a sharp rebuke. In fear, Simon repented of his greed and begged for forgiveness. But was it a genuine change of heart? Church fathers writing in the first and second centuries frequently speak of a group of heretics called Simonians. Scholars, however, debate whether this group was actually connected with the Simon of the Bible. We can say with certainty that Simon's story contributed a word to our English language—"simony," the deplorable practice of buying or selling a church office. (See Acts 8:9–24.)

The Carnal Corinthian

Hostility and indifference are what most people expect from enemies—but not from one's friends, neighbors, or fellow church members. Sadly, the apostle Paul endured all sorts of ill treatment from the Corinthian church. One man, in particular, had divided the assembly with his controversial deeds. Paul does not mention his name or specify what he did. However, it is clear that Paul wrote a strong letter to the Corinthians urging them to discipline the offender. Some Bible scholars identify the troublemaker with the man who shamelessly slept with the wife of his own father, a scandal that Paul sternly condemned in his first letter to the Corinthians (1 Corinthians 5:1). Most scholars, however, believe the offender was yet another agitator in the controversy-stricken Corinthian church. Paul's letter apparently had a great effect, because in his second letter to the Corinthians, he implores the church to reconcile with the man, who had come to recognize his error. (See 2 Corinthians 2:5–11.)

Diotrephes the Dictator

Churches typically bring out the more charitable, caring, and generous side of people. But some people are incurably power hungry—even in a house of worship. Diotrephes was one such character. His desire for complete authority brought him into conflict with the apostle John. His tool for controlling others was ostracism. Any member of his church who housed a traveling missionary or a messenger from John faced expulsion. Diotrephes thought it better to see a missionary sleep on the streets than to allow another person to influence his flock. To further insulate his followers, he spread rumors, malicious gossip, and outright lies about outsiders. John urged his fellow Christians not to be influenced by this bad example and promised to report Diotrephes' behavior to church authorities. (See 3 John.)

THE SEVEN SEALS OF REVELATION

The seven seals that are opened in the book of Revelation are some of the best-known symbols of judgment and apocalypse in all literature. The symbolism has appeared in art and prose through the centuries. But what do the seals mean?

SEAL/SYMBOL	DESCRIPTION	REFERENCE	POSSIBLE MEANING
First Seal: The White Horse	Its rider wears a crown and carries a bow. He marches out to seek victory in battle.	Revelation 6:1–2	Many scholars have concluded that it stands for the outbreak of violence in the coming tribulation.
Second Seal: The Red Horse	Its rider is given a large sword and has the power and authority to take peace from the earth.	Revelation 6:3–4	The red horse symbolizes a judgment of killing and warfare, accompanied by other disasters.
Third Seal: The Black Horse	Its rider holds a pair of scales while proclaiming the dearth of food and wine.	Revelation 6:5–6	The black horse symbolizes the panic and misery caused by famine.
Fourth Seal: The Pale Green Horse	The rider's name is Death and its companion is the Grave. They inflict suffering and death on a quarter of the world's population.	Revelation 6:7–8	The pale green horse is death in various brutal forms.

SEAL/SYMBOL	DESCRIPTION	REFERENCE	POSSIBLE MEANING
Fifth Seal: The Souls Under the Altar	On and beneath the altar are the souls of those who were killed for preaching God's word.	Revelation 6:9–11	The events of the fifth seal, unlike the previous four, take place in the realm of the spirit. The breaking of the seal announces God's vindication of saints who have suffered martyrdom.
Sixth Seal: The Great Earthquake	The earth is overwhelmed with natural calamities, each so devastating that people flee to escape God's wrath.	Revelation 6:12–17	The earthquake reveals the wrath of the Lamb, whose anger cannot be withstood. Humans choose to be crushed by mountains rather than face the one they have rejected.
Seventh Seal: Silence in Heaven	The opening of the seal begins with a long silence in heaven but culminates with seven judgments.	Revelation 8:1	The seventh seal begins the final cycle of judgments that ushers in the final battle between Christ and the forces of darkness.

SECTION THREE

FAQs

Angels

Do angels really exist?

Most of us haven't seen an angel and in this life probably never will. Does that mean angels do *not* exist? Some have answered this question with a resounding "Yes!" For these people, seeing is believing; human experience defines reality. But many people—including those mentioned in the Bible—know that reality cannot be limited to the narrow confines of human experience. There is a supernatural world, a world that exists beyond space and time. God occupies this world because he is a Spirit (see John 4:24). But he has also created spiritual beings called angels. These beings are his messengers. The Bible describes angels appearing to all sorts of people—from Balaam and his donkey to Gideon, to Samson's father and mother, to Mary (see Numbers 22:21–35; Judges 6:12–24; 13:2–24; Luke 1:26–38). These angels left a host of startled people and left changed lives behind as evidence of their comings and goings.

Do people have guardian angels?

God has assigned some angels to stand watch over those who trust in the Lord (see Psalm 34:7; 91:11). The Bible, however, doesn't say that every individual is assigned an angel. Jesus did say that there were angels who watched over children (see Matthew 18:10). Jewish tradition taught that people's guardian angels looked like them. This belief may have been expressed by the Christians who gathered to pray at Mary's house for Peter's release. When Peter showed up at the door, they didn't believe it was him! They said, "It must be his angel" (Acts 12:15).

Why doesn't God just appear to people? Why does he send angels?

The Bible says that no one has seen God (see John 1:18; 1 John 4:12), because he lives in unapproachable light (see 1 Timothy 6:16). Anyone who does see God will die (see Exodus 33:20; Judges 13:21–22). Because of this chasm between humans and God, the Lord uses angels as messengers. He usually sends angels when he wants to impress on a person that the message that person is hearing is a direct order from God himself (see Gideon's experience in Judges 6:11–27).

Was there any common experience that people who were visited by angels shared?

The Bible records a number of incidents when people have encountered angels (see Genesis 16:7; 19:1; 28:12; Exodus 3:2). The one common response of all these people is utter fear. The guards at Jesus' tomb shook in fear when a shining angel appeared (see Matthew 28:4). Cornelius, a Roman centurion, stared at an angel with sheer terror (see Acts 10:2–4). Zechariah was frightened when an angel appeared to him in the temple (see Luke 1:11–12). These people were justifiably afraid, for angels are God's servants empowered to do his will on this earth. Those who insist on opposing God's will can only expect to face an angel's sharp sword of punishment, as did Balaam and other enemies of God (see Numbers 22:23–34; 2 Kings 19:35). It is only when an angel says, "Don't be afraid," that a person knows for certain that the message the angel bears is one of peace and not judgment (see Luke 1:13, 30).

DID YOU KNOW?

What do angels eat?

Angels are usually pictured as flying, blowing trumpets, and speaking to startled men and women. Artists rarely depict angels eating, although the Bible plainly mentions the feast and sacrifices that were presented to heavenly visitors. Abraham offered a roasted calf, cheese curds, and milk to the three angelic men who visited him (see Genesis 18:6–8). Lot set a great feast, complete with fresh bread, before the two angels that visited him (see Genesis 19:1–3). Manoah, Samson's father, offered a roasted goat to an angel, but the angel refused to eat it, telling Manoah to sacrifice the goat as a praise offering to God instead (see Judges 13:15–16). Although it is not clear whether angels eat in heaven, the Bible does hint at heavenly food. Psalmists describe manna—the white, crisp wafers the Israelites ate in the wilderness—as the food of angels (see Psalm 78:24–25).

Collective Judgments

Did God really want the Israelites to kill off other people?

Some passages in the Bible contain specific commands for the Israelites to wipe out entire populations. In Numbers 31, for instance, we read of a campaign of vengeance against the Midianites that spared few. God knew that the people of Canaan had become so immersed in sin that they posed a dangerous influence on the morality of the nation. Mercy was shown, however, to those willing to accept the God of Israel and live according to the law of Moses. Rahab, the prostitute of Jericho, harbored Hebrew spies in her home and was spared when the city was sacked (Joshua 2; 6:17–25). She is remembered approvingly in the New Testament (Hebrews 11:31; James 2:25).

Why do some of the psalms seem to rejoice in the destruction and suffering of enemies?

Sometimes called the *imprecatory* psalms, these hymns request God's help in destroying an enemy. A good example is Psalm 109, in which the author implores God regarding his enemies: "May his children become fatherless, and his wife a widow" (Psalm 109:9). Although seemingly cruel, the point of such psalms is often missed. Rather than rely on his own power, the speaker trusts in God to carry out justice that is perfect and appropriate. This theme appears in all the imprecatory psalms. God will aid those who are right and just, not those who simply wish to settle a score with an enemy.

Why would entire families be executed for the actions of one person?

In 2 Samuel 21, we read the account of seven relatives of Saul who were executed for no crime on their part. Their forebear, long since dead, had killed a number of Gibeonites who were supposed to be protected according to an oath made with Israel. Thus Saul had incurred blood guilt on himself and his house for his violation of this oath. Blood guilt allowed a family of a victim to exact retribution, even taking the killer's life if the deed was premeditated. The customs of the day also allowed for relatives of the killer to be put to death under certain circumstances, especially if the crime had not been addressed or punished adequately.

If the Israelites were God's chosen people, why did they suffer so much oppression?

Israel's history reached lofty heights and fell to abysmal pits. Times of great achievement were followed by abject captivity and desolation. The writers of Scripture usually identified oppression with disobedience to God's law. According to Jeremiah, the Babylonian captivity of 586 B.C. was a direct result of Israel's flirting with idolatry and refusing to listen to God's prophets. The times of exile, harsh as they were, were meant to bring the people back to their foundation—a pure, holy life centered in God.

The Cup of Wrath

Prophets sometimes foretold the fate of entire nations. Yet few prophecies were as sweeping as the series of judgments on the nations that Jeremiah announced shortly before 600 b.c. These predictions and their uncanny outcomes are described in the chart below.

Nation Under Judgment	Outcome	Reference
Egypt	The Egyptian pharaoh Neco lost a decisive battle at Carchemish in 605 b.c. With that defeat, Egypt's power in the Middle East waned, and Babylon became the dominant power of the region.	Jeremiah 46
Philistia	The independence of the Philistine city-states declined as Assyria, Babylon, and then Greece swept through their land. The Maccabees conquered the remnants of this people in the second century b.c.	Jeremiah 47
Moab	Nebuchadnezzar occupied their land and effectively destroyed the nation in the years after 600 b.c.	Jeremiah 48
Ammon	A constant foe of Israel, Ammon was likely absorbed by the invading Babylonians, though no definite date is recorded.	Jeremiah 49:1–6
Edom	Edom, whose ancestor was Esau, brother of Jacob, incurred judgment for its cruelty to Israel. It came under the domination of Babylon, Persia, and later Greece, and eventually disappeared.	Jeremiah 49:7–22

Nation Under Judgment	Outcome	Reference
Damascus	Nebuchadnezzar defeated and occupied the city around 605 B.C.	Jeremiah 49:23–27
Kedar and Hazor	Kedar and Hazor were nomadic tribes that lived in the wilderness of the Middle East. Their relative seclusion offered no protection against the invading Babylonians.	Jeremiah 49:28–33
Elam	Elam would be conquered by Babylon but would rise again. Its chief city, Susa, became the center of the Medo-Persian empire after Babylon's decline.	Jeremiah 49:34–39
Babylon	Jeremiah told the people of Judah that Babylon would be God's agent for judging their sin, but that Babylon itself would be judged as well. Jeremiah also predicted the return of the exiles from captivity.	Jeremiah 50:1–51:64

Demons and
Demon Possession

Isn't believing in demons superstitious?

Certainly the writers of the Bible took demons seriously. Jesus, the disciples, and the early Christians confronted them frequently and warned other believers about their power to resist God's work. The descriptions one finds of demonic activity in the Bible cannot be explained away as mere physical or emotional illnesses (see, for instance, Mark 5:1–13). Moreover, there are many well-documented cases of supernatural activity in many cultures today that bear a striking similarity to the demonic accounts in the New Testament.

Where did demons come from?

The Bible does not say for sure. The presence of evil, however, is evident from Creation, when the serpent tempted Eve (see Genesis 3:1–5). The prophet Isaiah described a being called "shining star, son of the morning," whose pride and lust for power caused him to challenge the Most High (Isaiah 14:12–21). His rebellion resulted in his being hurled to the pit. Some scholars have suggested that this "son of the morning" was, in fact, Satan and that demons are angels who followed his rebellion and were banned from God's presence.

Are demons active in the world today?

The Screwtape Letters, one of C. S. Lewis's most popular and imaginative works, is based on the assumption that demons are indeed active in our world. But how can we see the evidence? Scripture describes several signs of demonic work, including human possession, occult rituals and sacrifice, supernatural disturbances, and deceitful teachings. Demons may also resist the work of God's angels.

What will happen to demons at the end of the world?

Jesus said they would be thrown into an eternal fire (see Matthew 25:41). The vision of John contained in the book of Revelation uses vivid language to describe the doom of Satan, who is hurled into the lake of fire and burned day and night without end.

Why wouldn't Jesus let demons talk?

A couple of times during Jesus' ministry, demons spoke to him, saying things like, "I know who you are—the Holy One sent from God!" (Mark 1:24). Immediately, Jesus would silence them. Why? The demons were speaking the truth, weren't they? Two basic explanations have been offered as to why Jesus silenced the demons. First, Jesus did not want the crowds to think of him as a wonder worker and sensationalist; the encounters with the demons, who often shrieked and shouted in his presence, could have distracted Jesus' audience from his teaching. Second, Jesus clearly wanted to reveal his identity and mission according to God's timetable, not Satan's. To disclose that news too soon may again have encouraged the wrong expectations—namely, that his ministry of healing was more important than his work of salvation.

How does a person become possessed?

In the book of Acts we find an account of demon possession that was linked to fortune-telling, an activity strictly forbidden by Old Testament law. Paul also speaks of sacrifices of pagans "offered to demons" (1 Corinthians 10:20). Both cases suggest that possession may occur from involvement in cult or occult activities, including sacrifices and spiritualism, or through prolonged exposure to harmful, self-destructive habits. Those who have studied contemporary instances of demon possession affirm this idea. (Interestingly, many of the cases of possession in the New Testament happen in areas where pagan worship and Jewish practice overlapped.)

How much power do demons really have?

In the book of Job, Satan had to ask God's permission to harass Job. In any event, we can say that demons have the power to make all manner of trouble—but only what God allows—and they are shrewd and know the vulnerable points of human behavior. In his letter to the Ephesians, Paul urged Christians to put on spiritual armor to resist the attacks of the devil. "For we are not fighting against flesh-and-blood enemies, but against evil rulers and authorities of the unseen world, against mighty powers in this dark world, and against evil spirits in the heavenly places" (Ephesians 6:12). It seems logical to conclude that such spiritual warfare is fought in human hearts and minds. Those who take faith as their shield will be able to ward off the fiery arrows of Satan (see Ephesians 6:16).

Do exorcisms happen today?

Fortunately, cases of demon possession are relatively rare. Yet many Christian denominations recognize that demonic activity is real and sometimes rely on skilled spiritual experts to confront and expel demons. Exorcisms (also called services of deliverance) clearly require discernment and must be performed with great caution. We find in the New Testament at least two incidents of exorcisms that failed because of disbelief or lack of spiritual understanding (see Matthew 17:14–18; Acts 19:13–16).

PORTRAITS OF SATAN

The first image of Satan most people have is of a man in a red suit with horns and a pitchfork. That portrayal of Satan may not be completely accurate; the Bible insists he can change forms—even transforming himself into a beautiful angel of light. Here are some other snapshots of Satan.

SATAN SNAPSHOT	REFERENCE
Satan, in the form of a serpent, tempted Adam and Eve.	Genesis 3:1–14
Satan appeared before God in order to get permission to destroy Job by taking away his money, his family, and his good health.	Job 1:7–2:10
Before his fall from heaven, Satan used to be an angel (some Bible versions say his name was Lucifer).	Isaiah 14:12
Satan wanted to be God.	Isaiah 14:14
Satan is called the Leviathan, a swift serpent-dragon of the sea.	Isaiah 27:1
Before his fall, Satan was perfect in wisdom and in beauty.	Ezekiel 28:12
Before his fall, Satan was in Eden. Satan's clothing was covered with jewels.	Ezekiel 28:13
Satan was a mighty angelic guardian with access to the holy mountain of God.	Ezekiel 28:14
Satan is a murderer, a hater of truth, and the father of lies.	John 8:44
Jesus called him "the ruler of this world."	John 14:30
Satan disguises himself as an angel of light in order to deceive people.	2 Corinthians 11:14
Satan is called the commander of the powers in the unseen world.	Ephesians 2:2
Satan tries to tempt people by strategies and tricks.	Ephesians 6:11
Satan is called the tempter.	1 Thessalonians 3:5
Satan wants to enslave people.	2 Timothy 2:26
Satan has the power of death.	Hebrews 2:14
Satan is an angel from the bottomless pit; he is called *Abaddon* and *Apollyon*, which mean the Destroyer.	Revelation 9:11

Satan Snapshot	Reference
Satan is depicted as a red dragon with seven heads, seven crowns, and ten horns.	Revelation 12:3–4
Satan has a host of demons at his command.	Revelation 12:7
Satan has deceived the whole world.	Revelation 12:9
Jesus has defeated Satan in battle.	Revelation 12:11
Satan will eventually meet his doom in a lake of fire and brimstone.	Revelation 20:10

Family Customs

Why do so many people in Bible stories marry close relatives?

Most incidents of a person marrying a close relative occur in the earliest times of biblical history, when populations were relatively small. In some cases, marrying a relative was a favorable alternative to a bond with a pagan spouse. Rebekah, for instance, sent her son Jacob to her brother Laban for a wife because she was fearful of the influence of Hittite women (see Genesis 27:46). Likewise, her son Esau married a relative for much the same reason (see Genesis 28:8–9). Recall too that the law of the kinsman-redeemer (seen in the story of Ruth) provided that a man could marry the widow of his brother or other relation to preserve the property holdings of the family.

If monogamy was God's design for marriage, why did he allow kings like David and Solomon to practice polygamy?

The pattern of monogamy appears to have God's approval from the beginning (see Genesis 2:21–24; Mark 10:6–9), but the practice of taking more than one wife occurs throughout the Old Testament. Lamech, Jacob, Esau, Elkanah, David, Solomon, Rehoboam, Abijah, and others had at least two wives, and sometimes many more. Especially among royalty, polygamy was a symbol of wealth and power, and the tolerance of polygamy may have been a grudging concession to custom. It should be stated that multiple marriages often caused formidable problems for families. David could not control his children, whose crimes included rape, murder, and rebellion. The writer of 1 Kings claims that Solomon's wives led him into idolatry and spiritual indifference (see 11:1–8).

Why did the Israelites circumcise males?
Circumcision was a sign of God's covenant with Abraham and his descendants (see Genesis 17:10–14). The ceremony was performed eight days after the child's birth. In the early church, circumcision became a hotly debated issue. Some Jewish Christians insisted that all male converts be circumcised, but a more conciliatory group, led by Paul among others, refused to make it a requirement. Their position eventually won the day.

What was the Nazirite vow?
Part of the law handed down to Moses included a voluntary pledge of dedication to God's service. Like monastic vows practiced centuries later by some Christians, the Nazirite abstained from certain practices during this pledge. He or she could not drink wine or eat grapes, cut his or her hair, or touch a dead body (see Numbers 6). Perhaps the most famous (and unusual) Nazirite was Samson. His case was atypical because his parents made the vow on his behalf, apparently for his entire life. From hints we find in Scripture, some have suggested that Samuel, John the Baptist, and the apostle Paul also took this vow at some time in their lives.

Why weren't the Israelites supposed to marry outside their clan? Does this mean that God is opposed to interracial marriages?
The prohibition against intermarriage was primarily a spiritual safeguard, not a separation demanded for racial or ethnic purity. Because the Israelites alone had received God's revelation, they feared that intermarriage would soften resistance to behavior considered sinful. By and large, this fear proved to be well founded. Bad company corrupts character, so the saying goes, and incidents of intermarriage tended to erode the moral foundation of Israel much more

frequently than they uplifted the culture of neighboring peoples. So serious was this problem during Judah's return from exile that the prophet Ezra ordered Judah's men to send their foreign wives and children away (see Ezra 9–10).

What is a concubine?

A concubine was in many ways a second-class citizen, a woman entitled to some but not all the privileges of marriage. A man could acquire a concubine either as a spoil of war or by purchasing her; it follows that concubines were often the reserve of wealthy or privileged men. A concubine had some legal rights, but she was still considered property rather than an equal partner. It is sad but not surprising to encounter stories of a master treating a concubine callously: witness Hagar's abrupt dismissal by Abraham (see Genesis 16:6) and the Levite's coldhearted offering of his concubine to the perverse men of Gibeah (see Judges 19:25–28).

Fire and Brimstone

You can't expect me to believe in a place where horned devils jab people with pitchforks. Is that what the Bible says about hell?

Many of the popular images of hell are often misinformed. Complicating the issue is the language used to describe hell—are we to take such images literally, or are they devices that convey the misery of such a place? We can reach some conclusions, however. Clearly it is a place of torment and suffering. Peter describes hell as containing "gloomy pits of darkness" that hold those awaiting judgment (see 2 Peter 2:4). Jesus referred to hell several times, calling it a place with "unquenchable fires" (Mark 9:43).

Does the Bible tell about anyone who went to hell?

In his first letter, Peter tells us that Jesus suffered a physical death and "preached to the spirits in prison"—perhaps a reference to a liberation of hell (see 1 Peter 3:19). However, the parable of Lazarus and the rich man tells the story of a soul in torment (see Luke 16:19–31). The rich man's sin was the neglect of God and of his neighbor, the beggar Lazarus. In hell, the man finds himself engulfed in flames, writhing with an unquenchable thirst. He is able to see Lazarus, comforted by and talking with Abraham in heaven. A great chasm divides hell from heaven, and the souls in one place cannot cross over to the other.

What is Sheol?

Sheol is a Hebrew word used in some Bible translations, commonly translated as "the pit" or "the grave." In Old Testament writings, Sheol harbored the souls of the dead and was thought to be deep in the earth itself. Although it is variously described as a devouring beast that is never satisfied (see Proverbs 27:20) and a gloomy abode (see Job 10:21), it was not a place of punishment, but rather the destiny of all human souls. Several passages in the Old Testament describe God's power to raise souls from Sheol and hint at the Christian understanding of the afterlife.

What is brimstone, and why is it associated with hell?

Some Bible versions use the word "brimstone" to describe a natural form of sulfur, a yellowish mineral that easily ignites and burns. This mineral can be found today near and around the Dead Sea. Its association with divine judgment likely comes from the fate of Sodom and Gomorrah, destroyed by a heavenly rain of "fire and burning sulfur" (see Genesis 19:24). The book of Revelation also depicts the punishment by fire and burning sulfur of those who worship the Antichrist (see Revelation 14:10).

HEAVEN AND HELL

The pit, the lake of fire, the second death—these are the vivid images that the Bible associates with hell. Scripture also gives us a glimpse of the beauty and peace of heaven. Even so, our understanding of the afterlife is cloaked in mystery. What facts does the Bible disclose about the eternal destiny of the human race?

FACTS ABOUT HELL	REFERENCE
Fire burns in it day and night.	Matthew 18:8; Mark 9:43
It is engulfed in darkness.	Matthew 25:30; 2 Peter 2:17
It is a place of punishment for the spiritually indifferent or neglectful.	Matthew 25:46
It is a place of suffering and thirst.	Luke 16:19–31

FACTS ABOUT HELL	REFERENCE
Those present in hell are separated from God.	2 Thessalonians 1:7–9
It is likened to a lake of fire, a place of torment for Satan and his angels.	Revelation 20:14

FACTS ABOUT HEAVEN	REFERENCE
Human relationships will be transformed and marriage will cease.	Matthew 22:29–32
It will be a place prepared by God for his children.	John 14:2–3
The human body will be renewed and perfected.	John 20:19, 26; 1 Corinthians 15:36–49
The redeemed will resemble Jesus.	1 John 3:2
The heavenly city exudes beauty and wonder.	Revelation 21:1
Death will be abolished.	Revelation 21:4
Sorrow and mourning will disappear and tears will no longer flow.	Revelation 21:4
God's brilliant presence so fills heaven that there is no need for light or the sun.	Revelation 21:23

Miracles

Doesn't the idea of miracles conflict with the natural laws that govern this world?

In recent centuries science has made great strides in understanding how our world works. From Newton's discovering the law of gravity to Einstein's discovering the theory of relativity, science has explained and defined the laws that govern the universe. Coupled with the astonishing progress of science, however, has been a growing skepticism of the supernatural and supernatural events, such as miracles.

Some of this skepticism is misguided. The existence of natural laws does not preclude the reality of miracles, and vice versa. There are several different ways to understand what miracles are, but none of these explanations discount the existence of natural laws. A miracle is, by definition, an event that is not natural or ordinary. These events are direct acts of God that either counter ordinary natural forces or break the natural laws in place. Some have suggested that miracles might even be a manifestation of unknown natural laws, which God uses to show his power.

In any case, a miracle is an exceptional event that originates in God's will and points to God (see Psalm 77:14; Hebrews 2:4). Since a miracle is not a part of our ordinary experience, it has not been subject to the same type of scrutiny natural phenomena have endured. This is why science doesn't have an explanation for miracles—and probably never will.

Why did Jesus perform miracles?

The Bible records a number of miracles performed by Jesus—from making water turn into wine to healing the lepers and the blind (see John 2:1–11; 9:1–41). Through these miracles, Jesus changed people's lives forever. A blind person could see. A leper was healed and then reunited with mainstream society. The results pointed to the type of God Jesus was revealing—a compassionate God who loved to liberate people and reconcile them.

A miracle's primary purpose, however, was to function as a sign of the divine origin of Jesus' message. Jesus performed many miracles among the people in order to prove to them that he was from God—in fact, that he is the Son of God (see John 2:11; 6:14; Acts 2:22–33).

Some gospel passages say that Jesus didn't perform miracles because the people didn't have faith. What is the connection?

In his hometown of Nazareth, Jesus didn't perform miracles because the people of his hometown lacked faith (see Matthew 13:53–58). Later, Jesus enabled Peter to walk on the water. But the text states that Peter's doubts caused him to sink. When Jesus helped Peter out of the water, he rebuked Peter for having "little faith" (see Matthew 14:31). Why was Jesus' ability to perform miracles hindered by a lack of faith or trust in God? The explanation lies in the purpose of miracles. They are signs from God either to authenticate a person as God's special servant or the message being preached (see Hebrews 2:1–4). If the one benefiting from the miracle does not acknowledge God as the originator of this great event or seek out God's assistance, then a supernatural event is pointless. If a person is unwilling to recognize a miracle as a sign of God's presence, God's extraordinary activity will go completely unnoticed. This is why Jesus made it clear that his miracles were tied to a person's faith in God (see Matthew 9:2, 22–29; 15:28; Luke 17:5–6, 19; 18:42).

THE FASCINATING MIRACLES OF JESUS

All miracles are astounding. But the miracles Jesus performed were not supernatural sideshows. They were intended to confirm God's faithfulness among his people. Moreover, those who were healed or delivered from oppression often had to first display faith. Jesus often would not perform miracles among disbelieving audiences. The miracles recorded in the Gospels are summarized below.

MIRACLE	REFERENCE
He healed a leper in Galilee.	Matthew 8:2–4
He healed a woman who had a bleeding disorder.	Matthew 9:20–22
He restored sight to two blind men in Capernaum.	Matthew 9:27–31
He cast a mute spirit out of a man in Capernaum.	Matthew 9:32–34
He restored a man with a withered hand in Galilee.	Matthew 12:9–13
He cast a blind and mute spirit out of a man in Galilee.	Matthew 12:22–32
He cast a demon out of a girl in the region of Tyre and Sidon.	Matthew 15:21–28
He fed over four thousand people with just seven loaves of bread and a few small fish.	Matthew 15:29–38
He caused money to be found in the mouth of a fish.	Matthew 17:24–27
He cursed a fig tree and caused it to wither.	Matthew 21:18–19
He caused a paralyzed man to walk.	Mark 2:1–12
He calmed a storm on the Sea of Galilee.	Mark 4:35–41
He walked on water in the Sea of Galilee.	Mark 6:45–52
He healed a deaf person with a speech impediment.	Mark 7:31–37

Miracle	Reference
He healed a blind man in Bethsaida.	Mark 8:22–26
He restored sight to Bartimaeus.	Mark 10:46–52
He healed Peter's mother-in-law of her fever.	Luke 4:38–39
He directed Peter, James, and John to an enormous amount of fish.	Luke 5:1–11
He healed a centurion's sick servant in Capernaum.	Luke 7:1–10
He raised a widow's only son from the dead in Nain.	Luke 7:11–17
He cast a demon out of a man in the region of the Gerasenes.	Luke 8:26–39
He raised Jairus's daughter from the dead.	Luke 8:41–56
He cast a demon out of a boy who was having seizures.	Luke 9:37–42
He healed a woman who had been crippled for eighteen years.	Luke 13:10–17
He healed a man who suffered from dropsy.	Luke 14:1–6
He healed ten lepers in Samaria.	Luke 17:11–19
He reattached Malchus's ear after Peter cut it off.	Luke 22:49–51
Jesus turned water to wine, beginning his ministry.	John 2:1–11
He cured an official's sick son in Capernaum.	John 4:46–54
He healed an invalid at the pool of Bethesda.	John 5:1–15
He fed over five thousand people with just five loaves of bread and two fish.	John 6:1–14
He restored sight to a blind man in Jerusalem.	John 9:1–7
He raised Lazarus from the dead.	John 11:1–44

MIRACLE	REFERENCE
He caused Peter, James, and John to catch 153 large fish.	John 21:1–13

DID YOU KNOW?

Why were Jesus' healings of lepers so remarkable?

An incurable and disfiguring malady called leprosy caused inflammatory skin ulcers that often became infected and sometimes killed their victims. The only treatment for lepers was a strict quarantine. Lepers were despised and widely shunned in ancient Israel. Few God-fearing Jews would have anything to do with lepers. Not only was the disease contagious, but anyone who touched a leper was considered ceremonially unclean and not allowed to participate in worship or have social contact for an extended time. But Jesus refused to heed the common taboos and healed many lepers. Nor did he ever contract the dread disease. His amazing work brought both physical and spiritual relief to a group languishing in neglect and hatred.

Prophecies

Is prophecy just another name for fortune-telling?

Prophecy involves much more than foretelling events. Prophets were God's spokespersons, just as Aaron was a spokesman for Moses (see Exodus 7:1–2). Their words were God's word (see, for instance, Jonah 1:1).

Many of the prophecies in the Bible were conditional, depending on the response of those who heard the prophecy. If the people turned to God, the prophets would predict peace and God's lavish blessings. If they stubbornly persisted in sin, the prophets would predict suffering and destruction (see Deuteronomy 30:15–18). In addition to this basic message of repentance, prophets of the Bible did predict the future. In many cases, these prophecies spoke of a coming Savior who would deliver God's people and defeat all wickedness (see Isaiah 9:1–7). In a few cases, time periods (see Daniel 9:24–27), specific locations (such as Bethlehem for Jesus' birth in Micah 5:2), and specific names (Cyrus in Isaiah 45:1, 13) are mentioned in Bible prophecies. But in general, the prophet's message was a consistent and clear call for repentance.

How should I respond to those who claim they have a message directly from God?

Not everyone who claims to be a prophet speaks for God. All of us must test a prophet to see if he or she speaks the truth. The first test for a prophet is Scripture. God never contradicts himself. If someone says something that is against the Bible, then that person is a false prophet. The Bible clearly states that if a prophet encourages people to worship a god other than the God of Israel, then that person is a deceiver (see Deuteronomy 13:1–3). The second test for a prophet is whether the prophet's predictions come true. If a prophet predicts a certain date for some event and that date passes without its coming true, then that prophet is a false prophet (see Deuteronomy 18:21–22). There will always be people who claim to speak for God. It takes careful discernment to know who to listen to and who to ignore.

Should I believe anyone who claims to know when God is coming to the earth?

No one knows when the world will end. Not even the angels know when God will end history as we know it (see Matthew 24:36). The Bible says that false prophets claiming to be God will try to deceive people (see Matthew 24:24–28). But no one should believe those who claim to be God. When God comes to this earth, all will know with certainty that he is God. His arrival will be announced with a loud trumpet call, and he will appear so that all can see his glory (see Matthew 24:27–31). God will come, and his coming will be unmistakable. The Bible warns us to make sure we are prepared for his coming (see Matthew 24:42, 44; Luke 12:40; 1 Thessalonians 5:2; 2 Peter 3:10).

CONFIRMED PROPHETIC PREDICTIONS

Every tabloid seems to proclaim bold predictions about the future of popular figures. But while prophetic statements remain as popular as ever in culture, few "prophets" today would readily submit to the tests of prophecy that God demanded. Any prophet who claimed a source for knowledge other than God or who proved by error not be a real prophet from God was to be killed (Deuteronomy 18:20). God-given prophecies were to be marked by precise fulfillment. The following chart includes a sample of biblical prophecies and their fulfillment.

PROPHECY	PROPHET	FULFILLMENT	REFERENCE
A great nation would come from one man's family, eventually blessing the whole world.	God gave this prophecy to Abraham when he invited the patriarch to leave home and trust God.	By the time Israel arrived in the Promised Land, they had become a great nation (see Numbers 23:10). The ongoing, miraculous survival of the Jewish nation bears tribute to God's integrity.	Genesis 12:1–2
God gave Canaan to Israel as a permanent inheritance.	God gave this promise to Abraham when Abraham returned to Canaan following a brief visit to Egypt.	The invasion and conquest of the Promised Land under Joshua established that ownership (see Joshua 21:43–45).	Genesis 13:15
A woman would defeat the powerful general Sisera.	Deborah the judge delivered this prophecy to Barak because he wouldn't take her word that God would lead the Israelites to victory over Sisera.	Jael, the wife of Heber, offered Sisera a hiding place in their tent, but when the general was sleeping, she drove a tent peg through his temple.	Judges 4:1–23
A childless woman's humble prayer would be answered.	A priest named Eli uttered this prophecy without actually knowing the content of Hannah's prayer.	Israel's great prophet, priest, and judge Samuel was born.	1 Samuel 1:9–28

PROPHECY	PROPHET	FULFILLMENT	REFERENCE
A childless woman from Shunem would bear a son in a year.	The prophet Elisha gave this prophecy as an expression of gratitude for the unselfish hospitality the woman's family had extended to him.	The woman gave birth to a son.	2 Kings 4:8–17
Though besieged and starving, the city of Samaria was promised abundant food within twenty-four hours.	Elisha gave this prophecy to king Joram during a siege of Samaria by King Ben-hadad of Aram.	Four desperate lepers ventured out of the city in hopes of begging some food from the Arameans, or dying. They discovered the well-stocked camp abandoned by an army that had panicked and fled, thinking they were under attack.	2 Kings 6:24–7:20
When the promised Savior comes, his own people will reject him.	Isaiah prophesied Jesus' suffering and death hundreds of years before Jesus was born.	The description of the rejection of Jesus captures the fulfillment of Isaiah's prophecy (Luke 23:13–25).	Isaiah 53:1–9

PROPHECY	PROPHET	FULFILLMENT	REFERENCE
The Messiah will be born in Bethlehem, in Judea.	Micah gave the exact location in which the promised Savior would be born.	Jesus was born in Bethlehem because the Roman emperor imposed a census. This required Mary and Joseph to travel to Bethlehem to register. While they were there, Jesus was born (Matthew 2:1–12; Luke 2:1–7).	Micah 5:2
The powerful and proud city of Nineveh in Assyria (present-day Iraq) would be completely destroyed.	Nahum gave this prophecy almost fifty years before the event, when Assyria appeared invincible.	Nineveh was defeated and destroyed by the Medes in 612 B.C.	The book of Nahum
The beautiful city of Jerusalem would be destroyed by rampart-building forces who would "not leave a single stone in place" (Luke 19:44).	Jesus gave this prophecy during his last visit to Jerusalem.	The Romans decided to wipe out Jerusalem as a rebellious outpost in A.D. 70, some forty years after Jesus' death and resurrection.	Luke 19:41–44
A disciple would deny knowing Jesus.	Jesus predicted Peter's denial during the Last Supper with his disciples the night before his crucifixion. Peter vehemently protested.	After Jesus' arrest, in the courtyard of the high priest, Peter three times denied knowing Jesus.	Luke 22:31–34; John 13:37–38

DID YOU KNOW?

What is the "sacrilegious object that causes desecration"?

In the book of Daniel and in the Gospels, we find mention of the "sacrilegious object that causes desecration" (some Bible versions say "abomination of desolation") that will appear in Jerusalem's temple during the last days. Bible students ever since have debated the meaning of this terrible event. Some have suggested that it refers to vainglorious rulers like Antiochus Epiphanes who attempted to deify themselves, or to Emperor Titus, who destroyed the temple and much of Jerusalem in A.D. 70. Others see the statement as a metaphor for the unsuccessful attempts of heathenism to undo the spiritual victory of Jesus over Satan. (See Daniel 11:31; 12:11; Matthew 24:15; Mark 13:14.)

Topical Index

A

Aaron
creation of golden calf, 160
creation of plague, 168
criticism of Moses' marriage, 164
death of sons, 178
Hebrews challenging, 30
Korah, Dathan, and Abiram challenging, 29
staff blossoming with almonds, 162
Abednego, 77, 78
Abihu, death of, 178
Abimelech, 49–50
Abiram, death of, 29
Abomination of desolation, 279
Abraham
angel visiting, 35
children of, 139
desert visitors and, 9–10
fathering Isaac at 100 years old, 141
Melchizedek ministering to, 7
offering meal to angels, 253
sacrifice of Isaac, 146

Abram, longevity of, 4
Absalom, death of, 153
Achan, stoning of, 180–181
Adam and Eve
curse of, 129
exile from Paradise, 131
Adultery, 129–130
Ahab
beheading of sons, 195
claiming Naboth's vineyard, 155, 181
death of, 206, 216
death of family, 13
warning of drought, 143
Ahijah, 215
Alexander the Great, 75
Altar
death of Joab, 201
Moses building, 172
named "Witness," 146
sacrifice of Isaac, 146
Amalekites, 13, 172
Ammonites
death of, 13, 208
judgment of, 256
Amorites
death of, 13

Joshua's victory over, 172–173
Ananias
death of, 112–113, 179, 203
visiting Saul, 114
Angel
as cherubim guarding Paradise, 131
of death, 132
Elijah and, 157
existence of, 251
fear of, 253
food for, 253
as mysterious messengers, 35–39, 132–133
providing food and water for Elijah, 220
sent by God, 252
sword-bearing, 131–132
Animal
sacrifice of, 229
stories of, 175–176
Apostles, angel visiting, 38, 39
Apparition, 89–90
Aramean soldiers, blindness of, 173
Araunah, 132

Ark of the covenant
  capture by
    Philistines, 200
  death of 70 Israelites,
    194
  disappearance of,
    25–26
  moving of, 179
  mysterious deaths
    linked to, 27–28
  return of, 201
Army
  Gideon's, 47–48
  Roman, 213
Asherah, 147–148
Assyrians, 75, 232
Athaliah, execution of,
  155
Axe head, floating of,
  162–163

B
Baal
  death of worshippers
    of, 201
  Elijah's victory over,
    157, 189
  Jerub-baal, 147
Baal-zebul, 109
Babylon
  blackened reputation
    of, 75–76
  destruction of, 137
  judgment of, 257
  then and now, 75–76
Babylonians
  destroying ark of
    covenant, 25–26
  destroying Ninevah,
    138
  destruction of
    temple, 212
  invading Israel, 74

Balaam
  angel visiting, 36
  blessing Israelites,
    34–35
  encouraging Moabite
    women to seduce
    Israelite men, 40
  King Balak sending
    for, 33
Balak, King, 33–35
Barabbas, 203
Bar-Jesus, 169
Barnabas, 169
Bath, healing, 224
Bathsheba, 59–60
Bear, 176
Beelzebub, 109
Behavior
  fermented beverage
    causing bizarre,
    86–88
  God's displeasure
    with, 4
Belshazzar, King, 83–84
Ben-Hinnom, 44–45
Beth-shemesh
  death of people, 28
  returning ark of the
    covenant to, 194
Betrayal, Judas of Jesus,
  96
Bible
  history of, 157–158
  reading with curious
    mind, xi
Biblical blessings, 16
Birth, miraculous,
  141–142
Black art, 169
Blasphemy, 180
Blessings
  biblical, 16
  mountain of, 41–43

Blindness
  of Aramean soldiers,
    173–174
  of Elymas, 169
Blood
  composition of, 20
  turning Nile River
    to, 19
  wiping on doorpost,
    21
Blood guilt, 255
Books, phantom,
  232–233
Bread
  as Communion/
    Eucharist, 151
  feeding thousands of
    families, 151
  for thousands
    gathered, 238
Bread from heaven,
  23–24
Brimstone, 267
Bronzed snake, 31–32
Burning bush, 156
Burnt scroll, 232
Bush, burning, 156

C
Caiaphas, 203
Cain, 5
Calf, golden, 160
Casting, of lots, 184
Children
  first born, first to
    die, 21
  Jephthah's vow,
    51–52
  penalty for
    disobeying parents,
    176
  sacrifice of, 45–46
  struggle for, 139–140

Christian blessings, 16
Christian Church
    birthday of, 111
Christianity, spreading
    word of, 115
Christians
    Saul's hatred for, 114
Church, donation to,
    112–113, 179
Circumcision
    controversial, 166–
    167
    of male Israelites, 264
    of son of Moses and
    Zipporah, 169
Cleopas, 102–103
Communion, 151
Concubine, 265
Corinthian church,
    letter to, 245
Cornelius, 39
Covenant, ark of, 25
Craftsmen, 193
Crucifixion
    Jesus' appearance
    following, 103,
    103–104
    shadows of, 91
Curse
    of adulterous woman,
    129–130
    of the garden, 129
    of Isaac, 14–15
    on Jericho, 53–54
    Jotham's, 49–50
    mountain of, 41–43
    on people of Gibeon,
    130
Cyrus, 214

D

Dagon, 56
Damascus, 257

Daniel
    angel visiting, 37
    as interpreter of
    dreams, 84
    lions ignoring, 176
    sentencing to lion pit,
    85–86
Darius the Mede, 85
Dathan, 29
David, King
    Absalom's death, 153
    affair with Bathsheba,
    59–60
    angel of death, 132
    angel visiting, 37
    collecting foreskin as
    dowry, 166–167
    conquering
    Edomites, 15
    defeating Goliath, 188
    division of land, 210
    killing of Goliath, 162
    mighty men of, 188
    Nathan confronting,
    215
    slicing edge of Saul's
    robe, 57–58
    war on Annonites, 208
Daylight savings,
    172–173
Dead, rising from, 91–
    92, 102, 226–228
Death
    of 70 people, 194
    of Ananias and
    Sapphira, 112–113
    angel of, 132
    close encounters
    with, 143–145
    dowry of, 151
    of firstborn, 21–22
    Hebrews swallowed
    alive, 29–30

instant, 178–179
    of Judas, 97
    linked to ark of
    covenant, 27–28
    as rite performed
    to pagan gods, 44
    by stoning, 175,
    180–181
Decalogue, tablets of,
    25
Deception, 14–15
Delilah, 154–155
Demetrius, 193
Demons
    attacking sons of
    Sceva, 209
    belief in, 258–260
    entering body of
    pigs, 100–101
    invading human
    body, 204–205
    Satan as prince of,
    109
Desecration, 44
    sacrilegious object
    that causes, 279
Desert visitors, 9–10
Desolation,
    abomination of,
    279
Destruction, of cities,
    137–138
Dinah, 152
Diotrephes, 245
Disguise
    people hiding
    identities with,
    217–218
    prophet in, 216
Dog, consuming body
    of Jezebel, 207
Donkey, talking, 34–35,
    175

Dorcas, rising from
dead, 228
Dowry, foreskin as,
166–167
Dreams, interpreter of,
17, 84

E
Earthquake
destroying prison,
122–123
God revealing
himself through,
157
in Jerusalem, 91–92
Edom
descendents of Esau,
149
judgment of, 256
Edomites, 15
Egyptians
death of firstborn,
12
drowning of soldiers,
12
judgment of, 256
Elam, judgment of,
257
Eleazar the One, 188
Eli, 140
death of, 178–179
death of family, 27
death of sons, 178–
179
Elijah
angel providing food
and water, 220
angel visiting, 37
as apparition on
mountaintop, 90
ascending to heaven,
71–72
destroying credibility

of Baal worship,
189
endless bread during
famine, 219–220
fire from the sky,
67–68, 69
hiding in cave, 143
letter to King
Jehoram, 231
running faster than
horse, 70
Elisha
bears mauling
detractors of, 176
blinding of Aramean
soldiers, 173–174
bringing boy back
from dead, 226
dead man rising from
touching, 226–227
floating axe head,
162–163
as follower of Elijah,
71–72
poisoned stew, 220
riddles of, 216–217
Elizabeth, 141–142
Elkanah, 140
Elymas, blindness of,
169
Ephesus, 193
Ephod
of Gideon, 192
of Micah, 192–193
Esau
the deception, 14
expensive meal, 149
God's destiny for, 15
Escapes, great, 78–80
Esther, Queen, 149–
150
Ethiopians, death of,
13

Eucharist, 151
Eutychus, rising from
dead, 228
Exodus, 23
Exorcism, 205, 209, 260
Ezekiel
temple of, 213
siege in Jerusalem,
235

F
Family, fish and bread
feeding, 151
Famine, 219–220,
221–223
Financial resources,
using wisely,
242–243
Fire
coming of God's
spirit, 110–111
pillar of, 22
from the sky, 67–68
valley of, 41–43
Firestorms, 229–230
Firstborn, death of,
21–22
Fish
feeding thousands of
families, 151
stories of, 237–238
Fleece, wet to dry, 134
Food
bread and fish for
thousands, 238
famine, 219–220,
221–223
Moses surviving
without, 157–158
mysteries
surrounding,
219–220
Fräulein, Saline, 11

G

Gabriel, 141–142
Gamaliel, 114
Garden
  cherubim guarding,
    131
  curse of, 129
Gehenna, 44–45
Genesis, giants in, 5–6
Genesis 3, 108
Ghost, 89–90
Giants
  Nephilites as, 5
  of Old Testament,
    182–183
Gibeon
  curse on people of,
    130
  sun shining over, 173
Gideon
  angel visiting, 36
  army of, 47–48
  building altar, 147
  dried fleece, 134–135
  ephod of, 192
  victory over
    Midianite army,
    173
God
  angels enduring
    wrath of, 6
  blessings from, 16
  displeasure with
    human behavior, 4
  final plague, 21–22
  generosity of, 242
  love of sinful people,
    236
  neglecting or defying
    power of, 12
  people claiming
    messages from,
    274–275

release of Hebrew
  slaves, 18
revealing presence to
  Elijah, 157
revealing presence to
  Moses, 90, 156–157
sending angels, 252
sons of, 5–6
using dreams to
  communicate, 18
God's mountain, 156
Gog, 76
Golding, William, 109
Goliath
  death of, 162
  defeat by David, 188
  as giant, 182–183
Gomer, 236
Gomorrah, 10, 137–138
Good News, 110, 125
Guardian angel
  existence of, 251

H

Hagar
  angel visiting, 35
  brush with death, 143
  dismissal of Abraham,
    265
  mother of Ishmael,
    139
Hallucination, 115
Haman
  death of, 143–144
  second banquet,
    149–150
Hammurabi, King, 75
Hananiah, 210–211
Handwriting on palace
  wall, 83–84
Hannah, 140
Hanun, 208
Hapi, 160

Hazor, 257
Headache, splitting,
  152–153
Healing, miraculous,
  224–225
Heathenism, 279
Heaven, bread from,
  23–24
Hebrews
  being swallowed
    alive, 29–30
  freedom of, 22
  plague causing death
    of, 30
Hell, 266–268
Herod Antipas
  death of, 120–121
  Herodias dancing for,
    150
  Peter escaping from
    prison, 119
  rebuilding temple in
    Jerusalem, 213
Herodias, 150
Hezekiah
  angel visiting, 37
  letter from
    Sennacherib,
    231–232
  shadow moving
    backward, 135
Hiel, 130
Hittites, 75
Holy Place, 91
Holy Vengeance, 12
Hophni, death of,
  178–179, 202
Horeb, Mount, 156
Hosea, 236
Human behavior, 4
Human hand,
    appearance of,
    83–84

Human sacrifice, 45,
51–52, 180
Humiliation
of Isaiah, 233
of Roman guards,
211
Hurricane, 124–125

I
Idolatry
Gideon against, 147
Israel flirting with,
255
practicing in
Ninevah, 138
tragic endings of,
192–193
Imprecatory psalm, 254
Indigestion, 149–150
Intermarriage,
prohibition of,
264–265
Intoxication, examples
of, 86–88
Isaac
Abraham fathering at
100 years old, 141
blessings from, 16
the deception, 14
sacrifice of, 146
Isaiah
nakedness of, 234
prophecy of, 214
shadow moving
backward, 135
Iscariot, Judas. See
Judas
Ishbi-benob, 183
Ishmael
brush with death, 143
son of Hagar and
Abraham, 139
Ishtar, 73

Israel
descendants of Jacob,
149
invasion by
Babylonians, 74
Israelites
angel visiting, 36
battle with giants, 6
battling Amalekites,
172
Beelzebub, 109
circumcision of
males, 264
as Gideon's army,
47–48
killing others for
God, 254
neglecting or defying
power of, 12–13
oppression of, 255
Pharaoh refusing to
free, 21
sacrifice of children,
45–46
saved by bronzed
serpent, 31–32
stoning for gathering
wood on Sabbath,
180

J
Jacob
angel visiting, 36
children of, 139–140
the deception, 14
expensive meal, 149
God's destiny for, 15
Jael, 152–153
Jairus, daughter rising
from dead, 227
Jambres, 168
Jannes, 168
Jehoash, King, 216

Jehoiakim, King
caring for Joash, 155
death of, 232
rebelling against
Babylon, 74
Jehoram, King, 231
Jehu, 195, 201
Jephthah, vow of,
51–52
Jeremiah
arrest and flogging,
202–203
confrontation with
Hananiah, 210–211
rotted loincloth, 234
scroll to King
Kehoiakim, 232
wearing yoke, 234–
235
Jericho, curse on,
53–54, 130
Jeroboam, 63–64,
215–216
Jerusalem
earthquake in, 91–92
siege in, 235
Jesus
apparition encounter
on mountaintop,
89–90
appearances after
resurrection,
103–104
breaking bread with
disciples, 103
changing water to
wine, 105–106, 150
death on cross, 91–92
exorcising vagrant of
demons, 100–101
healing of lepers, 273
Judas luring, 96
miracles of, 269–273

paying tax collector,
237–238
phenomena
surrounding death
of, 91
resurrection from
dead, 102
salvation through,
110
start of public
ministry, 150
widow's son rising
from dead, 227
Jewish dew, 24
Jewish nation, 146
Jewish Passover, 110
Jezebel
body consumed by
dogs, 207
causing stoning of
Naboth, 181
death of, 155
demanding death of
Elijah, 157
Joab, death of, 201
Joash, 155
Job, 230
John the Baptist
beheading of, 150
ill-treatment by
Diotrephes, 245
son to aged Zechariah
and Elizabeth,
141–142
Jonah
death of, 185
fish swallowing,
237
reform of Assyrian
city, 138
Jonathan
defeating Philistines,
187–188

defying Saul's fasting
order, 184–185
Joseph
angel visiting, 38
imprisonment of, 154
as interpreter of
dreams, 18
sold into slavery, 17
Joshua
casting of sacred lots,
184
curse of, 53–54
cursing Jericho, 130
cursing people of
Gibeon, 130
victory at Jericho, 131
victory over
Amorites, 172–173
Jotham, curse of, 49–
50, 194
Judah
falling darkness on, 74
worshipping Queen
of Heaven, 73
Judas (Iscariot)
conspiring with
religious leaders,
96
mysterious death
of, 97
remorse over arrest
of Jesus, 97
replacement of, 185
Judgment, nations
under, 256–257
Julius, 124–125

K

Kedar, 257
Kinsman-redeemer,
260–262
Kishon Valley, 189
Korah

death of, 29
neglecting or defying
power of, 12

L

Laban, 139–140
Lake, miracles of,
239–241
Last Supper, 151
Lazarus, rising from
dead, 227–228
Leah, 139–140
Leper, healing of, 273
Leprosy
instant, 164–165
Naaman suffering
from, 224
Letters, grim, 231–232
Leviathan, 177
Levite, offering
concubine, 265
Lewis, C. S., 107,
258–259
Liars, 210–211
Life expectancy, 4
Lights, strange, 114–115
Lion, 176
Loincloth, rotted, 234
Longevity
factors to, 4
of people in Bible, 3
Lost ark, 25–26
Lot
angel visiting, 36
escaping destruction
of Solom, 10
leaving city of
Sodom, 137–138
offering meal to
angels, 253
wife transformed to
block of sodium
chloride, 11

Lots, casting of, 184
Lying
    about proceeds of
        land, 112–113
    of Judas to Jesus,
        96–97

M
Magician, 168
Magog, 76
Manna
    as food of angels, 253
    sustaining Israelites,
        23–24
Manoah
    angel visiting, 37
    offering meal to
        angels, 253
Mark, nakedness of,
    208–209
Marriage
    of relatives, 263–265
Mary
    angel visiting, 38
    virgin mother of
        Jesus, 141
Massah, 170
Matthias, 185
Meal, most memorable,
    149–151
Medes
    occupying Babylon,
        75
Medium, 169
Melchizedek
    blessings from, 16
    ministering to
        Abraham, 7–8
    as priest forever, 8
Menelik I, 61
Mephibosheth, 210
Meribah, 170
Meshach, 77, 78

Meshech, 76
Messengers,
    mysterious, 35–39
Methuselah, longevity
    of, 3
Micah, 192–193
Michal, 166–167
Midianites
    death of, 47–48
    Gideon's victory over,
        173
Miracle, of Jesus,
    269–273
Miriam, leprosy of, 164
Moabites
    death of, 13
    invading Israel,
        226–227
    judgment of, 256
Molech, worship of, 45
Monastic vow, 264
Money
    donating to church,
        112–113, 179
    helping others find
        Christ, 242–243
Monogamy, 263–264
Moriah, Mount, 229
Moses
    angel visiting, 36
    as apparition on
        mountaintop, 90
    burning bush, 156
    circumcision of son,
        166
    creation of plague, 168
    forty days without
        food and water,
        157–158
    as great leader of
        Hebrews, 19
    Hebrews challenging,
        30

Korah, Dathan,
    and Abiram
    challenging, 29
    leprosy of hand, 164
    mysterious ceremony,
        41–43
    Pharaoh refusing to
        free, 21
    Ten Commandments,
        156–157
    water coming from
        rock, 161, 170–171
Most Holy Place, 25,
    91
Mountain
    of blessings and
        curses, 41–43
    encounter with Jesus
        on, 89–90
    God's, 156
Mount Horeb, 156
Mount Moriah, 229
Mount Sinai
    Elijah journeying to,
        157
    as God's mountain,
        156
    water coming from
        rock, 161, 170–171
Murderer, in Israel,
    195–199
Mysterious messengers,
    35–39

N
Naaman, 224
Naboth, stoning of, 181
Nadab, death of, 178
Nakedness, in
    Scripture, 208–209
Nathan, 215
Natural, 269
Nazirite vow, 264

Nebuchadnezzar, King
  as conquerer of
    Jerusalem, 74
  death of, 75
  fourth man in the
    fire, 77
  loss of sanity, 81–82,
    235–236
  return of sanity, 82
Nephilites, 5, 182
New Testament
  appearance of Satan
    in, 108
  beginning and ending
    with salvation epic
    of Jesus, 103
  demonic possession,
    204–205
  Mount Sinai, 156
  phantom books from,
    233
  Rahab, 252
Nicolaitans, 39–40
Nile River
  theory of turning
    red, 20
  turning to blood, 19
Nimrod, 75
Nineveh, destruction
    of, 138
Noah
  life expectancy after,
    4
  rainbow from God,
    134

O
Og, King, 182
Old Testament
  appearance of Satan
    in, 108
  coming of God's
    spirit, 110

existence of, xi
giants of, 182–183
Jesus explaining
  prophecies in
  Scriptures, 102
Mount Sinai, 156
phantom books from,
  232–233
polygamy, 263–264
Sheol, 267
Ophrah, 192
Oxen, stoning of, 175

P
Pagan gods, 44
Paphos, 169
Parables, 242–243
Paradise, exile of Adam
  and Eve, 131
Paralyzed man, healing
  of, 224–225
Pashhur, 202–203
Passover, 110, 132
Paul
  angel visiting, 39
  becoming blind, 114
  bringing Eutychus
    back from dead, 228
  brush with death,
    144, 145
  changing name from
    Saul, 114–115
  circumcision of
    Timothy, 167
  craftsmen blaming
    for troubles, 193
  death of, 205
  encounter with
    Ba-Jesus, 169
  God freeing from
    prison, 122–123
  letter to Corinthian
    church, 245

near-death in Lystra,
  181
removing demon
  from girl, 205
shipwreck, 124–125
slapping of, 203
spreading the word of
  Christianity, 115
Peninnah, 140
Pentecost, 110
Persians, 75
Peter
  angel visiting, 39
  becoming fisherman,
    238
  bringing Tabitha back
    from dead, 228
  catching fish to
    pay tax collector,
    237–238
  escaping from prison,
    118–119
  healing sick and
    crippled, 225
Pharaoh
  appointing Joseph
    as second in
    command, 18
  hardening of heart, 21
  imprisonment of
    Joseph, 154
  releasing Hebrew
    slaves, 22
Philistines
  capture of ark of the
    covenant, 200
  death of, 13, 27
  defeat by Eleazar, 188
  defeat by Jonathan,
    187–188
  defeat by Shamgar,
    187
  judgment of, 256

Philistines (cont.),
  killing Hophni and
    Phineas, 178–179,
    202
  returning ark of the
    covenant, 201
Phineas, death of,
  178–179, 202
Pigs
  demons entering
    bodies of, 101
  jumping off cliffside,
    100
Pillar of fire, 22
Plague
  death of Assyrian
    soldiers from, 232
  dying from, 12–13
  Hebrews succumbing
    to, 30
  Moses and Aaron
    creating, 168
Polygamy, 263–264
Pompey, 212
Pontius Pilate, 203
Potiphar
  advances toward
    Joseph, 154
  Joseph as servant
    of, 17
Priest, 202–203
Prison
  earthquake
    destroying, 122–
    123
  Peter escaping from,
    118–119
Prophecy, 274–278
Prophet
  abused, 65–66
  in disguise, 216
  mistake of, 63–65
  parable of, 59–60

slaughtering in
  Kishon Valley, 189
Psalm, imprecatory, 254

Q
Queen Makeda, 61–62

R
Rachel, 139–140
Rahab, 252
Rainbow, 134
Real estate transaction,
  112–113
Rebekah, 15
Rephaites, as giants, 182
Resurrection,
  appearances of
  Jesus after, 103–104
Revelation, seven seals
  of, 246–247
River, miracles of,
  239–241
Rock, water from, 161,
  170–171
Roman army,
  destruction of
  temple, 213
Roman guards,
  embarrassment
  of, 211

S
Sabbath
  harvesting manna,
    23–24
  stoning for gathering
    wood on, 180
Sacrifice
  animal, 229
  of children, 45–46
  death by stoning, 180
  human, 51–52
  of Isaac, 146

Sacrilegious object that
  causes desecration,
  279
Saline Fräulein, 11
Samson
  Delilah's betrayal,
    154–155
  hair as source of
    power, 200
  strength of, 55–56
  water appearing from
    ground, 171
Sapphira, death of,
  112–113, 179
Sarah
  mother of Isaac, 141
  struggle for a child,
    139
Satan
  appearance in Bible,
    107–108
  as Beelzebub, 109
  fiery end, 230
  Gog and Magog
    deceived by, 76
  portrayal of, 260–262
  as prince of demons,
    109
Saul, king of Israel
  casting of lots,
    184–185
  death of, 169
  defeating Philistines,
    187–188
  evil spirit invading
    body of, 204
  execution of family,
    255
  jealousy of David,
    57–58
  ordering foreskin as
    dowry for Michal,
    166–167

Saul of Tarsus. *See* Paul
Sceva, 209
Science, 269
The Screwtape Letters,
    258–259
Scripture
    destruction of Solom
        and Gomorrah, 10
    firestorms in, 229–
        230
    nakedness in, 208–
        209
    references to, xii–
        xiii
    upholding value of, xi
Scroll, burnt, 232
Sea monster, 177
Seleucia, 75
Sennacherib, 231–232
Serpent
    saving Israelites,
        31–32
    staff becoming, 161
Services of deliverance,
    205, 209, 260
Seth, 5
Seventy deaths, 194
Shadow, of crucifixion,
    91
Shadrach, 77, 78
Shamgar,
    accomplishments
        of, 187
Sheba, queen of, 61–62
Shechem, Prince
    dowry death of, 152
    Jotham's curse, 49–50
Shem, longevity of, 4
Sheol, 267
Shepherd's staff. *See*
    Staff
Shepherds, angel
    visiting, 38

Shipwreck, 124–125
Silas, 122–123
Simon, 244
Simony, 244
Sinai, Mount, 156
    Elijah journeying to,
        157
    water coming from
        rock, 161, 170–171
Sisera, death of, 152–
    153
Snake
    Paul bitten by, 145
    staff turning to, 161
Sodium chloride, 11
Sodom
    characteristics of, 11
    destruction of,
        137–138
Sodomites, 12
Solom, destruction of,
    9–10
Solomon
    fiery sacrifice, 229
    temple of, 212, 213
    visit from Queen
        Makeda, 61–62
    words of, 121
Sons, of God, 5–6
Sorcery, 168–169, 180
Soviet Union, 76
Spirit of Jesus, 103
Spring of the One Who
    Cried Out, 171
Staff
    becoming serpent,
        161
    blossoming with
        almonds, 162
    water coming from
        rock, 161, 170–
        171
Stew, poisoned, 220

Stoning
    death by, 180–181
    of oxen, 175
Supper, the Last, 151
Syncretism, 73

T
Tabernacle, death of
    Joab, 201
Tabitha, rising from
    dead, 228
Talking donkey, 34–35
Tax collector, 237–238
Temple
    destruction of,
        212–213
    fiery dedication of,
        229
Ten Commandments
    Moses receiving,
        156–157
    stoning for misusing
        name of Lord, 180
    storing in ark of
        covenant, 25
Terah, longevity of, 4
The Thirty, 188
The Three, 188
Thummim, 185–186
Timothy, circumcision
    of, 167
Traitors, turncoats, and
    treacherous types,
    97–99
Transfiguration, Mount
    of, 205
Tubal, 76
Tumor, dying from, 13

U
Urim, 185–186
Uzzah, death of, 28, 179
Uzziah, 165

V

Vagrant, Jesus
  exorcising of
  demons, 100–101
Vengeance, Holy, 12
Venus, 73
Voice
  of God, 135–136
  hearing, 115–117
Vow
  of Jephthah, 51–52
  Monastic, 264
  Nazirite, 264

W

Wailing Wall, 212
Warrior, 189–191
Water
  angel providing for
  Elijah, 220
  appearing from
  ground, 171
  changing to wine,
  105–106, 150
  coming from rock,
  161, 170–171

miracles of, 239–
  241
miraculous
  appearance of,
  170–171
Moses surviving
  without, 157–158
Weather,
  extraordinary
  events of, 92–95
Wedding, changing
  water to wine,
  105–106
Widow
  persistence of, 243
  son rising from dead,
  227
Wind, from God's
  spirit, 110–111
Wine
  changing water to,
  105–106, 150
  the Last Supper,
  151
Witness, altar name,
  147

Women
  angel visiting, 38
  of Moabite, 40
Writing on palace wall,
  83–84

X

Xerxes, King of Persia
  death of Haman,
  143–144
  second banquet,
  149–150

Y

Yoke, 234–235

Z

Zechariah
  angel visiting, 38
  father to John the
  Baptist, 141–142
Zedekiah, King, 74
Ziba, 210–211
Zipporah
  circumcision of son,
  166

Scripture Reference Index

Genesis 2:21–24	263	Genesis 21:14–19	35
Genesis 2:25	208	Genesis 22	52
Genesis 3	129	Genesis 22:1–19	52, 79, 133, 146
Genesis 3:1–5	258	Genesis 22:11–18	35
Genesis 3:24	131	Genesis 25:23	15
Genesis 5	4	Genesis 25:27–34	149
Genesis 6:1	5	Genesis 27	15
Genesis 6:1–8	6	Genesis 27:1–40	16
Genesis 6:1–8:22	79	Genesis 27:34–40	14
Genesis 6:3	4	Genesis 27:46	263
Genesis 8:20–9:17	134	Genesis 28:8–9	263
Genesis 9:1–11	16	Genesis 28:12	252
Genesis 10:2	76	Genesis 29:16–35	140
Genesis 11	137	Genesis 31:10–13	36
Genesis 11:1–9	75	Genesis 32:22–32	36
Genesis 14	8	Genesis 34:1–31	152
Genesis 14:18–20	16	Genesis 37:12–36	79
Genesis 16:6	265	Genesis 37:39–50	18
Genesis 16:7	252	Genesis 39:1–23	154
Genesis 16:7–13	35	Genesis 42–47	79
Genesis 17	139	Genesis 50:20	18
Genesis 17:10–14	264		
Genesis 18	35	Exodus 1:1–2:10	79
Genesis 18:1–15	141	Exodus 3:1–22	156
Genesis 18–19	10	Exodus 3:2	252
Genesis 18:6–8	253	Exodus 3:2–4:17	36
Genesis 19	11	Exodus 4:1–5	161
Genesis 19:1–3	253	Exodus 4:1–8	164
Genesis 19:1–29	36, 79, 252	Exodus 4:24–26	166
Genesis 19:24	12, 267	Exodus 7:1–2	274
Genesis 21	139	Exodus 7:14–25	20
Genesis 21:1–7	141	Exodus 8:26	180
Genesis 21:9–21	143	Exodus 11–12	20

Exodus 11:1–10	12	Numbers 20:1–13	171
Exodus 12:11–13	132	Numbers 21:4–6	12
Exodus 13:17–14:31	79	Numbers 21:4–9	32
Exodus 13:21–22	22	Numbers 21:7–9	32
Exodus 14:19–20	22	Numbers 22–24	35
Exodus 14:21–28	12	Numbers 22:16–17	34
Exodus 16	24, 219	Numbers 22:21–35	36, 251
Exodus 16:4	23	Numbers 22:21–36	175
Exodus 16:15, 31	23	Numbers 22:21–38	79
Exodus 16:31	22	Numbers 22:22	108
Exodus 17:1–6	161	Numbers 22:23–34	252
Exodus 17:1–7	22, 170–171	Numbers 22:31–34	132
Exodus 17:10–16	172	Numbers 22:33	35
Exodus 19:1–18	157	Numbers 25:1–9	12
Exodus 20:4–5	74	Numbers 25:1–4	40
Exodus 20:7	180	Numbers 26:10	12
Exodus 20:16	210	Numbers 27:21	186
Exodus 21:28–30	175	Numbers 31	254
Exodus 25	26		
Exodus 28–30	132	Deuteronomy 3:11	182
Exodus 28:30	186	Deuteronomy 13:1–3	275
Exodus 32	160	Deuteronomy 18:20	275
Exodus 32:15–28	12	Deuteronomy 18:21–22	275
Exodus 33:20	252	Deuteronomy 27–28	43
Exodus 34:1	135, 157	Deuteronomy 28:10	42
Exodus 39:42–43	16	Deuteronomy 30:15–18	274
Leviticus 10:1–3	178	Joshua 3	26
Leviticus 18:21	46, 51	Joshua 5:12	24
Leviticus 24:23	180	Joshua 5:13–15	132
		Joshua 6:2	130
Numbers 4:20	28	Joshua 6:17–25	254
Numbers 5:11–31	130	Joshua 6:24–26	130
Numbers 6	264	Joshua 6:26	53
Numbers 11:31–35	12	Joshua 7:1–26	181
Numbers 12:1–15	164	Joshua 8:30–35	43
Numbers 13:33	6, 182	Joshua 9:3–27	130
Numbers 14:36–37	12	Joshua 10:9–14	173
Numbers 15:32–35	180	Joshua 10:11	13
Numbers 16	30	Joshua 15:8	45
Numbers 16:5	29	Joshua 18:1–10	184
Numbers 17:1–11	162	Joshua 18:16	45
Numbers 20:1–12	161	Joshua 22:10–34	147, 254

Judges 2:1–5	36	1 Samuel 14:1–23	188
Judges 3:31	187	1 Samuel 14:36–45	185
Judges 4:1–24	153	1 Samuel 15:1–7	13
Judges 5:24–31	153	1 Samuel 16:14–23	204
Judges 6:11–27	252	1 Samuel 17	162, 188
Judges 6:11–24	36	1 Samuel 18	27, 167
Judges 6:12–24	251	1 Samuel 19:1–20	204
Judges 6:17–22	134	1 Samuel 19:9–10	204
Judges 6:24–32	147	1 Samuel 19:11–18	79
Judges 6:33–40	135	1 Samuel 24	58
Judges 6–7	48	1 Samuel 24:1–22	79
Judges 7	173	1 Samuel 28	169
Judges 8:22–28	192	1 Samuel 28:6	186
Judges 8:27	192	1 Samuel 30:1–31	80
Judges 9	50, 194	1 Samuel 31	206
Judges 9:19–20	50	1 Samuel 42	204
Judges 9:57	50		
Judges 11	52	2 Samuel 1	37
Judges 11:36–37	52	2 Samuel 6	179
Judges 13–16	56	2 Samuel 6:6–7	28
Judges 13:2–24	251	2 Samuel 8:14	15
Judges 13:2–25	37	2 Samuel 10:1–5	208
Judges 13:15–16	253	2 Samuel 11–12	60, 215
Judges 13:21–22	252	2 Samuel 16:1–4	210
Judges 14:19	208	2 Samuel 18	153
Judges 15:14–15	13	2 Samuel 19:24–30	210
Judges 15:18–19	171	2 Samuel 21	255
Judges 16:1–21	155	2 Samuel 21:15–22	6, 183
Judges 16:4–30	200	2 Samuel 23:9–10	188
Judges 17:1–18:31	193	2 Samuel 24:10–16	13
Judges 19:25–28	265	2 Samuel 24:15–17	37
1 Samuel, book of,	200	1 Kings 2	201
1 Samuel 1	140	1 Kings 5–8	212
1 Samuel 2:12–26	202	1 Kings 8:6–11	212
1 Samuel 4	26	1 Kings 10	62
1 Samuel 4:1–22	202	1 Kings 11:1	61
1 Samuel 4:4–22	27	1 Kings 11:1–8	264
1 Samuel 5:1–12	13	1 Kings 11:5	45
1 Samuel 5:1–6	27	1 Kings 11:26–40	216
1 Samuel 5:12	27	1 Kings 12:20	216
1 Samuel 5:1–6:18	201	1 Kings 13	65
1 Samuel 6:19–20	28, 194	1 Kings 13:3	63

1 Kings 13:8–10	64	1 Chronicles 21:12–30	37
1 Kings 16:34	54, 130	1 Chronicles 28:2–3	212
1 Kings 16–21	155		
1 Kings 17:1–7	143	2 Chronicles 3–7	212
1 Kings 17:8–16	220	2 Chronicles 7:1–4	229
1 Kings 18	68, 70	2 Chronicles 14:12–13	13
1 Kings 18:3–4	65	2 Chronicles 16:7–10	65
1 Kings 19:1–18	157	2 Chronicles 18:12–27	65
1 Kings 19:1–3	65	2 Chronicles 20:22–24	13
1 Kings 19:1–8	220	2 Chronicles 21	231
1 Kings 19:5–7	37	2 Chronicles 24:20–22	65
1 Kings 20:23–43	216	2 Chronicles 26	165
1 Kings 21:1–22	181	2 Chronicles 28:3	45
1 Kings 21:17–19	206	2 Chronicles 33:6	45
1 Kings 22:10–28	65		
1 Kings 22:29–40	206	Ezra 1–6	213
		Ezra 1:1–4	214
2 Kings 1:2	109	Ezra 9–10	265
2 Kings 1:9–12	13		
2 Kings 2	72	Esther, book of	144
2 Kings 2:23–24	65, 176	Esther 2–7	80
2 Kings 4:32–37	226	Esther 3–7	150
2 Kings 4:38–41	220		
2 Kings 5	224	Job 1	108, 230
2 Kings 6:1–7	163	Job 3:8	177
2 Kings 6:8–23	174	Job 10:21	267
2 Kings 9:7–37	155	Job 41:1–34	177
2 Kings 9:30–37	207	Job 42:12–17	16
2 Kings 10:1–17	13, 195		
2 Kings 10:18–29	201	Psalm 1	16
2 Kings 11:1–15	155	Psalm 34:7	251
2 Kings 13:14–20	217	Psalm 51	60
2 Kings 13:20–21	227	Psalm 74:14	177
2 Kings 19:34–35	37	Psalm 77:14	269
2 Kings 19:35	252	Psalm 78:24–25	253
2 Kings 20:1–11	135	Psalm 91:11	251
2 Kings 20:8–11	214	Psalm 109:8	185
2 Kings 23:10	45	Psalm 109:9	254
		Psalm 110	8
1 Chronicles 10	206		
1 Chronicles 13	26	Proverbs 27:20	267
1 Chronicles 20:4–8	183		
1 Chronicles 21:1	108	Isaiah 6:1–13	214

Isaiah 7:14	142	Daniel 6:17–18	78
Isaiah 9:1–7	274	Daniel 6:22	37, 86
Isaiah 13–14	137	Daniel 8:15–27	37
Isaiah 14:12–21	258	Daniel 9:19–27	37
Isaiah 14:12	108	Daniel 9:24–27	274
Isaiah 20	234	Daniel 10:1–12:13	37
Isaiah 20:1–5	214	Daniel 11:31	279
Isaiah 36:1–37:28	232	Daniel 12:11	279
Isaiah 44:28	214		
Isaiah 45:1	274	Hosea 1–3	236
Isaiah 45:13	274	Hosea 1:2	236
Jeremiah 7:18	74	Jonah 1:1–2:10	80, 237
Jeremiah 7:31	45	Jonah 1:1	274
Jeremiah 13:1–11	234	Jonah 1:3–16	185
Jeremiah 20	203	Jonah 3	138
Jeremiah 22	232		
Jeremiah 25	74, 76	Micah 5:2	274
Jeremiah 26:20–23	66		
Jeremiah 27–28	235	Nahum, book of	138
Jeremiah 28	211		
Jeremiah 32:35	45	Matthew 1:18–24	38
Jeremiah 36	232	Matthew 1:18–25	142
Jeremiah 37:1–38:13	66	Matthew 2:13–23	38
Jeremiah 44:17–19	74	Matthew 5:1–12	16
		Matthew 8	101
Ezekiel 1:5–10	131	Matthew 8:28–34	205
Ezekiel 4–5	235	Matthew 9:1–8	225
Ezekiel 10:1–22	131	Matthew 9:2	270
Ezekiel 12:3–7	235	Matthew 9:18–26	227
Ezekiel 24:16–17	235	Matthew 9:19–22	225
Ezekiel 38:8	76	Matthew 9:22–29	270
Ezekiel 38:14–23	76	Matthew 12:24	108, 109
Ezekiel 40–43	213	Matthew 12:38–42	135
		Matthew 13:53–58	270
Daniel, book of	76	Matthew 14:1–12	150, 151
Daniel 3	78	Matthew 14:6–12	66
Daniel 3:1–30	80	Matthew 14:13–21	238
Daniel 3:24–25	77	Matthew 14:31	270
Daniel 4	80, 82, 235	Matthew 15	151
Daniel 5	84	Matthew 15:28	270
Daniel 6	86, 176	Matthew 15:32–39	238
Daniel 6:1–28	80	Matthew 17	90

Matthew 17:14–21	205	Mark 14:51–52	209
Matthew 17:14–18	260	Mark 16:12–13	103
Matthew 17:24–27	238		
Matthew 18:10	251	Luke 1:5–25	142
Matthew 20:1–16	242	Luke 1:11–20	38
Matthew 24:1–2	213	Luke 1:11–12	252
Matthew 24:15	279	Luke 1:13	252
Matthew 24:24–28	275	Luke 1:26–38	38, 142, 251
Matthew 24:27–31	275	Luke 1:30	252
Matthew 24:36	275	Luke 1:57–80	142
Matthew 24:42	275	Luke 2:8–15	38
Matthew 24:44	275	Luke 3:1–18	142
Matthew 25:41	259	Luke 4:14–30	80
Matthew 26	151	Luke 5:1–11	238
Matthew 26:1–27	203	Luke 5:18–26	225
Matthew 27	97	Luke 7:11–17	227
Matthew 27:4	97	Luke 8	101
Matthew 27:5	96	Luke 8:26–29	205
Matthew 27–28	92	Luke 8:40–56	227
Matthew 27:62–28:15	211	Luke 8:43–50	225
Matthew 28:2–7	38	Luke 9	90, 151
Matthew 28:4	252	Luke 9:37–43	205
		Luke 12:40	275
Mark 1:24	259	Luke 16:19–31	266
Mark 2:3–12	225	Luke 17:5–6	270
Mark 5	101	Luke 17:19	270
Mark 5:1–13	258	Luke 18:1–8	243
Mark 5:1–20	205	Luke 18:42	270
Mark 5:21–43	227	Luke 22	151
Mark 5:24–34	225	Luke 22:3	96
Mark 6	151	Luke 22–24	92
Mark 6:5–6	135	Luke 24:13–35	103
Mark 6:14–29	150		
Mark 6:30–44	238	John 1:18	252
Mark 8	151	John 2	106
Mark 8:1–10	238	John 2:1–11	270
Mark 9	90	John 2:3–11	150
Mark 9:14–20	205	John 2:4	105
Mark 9:43	266	John 2:11	270
Mark 10:6–9	263	John 3	245
Mark 13:14	279	John 3:8	108
Mark 14	151	John 3:14	32

John 4:12	252	Acts 19:21–41	193
John 4:24	251	Acts 20:7–12	228
John 6	151	Acts 22	115
John 6:1–15	238	Acts 23:1–5	203
John 6:14	270	Acts 23:12–35	80, 145
John 6:70	96	Acts 27–28	125
John 9:1–41	270	Acts 27:1–28:6	145
John 11	228	Acts 27:21–26	39
John 12:27–36	136	Acts 27:22–25	124
John 13–17	151		
John 14:30	108	1 Corinthians 5:1	245
John 19–20	92	1 Corinthians 7:5	108
John 21:1–10	238	1 Corinthians 10:20	259
		1 Corinthians 11:26	151
Acts 1:6–11	38		
Acts 1:18	96, 97	2 Corinthians 2:5–11	245
Acts 1:20–26	185		
Acts 2	110	Ephesians 2:2	108
Acts 2:22–33	270	Ephesians 6:11	108
Acts 5:1–20	179	Ephesians 6:12	260
Acts 5:1–11	179	Ephesians 6:16	260
Acts 5:12–16	225		
Acts 5:17–32	80	1 Timothy 6:16	252
Acts 5:17–20	39		
Acts 8:9–24	244	2 Timothy 3:8–9	168
Acts 9	115		
Acts 9:1–25	144	Hebrews 2:1–4	270
Acts 9:21–25	80	Hebrews 2:4	269
Acts 9:36–43	228	Hebrews 5–7	8
Acts 10:2–4	252	Hebrews 7	203
Acts 10:3–8	39	Hebrews 7:2	7
Acts 12	119, 121	Hebrews 7:3	8
Acts 12:1–19	80	Hebrews 11:31	254
Acts 12:1–11	39	Hebrews 13:2	35, 90
Acts 12:15	251		
Acts 13:4–12	169	James 2:25	254
Acts 13:22	60		
Acts 14:19–20	181	1 Peter 3:8–14	16
Acts 16	123	1 Peter 3:9	266
Acts 16:1–4	167	1 Peter 5:8	108
Acts 16:16–19	205		
Acts 19:13–16	209, 260	2 Peter 2:4	6, 266

2 Peter 3:10	275	Revelation 2:20	155
		Revelation 13:1–9	177
Jude 6	6	Revelation 14:10	267
		Revelation 18	76
Revelation 2:6	39	Revelation 20:7–10	108
Revelation 2:14	40	Revelation 20:8	76
Revelation 2:16	39	Revelation 20:9–10	230

Index to the Charts

Abused Prophets   65
Angel of the Lord   132
Ark of the Covenant Linked to Mysterious Deaths   27
Blessings   16
Confirmed Prophetic Predictions   275
Cup of Wrath   256
Famine and Hunger   221
Fascinating Miracles of Jesus   271
Great Escapes   78
Hearing Voices   115
Heaven and Hell   267
Holy Vengeance   12
Lakes, Oceans, Rivers, and Waters   239
Long and Amazing Life of the Bible   158
Masters of Disguise   217
Mighty Warriors   189
Murderers' Row: Killers in the Bible   195
Mysterious Messengers   35
Portraits of Satan   260
Postresurrection Appearances of Jesus   103
Seven Seals of Revelation   246
Traitors, Turncoats, and Treacherous Types   97
Under the Influence   86
Vanishing Books   232
Weird Weather   92

Index to "Did You Know?"

What was the pillar of fire?   22

Who were the Nicolaitans?   39

Why did the ancient Israelites sacrifice their children to Molech
    in the valley of Ben-Hinnom?   45

What is the strange land whose identity still eludes scholars
    and laypeople alike?   76

Why did the ancient Israelites use the obscure name "Beelzebub"
    to refer to Satan?   109

Who was the goddess Asherah? What were Asherah poles?
    Why did the prophets of Israel passionately denounce
    the worship of Asherah?   147

Who survived forty days without food or water?   157

Why would the Hebrews worship a calf?
    How could a golden statue inspire an orgy?   160

What ferocious beast mentioned in the Bible has defied
    scientific classification?   177

What were the Urim and Thummim?   185

How did a prophet know the name of the man who would
    order the exiles to return to Jerusalem and rebuild
    their temple?   214

What do angels eat?   253

Why were Jesus' healings of lepers so remarkable?   273

What is the "sacrilegious object that causes desecration"?   279